STUDIES

IN LAW AND POLITICS

BY

HAROLD J. LASKI

ARCHON BOOKS
1969

FIRST PUBLISHED 1932
REPRINTED 1969 WITH PERMISSION OF
GEORGE ALLEN & UNWIN LTD.
IN AN UNALTERED AND UNABRIDGED EDITION

SBN: 208 00731 8
LIBRARY OF CONGRESS CATALOG CARD NUMBER: 69-12933
PRINTED IN THE UNITED STATES OF AMERICA

TO

MR. JUSTICE BRANDEIS

WITH AFFECTION AND ADMIRATION

TYLER STATE COLLEGE LIBRARY

PREFACE

THESE essays have been published at various times and places in the last seven years. I reprint them, partly because the original sources of publication have been so diverse, and partly because friends have asked me for copies of a number of them which are now out of print. Though they treat of very different subjects, I venture to think that they are brought into something like unity by the fact that they express a general attitude in spite of their varying subject-matter. I should like here to express the debt the last essay owes to Sir Edward Parry, to whose admirable work I owe my interest in the subject of law reform.

I am grateful to Professor F. J. C. Hearnshaw, the Fabian Society, the Ethical Union, and the editors of the *Harvard Law Review*, the *Yale Law Journal*, the *Michigan Law Review*, *Economica*, and *Harpers' Magazine* for permission to publish material originally printed under their auspices.

I may add that the dedication is something more than a formal tribute. What I owe to the friendship of Mr. Justice Brandeis lies deeper than I can easily put into words.

H. J. L.

THE LONDON SCHOOL OF ECONOMICS
AND POLITICAL SCIENCE

CONTENTS

CHAPTER	PAGE
PREFACE	9
I. THE AGE OF REASON	13
II. DIDEROT	48
III. THE SOCIALIST TRADITION IN THE FRENCH REVOLUTION	66
IV. THE PROBLEM OF A SECOND CHAMBER	104
V. THE STATE IN THE NEW SOCIAL ORDER	125
VI. THE POLITICAL PHILOSOPHY OF MR. JUSTICE HOLMES	146
VII. THE TECHNIQUE OF JUDICIAL APPOINTMENT	163
VIII. THE PERSONNEL OF THE BRITISH CABINET, 1801–1924	181
IX. JUDICIAL REVIEW OF SOCIAL POLICY	202
X. PROCEDURE FOR CONSTRUCTIVE CONTEMPT	222
XI. LAW AND THE STATE	237
XII. JUSTICE AND THE LAW	276
INDEX	297

STUDIES IN LAW AND POLITICS

I

THE AGE OF REASON

THE study of the eighteenth century in France must begin by the admission of its complexity. Generalization is helpless before temperaments so various and ideas so disparate. If we make it the period of aggressive rationalism we are confronted by the dominating spectacle of Rousseau. If we find its significance in the emergence of romantic sensibility Voltaire, Holbach, and Montesquieu immediately arrest our attention. In a sense, it is the most French of all the centuries, French in its passion for logical abstraction, its taste for simplification, its determination to push principle relentlessly to its appointed end. Yet, in another sense, no epoch saw a wider influence attributable to foreign doctrine. If eighteenth-century France is the age of Voltaire, Montesquieu, and Rousseau, it is the age also of Locke and Richardson, of Ossian and Young. The Romantic movement, at least, has its roots deep in English soil.

The period, moreover, is not one of an unchanging temper. The first forty years are, for the most part, rationalist in outlook. But that rationalism is not of the eighteenth century in its origins, nor is it unique in its pervasiveness. It comes from the scepticism of Bayle and Fontenelle and Saint-Évremond, and this, in its turn, is linked at once to Descartes and the classical spirit on one side, and, on the other, to Rabelais and Montaigne, with their deep-rooted Renaissance humanism. Yet even here the faint beginnings of the Romantic temper can be discerned. There is a morality of the heart in Saint-Évremond, an emphasis upon the claims of passionate feeling in works like the *Lettres d'Héloïse et Abélard*, a defence of sentimental insight in the Abbé Dubos and in Toussaint, which presaged a wider development. Nor must we forget that both in this period and its successor there is an atmosphere in which experimental science seems to provide the mainsprings of social thought. When Diderot attended lectures on anatomy and physiology he was only doing what every great lady thought it a part of her education to do. Even Rousseau wrote a book on the principles of chemistry; and no one can read the works of Condorcet or Turgot or the Physiocrats without seeing that the influence upon them of scientific discovery was almost boundless. Another change is visible again after the publication of the *Nouvelle Héloïse* in 1762. The claims of reason seem to fade before the imperative demands of sentiment. Tenderness, intuition, sensibility, dethrone the empire of deductive rationalism. Yet even in this new phase the older system-making does not lose its prestige. If Julie enchants thousands, the average Frenchman continues, with Candide, to cultivate his garden. Abstract truth, the Voltairean common sense, with its power of destructive irony, the natural laws of Condillac and Quesnay—these still advance with pride to the conflict of ideas.

Yet one thing we can say of the period with conviction which would not be true of any earlier time. The nation discovered its own existence, and therewith its right to political power. It made the discovery because the philosophers destroyed altogether the association of social rights with aristocratic privilege. Seeking for themselves the right to follow the effort of intelligence, wherever it might lead, they found that the condemnation of the institutions of the *ancien régime*, political, religious, economic, was inherent in their effort. No one can seriously claim to-day that the philosophers caused the Revolution; that is a mythopoesis not even edifying to ourselves. But no one, either, is entitled to argue that, without them, it would have been the same

Revolution. They made it conscious of its purposes. They provided it with the intellectual armoury from which its main weapons were drawn. The young Marat declaiming the *Contrat social* in the gardens of the Tuileries, the still younger Marie Phlipon insisting that her life was different because she had read the *Nouvelle Héloïse*, were paying a conscious tribute to those who had shaped its destiny.

Let us try to put this from another angle. In the space of less than a hundred years the philosophers effected a transformation in the French mind which can, perhaps, be best explained by saying that Bossuet, Boileau, and Racine would not have understood either the methods or the aspirations of Diderot, Mably, and Rousseau. So widespread, indeed, was the empire of the new spirit that even its opponents were deeply infected by its presuppositions. If we take any characteristic apologist for Catholicism in the eighteenth century—the Abbé Gérard, for example—it is as obvious that he is the contemporary of Voltaire and Rousseau as that the groundwork of his defence would have been unintelligible to Bossuet or the "Great" Arnauld. The pervasiveness of this new spirit is remarkable. It is hardly less perceptible in the sermons of Massillon than in the *Encyclopædia* of Diderot, in the comedies of Marivaux than in the demographic studies of Sébastien Mercier.

Nowhere, indeed, is it simple or uniform. Partly it is a faith in the boundless power of reason, a faith reinforced by confidence in the prospects of scientific discovery, a trust in the power of rational inquiry to discover the structural principles of the moral universe. Thence comes, by a natural sequence, its profound optimism, its confidence in the certainty of human progress, which, as with the Abbé de Saint-Pierre and Condorcet, refuses to set limits to the perfectibility of man. Partly, also, it is a trust in intuition, a belief that the sentiment within most truly reveals the reality without, which enables us to insist not only upon the natural goodness of man, but also to make the discoveries of reason square with our own desires. In this realm the high-priest is Rousseau; and no other political thinker has even approached his power of externalizing his autobiography into a programme.

II

Certain characteristics of the eighteenth century stand out in startling contrast to the qualities of its predecessor. The seventeenth century was, despite the persistence of a libertine tradition, essentially Christian in outlook; not less certainly the eighteenth is profoundly hostile to Christian dogma of every kind. The seventeenth century was deeply nationalist, but little critical, a period of great art and an ardent love of order. The eighteenth century is cosmopolitan in outlook, and, as with Voltaire and Rousseau, nationalism in the realm of thought or institutions seemed to it a pitiful thing. It is above all things critical of tradition and rule, less interested in the form of its thought than in its substance. What explains these differences? Essentially, it is obvious, their explanation lies in the effects of Louis XIV's reign. The growing weakness of the Church was patent to everyone, and it was the primary architect of its own misfortunes. Its hostility to all inquiry, its zeal for persecution, its fanatic opposition to change, made it suspect on every side. The quarrel between Jansenist and Jesuit, between Bossuet and Fénelon, ended in part by sickening men of religion, and in part by making them aware of the intellectual weaknesses of the Church. The Revocation of the Edict was welcomed when it came; but it was not long before men felt that the economic price of religious unity was too high. The grim devotion by which Louis XIV, in his later years, sought to atone for the licence of his youth provoked an hypocrisy and a disgust of which the Regency was the inevitable price. By 1715 the renaissance in religion over which men like St. Francis of Sales had presided was in total ruin. A general scepticism was created, and in that atmosphere the seeds sown by men like Bayle naturally yielded an unlooked-for harvest.

The seventeenth century, moreover, was the epoch of monarchical absolutism. Opposition to Louis had ceased altogether; he was the unchallenged master of the lives and fortunes of his subjects. What had he done with his power? The answer to that question is to be found in the formidable literature of indictment framed against him by the most distinguished figures of the latter part of his reign. The economic devastation is shown by Vauban and Bois-Guillebert, in the dispatches of the Intendants, and in an unforgettable picture of the common people from the acid pen of La Bruyère. The political folly of Louis's system is insisted upon not only by great nobles like Saint-Simon, or lesser aristocrats like Boulainvilliers; it is shown with passionate accuracy by the despairing Protestants. I omit the prejudiced account of Jurieu, since he appears definitely to have been a spy in the pay of William III. But who can read the descriptions of the noble-minded Claude, of the cool and sceptical Bayle, of the author of the unanswerable *Soupirs de la France esclave*, without an irresistible sense of their truth? And their tale is amply confirmed by those letters and pamphlets of Fénelon which seem, in their noble indignation, to have recaptured the spirit and the eloquence of a prophet of old. Their case against Louis XIV is an unanswerable one. His unnecessary wars, his personal extravagance, his reduction of the aristocrat to the position of that courtier so exactly defined by Dr. Johnson, the complete breakdown of the financial and economic system, the capricious and largely ignorant use of literary and artistic patronage, the moral disaster of a social system which stifled initiative by impressing with increasing intensity as we descend in the social scale the sense of inferiority —all this was a heavy tribute to levy upon a nation. It is no cause for wonder that the death of Louis was welcomed on all hands as a release from burdensome trammels. He had broken the ancient alliance between the French monarch and his people. Never after him did the Royalist idea act as an institutional force upon the mind of France. It had so completely failed to justify its power that men no longer looked to it for leadership. The lesson of its failure was the lesson of self-confidence. Classes which had trusted to it for protection now found that they must trust to themselves. And the history of the eighteenth century is the growing realization of a class which, as a social group, had thus far played no part in the history of the *ancien régime* that its institutions were incompatible with its urgent need to control its own destiny. The whole temper we must seek to seize was thus not the sudden product of a group of bizarre thinkers, but the inevitable inference from facts of which grim experience had taught the inescapable burden.

It is, perhaps, symptomatic of the temper that develops that, whereas in the seventeenth century intellectual work is mainly built round the patronage of the Court, in the eighteenth century it practically ignores the necessity for that enslavement. Voltaire is the uncrowned king of a realm more real and wider by far in its influence than that of Versailles; d'Alembert and Rousseau, Diderot and Mably, in striking contrast with Boileau and Racine, call no man master. Where Vauban could not survive the hint of royal displeasure Marmontel and Morellet, Diderot and Voltaire, wear their imprisonment as a proof of quality and courage. Everyone knows the famous passages in which stout *bourgeois* like Barbier and retired officials like d'Argenson recount the rise of the power of public opinion. The memoirs of noblemen like Ségur reveal to us how the swelling tide of liberal sentiment captured the very class it was destined to engulf.

No one suspects Mme du Deffand of sympathy with the new ideas; and yet, because for her the whole quality of life resided in the contact of mind with mind, it was with the new forces that she had to build her life. In the seventeenth century she would have solaced her interminable darkness with the attractive preciosity of Voiture, or Chapelain, or Mme de Lafayette; in the eighteenth she is dependent upon d'Alembert and Voltaire and that Mlle de Lespinasse whom merely to read of is to love. In the seventeenth century no voice of authority is raised against the Revocation; in the eighteenth a whole multitude follows with reverent admiration Voltaire's vindication of Calas and de la Barre. The seventeenth century could not even have conceived the *Encyclopædia*; for its essence is a challenge to every principle by which the classical monarchy took its stand. But to the eighteenth century its suppression was a national misfortune which aroused the equal anger of conservatives like Barbier and liberals like Malesherbes —himself, let us note, the director of the censorship. One is tempted to remark that in the seventeenth century the great man of letters is, at most, a divine plaything; to its successor he is the spiritual leader of the nation. Clearly we are in the presence of a new world.

III

Let us try to trace, in such detail as we may, the character of its intellectual frontiers. There is a sense in which one of them, at least, is traced by the philosophy of Candide. He may experience the whole gamut of human misery, but in the end we leave him cultivating his garden. Why? Because he has courage enough still to believe in the power of reason to conquer the future. He is optimistic because he is rationalist. The world, as Voltaire said, may be the lunatic asylum of the planets, yet in the end it is governed by the sages

That is why the outstanding books—at any rate, until the emergence of Rousseau—are all of them deliberate essays in rationalism. The *Lettres anglaises* of Voltaire is not an account of England, but a description of what English rationalism is, and what triumphs, especially in the field of social affairs, may be accredited to its account. The *Lettres persanes* is the picture of contemporary France that a rational observer would draw; and the *Esprit des lois* is, above all, an attempt to find the nature of legal rationalism. The *Encyclopædia* itself is nothing so much as a huge repertory of all that rationalism has so far been able to establish.

What does this rationalism mean? It is essentially an attempt to apply the principles of Cartesianism to human affairs. Take as postulates the inescapable evidence of stout common sense, and reason logically from them to the conclusions they imply. That common sense, all the philosophers believed, will give everywhere the same results; what it is to the sage of Ferney it will be in Pekin or the woods of America. It is a kind of psychological geometry built upon the belief that human nature is everywhere the same. With La Mettrie or Helvétius, with Buffon or Condillac, we can trace from the characters we put one by one upon the *tabula rasa* of the mind what human nature is bound to be when it issues forth in social action.

With the obvious weaknesses of this method, which Diderot saw as early as 1754, I am not here concerned. It is more important for us to dwell upon its consequences in the event. It insists, first of all, upon the application of rationalism to religion. Diderot does not see why religions which proclaim their truth should not convince common sense of their adequacy by clear and obvious proof; for that is demanded of all the sciences. It is not often, indeed, that the demand is so definitely made. The more usual method is that of the *Encyclopædia*, which offers the authority of the Church for

THE AGE OF REASON 21

truths which it has already made impossible of acceptance by its method of stating them.

But once religion is asked to prove itself it cannot maintain its particular dogmas. It must submit to the demands of a universal common sense, which means that what is true of Christianity must be true also of Buddhism, or Islam, or the faith of the Incas. And, therefore, it is necessary to purge religious belief of absurdities due to ancient superstition, or priestly invention, and take as true only that which commends itself to the reason of universal man. There thus emerges the famous natural religion of the philosophers, the faith of Voltaire and Montesquieu, of d'Alembert and Condorcet. There is a God Who created the world. He gave to men a sense of right and evil and a soul which may or may not be immortal, and thus may or may not be punished or rewarded in the after-life. This is all that a rational man is entitled to believe, and any particular religious creed which adds its private dogmas thereto is merely building upon dupery and chicane. For the history of any particular religion—especially, Voltaire would add, the history of Christianity—shows us an ignorant mass, fearful of a mysterious power beyond, and willing to pay an exploiting priesthood for protection against its anger. Dogmatic religion is the armoury of that exploiting priesthood. And, accordingly, the rational man will regard dogma and its institutions as the infamous that he must crush at all costs.

Some, indeed, were willing to go farther. The eighteenth-century materialists are, relatively, a small school of thought, but their urgency of conviction and the ability with which they stated their case enabled them to drive their more timid colleagues to lengths greater than they might otherwise have been anxious to go. Helvétius shows us a philosopher hovering uneasily upon its confines; with Holbach and Diderot, with the Abbé Meslier and Naigeon, with

La Mettrie, we are in the midstream of materialistic atheism. The world, they say, is composed of a single element, matter; it appears in the most various forms, as vegetable or animal or mineral; it is organic and inorganic, living and dead. With Diderot the philosophy of materialism is no mere assertion, but a carefully built system made from observation and experiment. He notes the rigorous bond between body and soul, the way in which a change in physical constitution may affect our spiritual outlook. He concludes that matter and spirit are identical; that it is as illogical to postulate a spiritual principle to explain the mind as for a peasant to argue that a watch moves because some demon animates the hands.

The atheists, as I say, were small in numbers, and, in the case of Diderot at least, their influence was personal rather than public. What gave them power was their alliance with the more moderate school to demand religious toleration. Here, once more, what they had to say was in nowise new. Everything that can be said for tolerance is already said magistrally by Bayle. But the power of the Church was enormous even in the eighteenth century, and to batter down its defences was a formidable task. The philosophers, certainly, neglected no weapon they could use. They translated the English defenders of toleration, like Locke. They abounded in irony and invective against the proponents of persecution. Montesquieu, in the *Lettres persanes* and the *Esprit des lois*, d'Argenson, Voltaire in a hundred pamphlets, make the case for reasonableness overwhelming. Little by little they gained the day. Their triumph must have been manifest even to their opponents when young theorists of the Sorbonne, like Turgot and Morellet, agree among themselves that intolerance is impossible, and join their effort to that of the philosophers as soon as they enter the world. After 1760 persecution found but few defenders who, like the Abbé Caveyrac, were prepared to justify it;

and the feeling that fanaticism was contemptible was completed by such judicial tragedies as those of Calas and Sirven and de la Barre. One need not argue that the methods of their campaign were always honourable, or that the substance of their attack was invariably just. But it must be remembered that they were fighting an opponent whose methods were still those of the stake and the galleys. Huguenot ministers were still being hanged; Protestant children were still, at a tender age, being forcibly immured in convents. To make Joan of Arc the basis of an indecent poem, to attribute the Crusades to the meanest motives of which man is capable, to regard St. Francis of Assisi as no more than a mystic madman, these are indefensible errors of taste. But much is, after all, intelligible in men who were fighting the battle of reason against a power without mercy for its opponents.

The consequences of their victory were enormous. They not only won for rationalism an empire which had hitherto resisted the whole impact of its invasion. They made certain the victory of the principle that a political State cannot place itself at the disposal of a religious organization, at least within the confines of Western civilization. They saw with indisputable clarity the consequences of their victory. Deny the truth of revealed religion, and morality must discover other than religious foundations. Until their time it is not unfair to suggest that moral principle was regarded as essentially inherent in religious belief. They insisted upon the divorce of the two. Here, again, their effort was not new; they merely developed a doctrine already set out completely in Bayle's famous *Pensées sur la comète*, where he showed that a society of atheists would not necessarily be immoral. What Bayle said to the scandal of his generation they said, broadly speaking, to the satisfaction of their own. They were helped, doubtless, by influences on which Bayle could not rely. The writers of Utopias, like Fénelon and Ramsay, had already familiarized Frenchmen with the view that morality and paganism were not incompatible; and innumerable travellers had brought back accounts of tribes which, though innocent of Catholic dogma, led a life of notable virtue. Yet it was important to make the explicit affirmation of independence. What, asked Toussaint in his *Mœurs*, is virtue? "It is," he replies, "a faithful constancy in fulfilling the obligations Reason creates in us." Bayle apart, that could hardly have been said in the seventeenth century.

It is a little surprising to note how rapidly this view made its way, for, obviously, if it is true a large part of the utility of religious institutions disappeared. It makes an end of supernatural sanction and the revelation of divine law as the source of moral conduct. The problem of its proof was not an easy one. It was natural for Rousseau to argue that the moral sense was an instinct with an imperative claim, for he was but tenuously attached to the philosophic outlook; and there are even occasions when Voltaire, though with hesitation, was a partisan of this view. But to a generation which had learned from Locke to reject innate ideas the idea of a moral instinct was necessarily unsatisfactory. Morality is therefore explained, as by La Mettrie and Helvétius, as the natural consequence of social experience. We live the same lives, we encounter the same impressions. We learn therefrom the obvious convenience of accepting the same rules in the field of conduct. Morality is thus an experimental science. It is not built upon constraint. Man is no longer the product of original sin. He is entitled to be happy, and this involves the full enjoyment of his natural passions. But these can only give us happiness as they function in a social way. Voltaire, Mably, Diderot, Holbach, all combine, from their different standpoints, to explain that nothing more satisfies the individual passion than its devotion to social good. Mably, Holbach, and

Saint-Lambert write catechisms of lay morality whereby the legislator may teach men in these terms their duty to their neighbour and their country. For Rousseau, indeed, as the *Contrat social* shows, this view was utterly inadequate; but there is perhaps no point on which he was more clearly separated from his contemporaries than in his insistence upon the need for a religious foundation of civic action.

IV

Once the problems of religion and morals had come within the purview of the philosopher it was natural and logical that he should extend his survey to the political field. The problem of interpretation here is much more complex than in issues of religious or ethical controversy. The tradition of speculation, to begin with, was much more faint. Frenchmen had hardly discussed the foundations of politics since the epoch of the wars of religion. Among the innumerable pamphlets of the Fronde there are hardly more than half a dozen which demand more than the redress of particular grievances; and even the literature of protest under Louis XIV is innocent of any thoroughgoing radicalism. Bayle's political outlook is the essential conservatism of the scholar to whom disturbance is the supreme evil. Jurieu may preach the sovereignty of the people; but there is no sign that he desired to make the doctrine one of wide or profound application. It is notable that after Vauban and Bois-Guillebert had discussed the amazing economic distress they scrupulously abstain from any discussion of its impact upon matters of ultimate political constitution. The whole mind of Fénelon or Saint-Simon looks backward to a dead past for its inspiration, and ignores, almost completely, the living reality with which it was confronted. Barbeyrac, in his commentaries on Grotius and Pufendorf, was bolder; but, like Jurieu, he was living in exile. The little group which, under the leadership of the Abbé de Saint-Pierre, formed the Club de l'Entresol in the time of Fleury, to discuss political questions, does not seem to have made any startling affirmations, and it timidly accepted its suppression by the Minister as in the nature of things. Nor, at any rate until 1730, were English ideas influential. For England was long held in horror for the execution of Charles I, and such English treatises as were translated—Hobbes, for example— would not have aided the critical examination of a despotic system. It is not, I think, unreasonable to say that, until twenty years after their publication, the mind was rare which doubted the adequacy of Bossuet's political ideas.

Not, of course, that change is not in the air. Its presence may be discerned in the unforgettable bitterness of La Bruyère. It is apparent in the immediate inability of the monarchy under Louis XV to sustain either the prestige or the authority of its predecessor. There are countless passages in Marais and Barbier and d'Argenson which point to the definite existence of a new spirit, the precise extent of which men are not able to gauge. The Utopias of Vairasse and Sadeur would not be egalitarian if that aspiration did not correspond to a wide and felt need; for we could not otherwise explain their popularity. Obviously, too, a reason which believed both in its right and power to solve the problems of chemistry and physics, of ethics and religion, would insist on the extension of its empire. If Voltaire at thirty can express his mind in England, but not in France, being Voltaire, he is bound to ask why and to protest against the limitation. That insatiable curiosity which was Montesquieu was bound, also, after his famous visit to England and Holland, to probe the secret of its political method. Was there, he could not but ask, as Temple had inquired, half a century earlier, some mysterious affinity between prosperity and political freedom? Rationalism, accordingly, has its hands upon politics from the outset;

THE AGE OF REASON

and the degree of its analysis was merely a matter of time. Yet do not let us forget the timidity or the indirectness of the approach. Montesquieu may, in the *Lettres persanes*, discuss political and economic questions. But Usbek is a Persian writing to Ispahan, and he uses a thousand nuances and distractions to conceal the boldness of his ideas. Men, even after 1750, write always with a sense of excessive temerity upon these issues; and, until the very verge of the Revolution, the censorship does not fail to correct their liability to frankness. The censorship, indeed, is always a little ashamed and incomplete; and, as with Malesherbes, it has its moments of forgetfulness. But it is always there to remind the philosopher that the price of despotism is eternal constraint.

When the philosophers at last move to the citadel of politics what is in their minds? As one would expect, their ideas are a reflection of their situation. They are interested, above all, in social freedom, in the effort to secure for the individual protection from arbitrary interference in his private life. Their discussion of political institutions revolves always about that vital centre simply because that is the main experience they have known. What interests Voltaire in England is the boldness which can criticize without restraint (less admirable, in fact, than he knew) established institutions, the control of Parliament by the electorate, the power of the purse as an instrument for restraining monarchical authority. So with Montesquieu the ideal is a system in which, from the equilibrium of powers, social freedom necessarily emerges. All constitutions come within his ken; but the standpoint from which all his values are ultimately fixed is his belief in an individual citizen whose life is unfettered by wanton attack. There is little zeal for democratic institutions in the majority of writers. Meslier may propound in secret his passionate dithyramb to the Revolution; but his thoughts on the need for catastrophic change were unknown to his contemporaries. Mably and Morelly may be so impressed by the consequences of economic inequality as to propound communistic solutions, but neither is, I think, in the mainstream of political thought. They are significant, indeed, of a nuance of temper which gathered immense force after it had become evident that the Revolution was to profit but little the working-classes. For his own day, Morelly's Utopia was merely an attractive literary exercise; and the pessimism of Mably about his own ideals shows clearly that he himself considered them meat too strong for the digestion of his own contemporaries. His practical proposals, in fact, are remarkably moderate. Like his own master, Plato, he understood that his ideal republic was a pattern laid up in heaven, and, like him, he wrote a simpler version for a generation too little heroic to be capable of the larger sacrifices he desired.

If we omit Rousseau and the Physiocrats, who had each ideas quite special to themselves, we can generalize with some confidence about the common temper. All the philosophers, broadly speaking, combine to demand a constitutional government. They want religious toleration, civil freedom, the right to criticize, a rational jurisprudence, a fair system of taxation, the abolition of special privileges for the aristocracy. For the most part they do not condemn a limited monarchy, though Voltaire has his moments of ardent republicanism. They are not in the least democratic; on the contrary, as with Voltaire, they have a genuine fear of the multitude, and some of them, Voltaire included, are not even certain that popular ignorance is not a means to social security. This is not, indeed, true of Diderot, to whom the instruction of the people is the basis of social wellbeing. But, in general, the philosophers are conscious of themselves as an *élite* whose rights and capacities are different from those of the common herd. They are stout *bourgeois* to whom the rights of property are fundamental;

and it is amusing to note in Barbier the sense of that *juste milieu* which Guizot was later to make the basis of a disastrous adventure. It is important to examine the methods by which these results were reached; for they reveal more of the mind of the age than the conclusions themselves. Partly, at least, they are more like a psychological geometry than anything else. They postulate a human nature, and deduce from the laws with which they have endowed it the rules and ideals it ought to obey. Of time and space they make entire abstraction. Man, for them, is the same in Paris as in Pekin; and an ancient Roman would have recognized his habits in the predispositions of one of Mably's citizens. There is no sense of the historical element in politics. Variety of fact is not allowed to disturb their desire for ample and simple conclusions. Even Voltaire, who, in the *Essai sur les mœurs*, in some sort founded the modern study of history, writes as though an Iroquois or a Chinese was not very different from a sophisticated Parisian of eighteenth-century Paris.

Yet, by the middle of the century, the inadequacy of this purely *a priori* method is obvious to almost everyone. It was evident that diversity of fact made nonsense of simplicity of principle. It then became the fashion to seek for knowledge of what is original in the nature of men, to find the universal elements which seem, in fact, to be independent of time and place. Because these are universal they are accepted as legitimate, and the business of the political philosopher is then the discovery of reasonable means for their satisfaction. This method arose quite naturally from the voyages and Utopias of the time; and it is, of course, the method upon which Rousseau relied in the first two *Discours*. It is the method also of Helvétius and of Holbach, and its philosophic defence is derived from the psychology which Locke and Condillac had made the grand commonplace of the time. If we take, for instance, the *Politique naturelle* of Holbach (1773)—an unduly neglected book—we find the portrait of a man whose primordial needs can be known. These, because they are primordial, are natural, and reason can assure their satisfaction. We have an egoistic and an altruistic instinct which enables man to consent to sacrifice for the common interest. From these can be built, by the association of ideas, the whole complex mechanism of modern society. I use the word "mechanism" advisedly; for there is obviously a definite element of Cartesian automatism in this outlook. Society is here a machine constructed of parts which can be taken to pieces and put together again by reason; and reason, therefore, enables us to explain the rights of citizens, the functions of government, the method of education most fitted to the best results. One is irresistibly reminded of modern social psychology, which, with a bundle of denominated impulses, was prepared to correct the old world and boldly to plan a new.

Another aspect of this approach is analysis not by way of original and universal human nature, but of primitive society. That has many obvious merits. The problem of how an individual passes into a social tradition can be evaded; and by taking a society as given we do not fall into the difficulty which arises when political method is approximated to physical analysis. By searching the elements of primitive social organization the theorists are able, at the same time, to discover what is primitive, and therefore natural, in the society about them. The method is seen, perhaps at its best, in the second *Discours* of Rousseau. The notes he added to the text show that he had taken real care to acquaint himself with the existing accounts of primitive societies. They show, also, that for the end he had in view the amount of fact at his disposal is small. What, therefore, he does is to add to his knowledge inferences of what must, rationally, have been in order to complete the picture. We begin with a communistic society in which there is neither property nor the division of labour. Let a man once enclose a plot of ground, and, step by step, we can deduce by logic all that must have occurred in the development of inequality. From Rousseau's angle, particularly, the method is invaluable. It not only enabled him, with the support of innumerable travellers' tales—the relations, for example, of missionaries whose good faith was not suspected—to insist upon the superiority of the primitive over civilized life, to argue that, in fact, modern society is a deformation of human nature. It gave also to his hypothetical reconstructions a supposed groundwork in the facts of infinite value in its propagation as a system of ideas. When he and a hundred others—Morelly, Raynal, Brissot de Warville, even an enemy of the philosophers, like Linguet—vaunt the noble savage and nature's simple plan they are engaged upon the urgent task of justifying human nature to itself. We must not miss the effect of these ideas upon such theological dogmas as original sin, nor, in another field, miss their application, both widespread and influential, to the demand for the abolition of slavery.

From methods such as these two conclusions emerge. The philosophers are clear that an analysis of human nature is, at the same time, a solid proof of progress. If we compare, they say, Newton or Locke or Bacon even with the wisest of the ancients or the primitives it is evident that the advance is real. Let their spirit and its results pervade society, and we have the right, as d'Alembert and Condorcet both eloquently insist, to believe that reason can assure the happiness of men. And even the theory of primitive superiority leads to the elevation of rationalism. For what, it teaches, is wrong with modern society is those elements which are not the natural developments of its basic principles. Reason alone can distinguish between them, and reason alone, therefore, is the sovereign guide to well-being.

Rousseau, I need not say, would have rejected this view. But it is one of the explanations, for example, of the communism of Meslier and Morelly, and when sentiment becomes an operative agent in the control of ideas that type of thought becomes a factor of great importance. For, as certain strands of the Revolution showed, when it is linked to the facts of the economic *régime* it becomes, as supremely with Babeuf, a rallying-cry for the disinherited. It failed, of course, because it was before its time. Yet its intellectual affiliations show how deeply rooted it was in a fundamental attitude of the age.

Here, however, we must make an important distinction. Everyone knows Taine's famous picture of a nation made drunk by the classical spirit of abstract reason; and thinkers as eminent as Tocqueville and Cournot have spoken, if less excessively, in a similar sense. Let us, therefore, remember that the age of deduction is also an inductive age. What men have to say is built, after all, upon a fairly wide basis of direct observation. Everyone travels, Voltaire to England, Germany, and Switzerland, Montesquieu to Holland, Italy, and England, Diderot to Holland, Germany, and Russia. The passion for travel, and for reflection upon the diversity therein encountered, is one of the most real qualities of the time; the vast collections of voyages alone prove that. What M. Chinard has called *l'exotisme* is based, above all, upon a sincere appreciation of the need to recognize the ultimate stubbornness of variety. Often enough, doubtless, this *exotisme* is merely precious or attitudinizing; when it deals with Persia or Babylon or China one must, as a rule, throw up one's hands. But when geography is linked with history it produces the *Essai sur les mœurs* of Voltaire and the *Esprit des lois*. These, if they are anything, are careful generalizations built from a patient and laborious study of the best knowledge then available. With Montesquieu, they lead to a perception that reason has its limitations. Institutions, he sees clearly enough, are not infinitely malleable; they are a function of climate and race and tradition. His famous definition of law is already nothing so much as a perception that institutional truth is necessarily relative. Men who live differently think differently, and he knows well enough that a different thought is not necessarily an inferior thought. The good in law is for him not that which is common to all peoples, but that which best suits the particular people for whom it is intended.

Montesquieu, perhaps, is the supreme realist of the age; but we must not conceive of his revolt from the abstract as in any sense singular to himself. It is found in the natural sciences: positively, as in the experiments of Réaumur and Nollet; negatively, as in the scepticism of Buffon's vast edifice, which all the great scientists seem to have felt. It is found, too, in literature, where the discovery of English and German works makes it apparent that universal rules are dubious, that, as Diderot said, it is the happy influence of manners, habit, and climate which produces the great books. There is even doubt whether beauty is, after all, an absolute; and Diderot's article "Beau" in the *Encyclopaedia* is nothing so much as an indictment of Boileau and the classical spirit. The same may be said of educational practice. In this, the most obstinate of conservative strongholds, it is permissible to argue that *Émile* conquered its generation. When the Jesuits were expelled from France in 1762 the change in educational method which occurred in their transferred schools amounted to a revolution. Latin, doubtless, retained its pre-eminence, but at long last French became the usual vehicle for instruction, and the natural sciences won a place in the curriculum. Education begins to be conceived as essentially a guide to practical life. Nor must we forget the similar movement in the economic field. The work of Quesnay, of Mercier de la Rivière, of Dupont de Nemours, seems rigorously deductive enough. But we must set it in the context of agricultural experiments like those of Mirabeau *père*, of the innumerable studies of observation to be found in the *Éphémérides* and the proceedings of agricultural societies, of solid factual studies, like those of Forbonnais upon the history of French finance. The men who influenced the age were, for the most part, not merely men of the study. Montesquieu was judge as well as jurist; Turgot was a great Intendant as well as a defeated Minister; Helvétius was not only a farmer-general, but a great landlord deeply loved for his careful administration of his estate; few writers have shown more admirable qualities as man of business than Voltaire; and even Mably was secretary to the Minister for Foreign Affairs. Even those without such practical knowledge, Diderot, Rousseau, Condorcet, mingled with these men and shared their hopes and fears. When they wrote they were not spinning their webs from idle dreams, but building upon a knowledge of the reality about them.

That, I conceive, can be proved from the books themselves. It is obvious enough in Montesquieu and Voltaire; indeed, the impatience of the latter with all system-making in politics is notorious. It is clear from the chapters in which Holbach demonstrates that there cannot be an ideal form of government. Mably is abstract and rationalist enough; but even he insists that we must take account, in all our systems, of the passions and the ignorance of men. Condorcet may put on record his desire for a cosmopolitan society in which the law is made by an Areopagus of philosophers; but Condorcet is as ardent as any for experiment, observation, the recognition that we must square our desires with the facts. He is even doubtful whether the citizen without property is entitled to the rights of man. It would not be difficult to paint a Diderot whose political speculations shatter the foundations of all existing systems. But there is the realist Diderot of the *Encyclopaedia*, whose programme is simply the rejection of divine right, the limitation of privilege, the grant of a constitution, the recognition of civil liberty. Democracy, he thinks, is suitable only to small States, and he will not approve "the chimera of absolute equality." Rousseau is often cited upon the other side; and, in a sense, the *Contrat social* is the supreme proof of Taine's generalization. But alongside the Rousseau of the *Contrat social* we must put the Rousseau careful for Genevese tradition in the *Lettre à d'Alembert*, the Rousseau, conservative, realist, even timid, of the *Lettre à M. Buttafoco* and of the *Considérations sur le gouvernement de Pologne*, the Rousseau, finally, of the *Lettres écrites de la montagne*, who will have no traffic with his supporters who dream of a revolution in Geneva. Whatever the men of 1789 learned from their precursors, they could not have failed to find there an insistence upon the need for social discipline, a care for the difficulties of adapting principles to practice, which are notable and outstanding. Upon sober examination the abstract reason of the age turns out not to have been so very abstract after all.

V

Exactly as the rationalism of the eighteenth century was merely the logical development of the Cartesianism of its predecessor, so also its romantic aspect is easily discoverable in the preceding age. Reasonableness in religion may have been the dominant *credo* of Bossuet and Bourdaloue; but the mysticism of St. Francis of Sales, and the Quietist controversy, in which Fénelon was the protagonist, show clearly enough that other influences were at work. This effort to build a religion from the revelations of the heart rather than from the intimations of mind joins hands with the effort of those whom La Bruyère called "les esprits forts" to make pleasure a criterion of action which challenges the competence of reason to be the sole judge of the conduct a man should pursue. By the end of the century there has developed what may, perhaps, be termed a morality of sentiment hardly less important than the morality of reason. Its roots are extraordinarily complex. It is already fairly clear in Molière and La Fontaine. It is insistent in Saint-Évremond. Its thesis seems to be that life must be justified as it is, without the undue submission of its content to a body of rules imposed from without. To want passionately is to want rightly; to feel deeply is to feel truly. Long before Rousseau gave to romanticism its letters of credit it had become an integral part of the mind of the age.

Yet what it essentially became Rousseau made it, and it is in the terms of his attitude that we must consider its claims. For in his hands it became not merely a vague sense of the inadequacy of reason, but a very definite philosophy aimed to contest the supremacy of rationalism; as he himself said, "one must kill the other." With him, as always, the challenge is a product of the most intimate experience. He had wished to be a philosopher, but life had taught him that the promptings of his heart were superior to the logic of his mind. He found truth not in the discussions of the *salon*, but in those lonely wanderings round Montmorency, where, in the silent voice of nature, he seemed to be at one with its eternal principles. It is, therefore, to the inner revelation of conscience that he pins his trust. Reason, he concludes, can build nothing. It leads only to hopeless cynicism, as in Wolmar, and its foundations are a deceitful pride. But the heart leads us to God, and God, by the divine instinct of conscience, to virtue. We know therefrom, and, what is better, we feel, that there are rules of life which go deeper and remain truer than anything the logic of the philosophers can establish. The rules our conscience gives us satisfy our yearning for a harmonious existence. They cannot be demonstrated. But they make Julie live a life of virtue. They are true because their results are satisfactory.

I do not need to explain that this romantic outlook provoked an antagonism as passionate as any the orthodox religion had encountered. The pamphlets of Voltaire, the pastoral letter of the Archbishop of Paris, the famous persecution of Rousseau by the authorities at Geneva—these are merely incidents in a campaign of which the fury knew no bounds. What Rousseau was preaching was a Calvinism without dogma, a justification by a faith taught by incommunicable voices. It was an onslaught on reason and authority which went to the root of their claims. For it discovered the individual in society as the centre upon which all social action turns. Social rules, however established, were to submit themselves to a test of sentiment, which, in the end, became the sovereign judge of action. To the Church, not less than to the philosophers, this seemed the coronation of anarchy. To the one he opposed a religion of inner conscience which annihilated the validity of its official tradition; to the other a claim of the heart which began by denial of the right of reason to its empire. And from the rapid hold he obtained upon the mind of the generation it is clear that the revolution he wrought was more than due. The Voltairean method had exhausted its original potency; the criticisms of Moreau and Barruel, which now read to us so tediously, would not have had their success had it been otherwise. Rousseau came to affirm in an age where negation seemed to have triumphed, where, yet, its triumph had already brought a certain weariness of the spirit. There comes an immense revival of the belief in Providence and the simple virtues, a recreation of a Christianity of which the Savoyard Vicar is the noble embodiment. Bernardin de Saint-Pierre, Sébastien Mercier, even semi-philosophers like Marmontel, are only instances of the degree to which the new religion of the individual heart, the insistence on the truths of inner enthusiasm, established their dominion.

I do not mean, of course, to assert that Rousseau incarnated in himself the new creed. There are aspects of it with which he had no connection; Edward Young and Goethe, for instance, contributed to romantic sensibility elements to which Rousseau was entirely a stranger. There are sources which deepen its influence—the drama, for example, of Nivelle de la Chaussée in France and Lillo in England, with which he had no concern. And once the Romantic movement had entered its kingdom it became more various by far than its chief sponsors would have approved, or even deemed possible. In politics, assuredly, it begets traditions so different that it becomes an infinitely difficult task to trace them to their common source. Burke, for instance, is outstanding among the critics of Rousseau; yet there is nothing more fundamental in Burke than the sense in which he was Rousseau's disciple. Romanticism becomes a politics of the unconscious, an acceptance of tradition as the mastering influence in men's lives, which links it, through philosophic idealism, with the tactic of historic conservatism. But this is, relatively, a late development, dating essentially from Hegel, though it is already implicit in Rousseau himself. What is immediately important, in the social field, is its revolutionary side. There, not less certainly, it begat an amazing progeny. Babeuf, Fourier, and Lamennais in France, Shelley and Godwin in England, Marx, through Hegel, in Germany, are only instances of the impress that it made. We have to try, in some sort, to probe the principles out of which this revolutionary element emerged.

Their main source in Rousseau is, I think, obvious enough. You cannot exalt the dictates of the heart without insisting, at the same time, upon the dogma of equality in every field of social action. For if what my conscience dictates is the supreme arbiter of what I ought to do, no other can be rightfully the master of my person. Law, then, is justified not by its source, nor by what it contains, but by my judgment of it, by the degree, that is, to which it embodies my own sense of the things law ought to do. Romanticism, in this aspect, is obviously unfavourable to authority. It calls upon the latter to justify itself by proving the conformity of its ideals with those of the mass of men. Romanticism, that is to say, is democratic. It asks for the rule of the majority, the right, that is, of the consciences of the multitude to prevail. And here, of course, it is of supreme importance not only that Rousseau himself was of the people, but that, also, perhaps first among the great men of letters, he proudly defended the class from which he sprang. His own pathological sensitiveness makes it impossible for him to accept the hierarchical structure of the society he sought to conquer. To live according to nature becomes, for him, to make an end of those refinements of civilization which seemed, as he urged, to invite luxury, aristocracy, control, on the one side, and poverty and submission upon the other. Alongside the life of the *salon* or of Ferney he puts the life of the Hermitage or Les Charmettes as the life to which man has been called by nature. But that is a life within the power, as he believes, of the average man. It is not attainable within the confines of the society about him. If it is to be achieved there must be a revolution in the spirit of man, of which the *Contrat social* traces the basic programme. Establish, he seems to say, social institutions in which there are equal rights available to all and the goodness inherent in the hearts of men will reassert itself. It is even worth noting that what may be called the primitive elements in the *Contrat social*, the civil religion and the device of the legislator, are not without significance in this context. They are recognizable, I venture to believe, as the supreme source of that attitude to dictatorship which is an integral part of revolutionary romanticism. Once the ideas it maintained had become conscious of their power, it was inevitable that they should seek the means of direct translation into terms of social structure. They are a doctrine armed, a religion; and, like all militant creeds, they demand an army for their imposition.

One other remark must be made in this context. How central is the influence of Rousseau in this movement it is not necessary to insist. But it is important to bear in mind that with Rousseau it has a special character. It is not for nothing that he was a son of Calvinist Geneva, and I do not think we do injustice to his essential ideas if we call him the parent of Puritan romanticism. For he did not argue, as did others about him, that the rights of sentiment are unlimited. He did not conceive that there was an antinomy between the teaching of the heart and the principles of nature. The passion he exalts is always the passion for virtue, the zeal for duty, the enthusiasm for simplicity. It would even be true to say that the inner voice to which he listened taught him less the duty of revolt than the lesson of infinite resignation. It insists that he must restore the moral foundations of his epoch, revivify its religion, and purify its manners. No one who reads the innumerable letters of his correspondents can doubt that for them he was more than anything else a father-confessor whose principles had the force of a categorical imperative; and this is true whether the writer is prince in one country or humble student in another. There is, of course, something in Rousseau other than the preceptor of simplicity, even of asceticism. But that essential Protestantism in his work is the point of departure from which not the least part of his influence takes its origin. For himself, perhaps, it was more important than any other, and, because for himself, it is a reason for resignation; it is one of the reasons why the

THE AGE OF REASON 41

accusation that he was a protagonist of anarchy left him at once so embittered and so confounded.

VI

What both the philosophers and the romantics gradually built up may fairly be termed a religion of service to one's fellow-men. Their conception of the State is of an organization which owes itself to the well-being of its fellow-citizens; that is why Diderot, Holbach, Turgot, Condorcet, are insistent that the good legislator is, in Mably's phrase, above all a moralist. That is why, also, they are so anxious to maintain that social organization is founded upon an instinct of altruism. The sympathy which Adam Smith made the basis of his theory of the moral sentiments is, for them, at the basis of society. We cannot, they consistently maintain, be happy if others are unhappy; we are driven by an inner energy to share in their joys and sorrows. It is this outlook which makes humanitarian effort, what, after the Abbé de Saint-Pierre, the age liked to call *œuvres de bienfaisance*, so characteristic of the period. When Rousseau makes the Wolmars devote themselves to their dependents upon their estate they are pursuing an *œuvre de bienfaisance*. When the Abbé Baudeau outlines a scheme for the relief of the poor; when the Intendant Morfantaine crowns each year at Salency the best and most hard-working of the poor girls in the neighbourhood; when, at Canon, there is celebrated the "fête des bonnes gens"; when a forgotten economist can depict himself as "l'ami de ceux qui n'ont rien"; when the *Mercure de France* and the anti-philosophic *Année Littéraire* can have a section in which to canonize humanitarian effort, it is because the "sensitive heart" is responsive to a wider sense of social obligation. For whereas in the seventeenth century such effort as this would have been cast largely in a religious mould, in the eighteenth it has an aspect, hardly less important than the religious, which is purely secular in outlook.

We must not, however, imagine that the mentality I have been seeking to recapture was either widespread or established without opposition. We must not forget that the century of rationalists like Voltaire and Diderot is also the century of Mesmer and Cagliostro. We must not forget, either, that for every *salon* and provincial academy where the philosophic spirit raised its head there were a dozen where it would have seemed either insolent or blasphemous to take it at its own assumption. Hundreds of petty *seigneurs* and unnumbered lawyers and men of business remained to the end enfolded in their traditional life, as faithful as ever they were to Church and king. We are, in fact, liable to misjudge the proportions of the success won by the philosophers if we keep our eyes solely upon the fall of the *ancien régime*. If there are free-thinking nobles like d'Argenson, there are also religious like the Duc de Croy. If there are houses, like that of Holbach, in which the Church is the infamous, there are also those, like that of Necker, frequented, let us remember, by the philosophers themselves, in which religious institutions were held in profound respect. Abundant contemporary evidence testifies to provincial places where either men had never heard of the philosophers or had heard of them only to detest them. The Parlement of Paris might struggle against the despotic changes of Maupeou; but, for Voltaire, it is hardly less an engine of obscurantism than the Church itself.

And almost down to the very eve of the Revolution, certainly to the Edict, which recognizes the legality of Protestantism, the alliance between throne and altar continues, without shocking the mind of the generation. Indeed, it might be said without exaggeration that the alliance is intensified once it has been discovered that the philosophers are a party with principles which threaten

THE AGE OF REASON

the existing order. The edicts which forbid the printing of dangerous books are multiplied. The punishment of the humble booksellers who secretly traffic in forbidden literature grows stronger. In 1768 a woman was sentenced to imprisonment for life for selling Holbach's *Christianisme dévoilé*. Toussaint had to go into exile for his book on *Les Mœurs*. Montesquieu did not put his name on the title-page of his masterpiece. Helvétius, who did, was not only compelled to make a humiliating retraction, but was afraid to publish its sequel in his own lifetime. Buffon was driven to admit that the Sorbonne knew more than he of natural history. Voltaire was driven to a thousand expedients, some of them, at least, barely honourable, to conceal his authorship of his ablest polemical tracts. Few lampoons of the age were more successful than Moreau's attack upon the philosophers; and their loathing of Fréron is evidence enough that they were not entirely happy in the presence of his criticism. To the end of the *régime* the threat of imprisonment hung like a shadow on those who were unduly bold.

Yet it can hardly be doubted that, despite the counter-currents of traditional opinion, the new ideas made their way steadily. The protection of the Pompadour, the capture of the Academy, the apotheosis of Voltaire, the performance of the *Mariage de Figaro*, are all of them incidents of which it is impossible to escape the significance. Barbier may detest the revival of a Frondeur spirit in the multitude; but he cannot deny its power. D'Argenson may express contempt for the effort of *gens de rien* like Voltaire and Diderot to form opinion; but the whole ethos of his mind is the half-conscious recognition that they are, in fact, forming it. The Sorbonne may condemn *Bélisaire*, but its censure merely provokes a ribald amusement. The decline in the number of communicants, as at Saint-Sulpice, the growth of freemasonry and illuminism—though it is fatally easy to exaggerate their importance—the increase in the number of newspapers, the growth of provincial academies, all testify to a change in the public temper. The Academy of Amiens actually made Rousseau the subject of its prize for eloquence; and at that Toulouse where Calas had been condemned it was discussed whether the name of Bayle should serve a similar purpose. When one turns over the innumerable and forgotten pamphlets of the last half-century of the *ancien régime* the influential names, the ideas that have given stimulus and conviction, are almost always those of the philosophers. Punishment would have been discussed even if Beccaria and Voltaire had not written a line; the revision of judicial procedure, public education, the place of commerce in the State, these are themes which do not require the philosophers for their discussion. But they would hardly have been discussed either as widely or intensely had not the philosophers directed the mind of the age. Anyone who reads the details of Mme Roland's youth, the transition in her outlook from a traditional religion to an ardent rationalism, will note with interest how it is effected by the books which we ourselves read as the proof that a new age is about to be born. When a religiously minded man like Bergasse, whose books are evidence of the depth of his conviction, can feel it his duty to go on pilgrimage to Rousseau and can admire Voltaire without outrage to his conscience, we can hardly doubt the impress upon it of the rationalist attitude. Foreign travellers have a similar tale to tell; and when we learn of the degree to which the officers are influenced by the philosophic spirit its reality does not seem to need discussion.

A new spirit does not mean a revolutionary spirit. It is, of course, tempting to make it so, and Taine, very notably, succumbed to the temptation. When Barbier writes, in 1760, that there is "une grande fermentation dans les esprits au sujet de gouvernement" it is of economic misery due,

THE AGE OF REASON 45

mainly, to iniquitous taxation of which he is thinking. When d'Argenson predicts a revolution the phrase probably means little more than an expression of disappointed ambition. There is anger, there are local disorders, there is intense impatience, a decline in the vigour of the monarchical spirit, a widespread disbelief in aristocratic privilege. But what is demanded is reform, and it is still not untrue in 1789 to say that it was to the monarch that the nation looked for reform. Certainly it would be difficult to find an outstanding intelligence of the age who deliberately prepared, or consciously welcomed, catastrophe except Meslier; and his remarkable book was, on its political side, not only unknown to his generation, but was essentially a *cri de cœur* rather than a considered philosophy. No one knew better than Turgot the need for reform; but Turgot never seriously deviated from the principle of monarchical control. When Mlle de Lézardière wrote those eight notable volumes on French constitutionalism which made her the Mary Bateson of her time it was to the king that her father presented them as their obvious destination. It is, I think, true that the nation expected a constitution, that it was done with political and economic subjection, that it ardently favoured judicial reform. That there was a genuine undercurrent of revolutionary sentiment before 1789 can be seen in placards and songs which express a quite real demand for the overthrow of established authority. But neither the placards nor the songs were an organized effort; and where the philosophers mention them it is to condemn and not to approve. The revolutionary sentiment before the *débâcle* meant as much, or as little, as the Communist Party in England to-day. Of itself it had no power to move the masses; and in itself there is no evidence that it commanded widespread allegiance. Events, indeed, might well quicken into a new life and give it wider significance. But it would not, even then, find response from the philosophers.

They remained, to the end, quite definitely reformist in outlook. As late even as June 1789 Morellet could not conceal from a friend that the Third Estate had become "un peu outré dans ses vues et dans ses principes."

Yet the philosophers had done their task. They had discredited a whole system of ideas and institutions which no longer served the national advantage. They had made the principles of civil liberty and constitutional self-government the grand commonplaces of the time. We cannot, indeed, look to them for the causes of the Revolution; its roots, above all, lie deep in economic soil. Incurable financial mismanagement, an impossible system of taxation, bad harvests, violent fluctuations in the cost of living, a reckless pursuit of costly military adventure, these were the main agents of catastrophe. The *ancien régime* committed suicide; it was unable to cope with the consequences of its own ineptitude. It could not maintain its institutions in the face of its complete inability to pay its way. It was compelled, accordingly, to call the middle classes into counsel, and to accept their demands as the means of rehabilitation.

But it found that, in the process of time, the middle classes had become actuated by ideas incompatible with the traditional system of France. They had solid grievances to remedy. They had grown into a new self-respect and a new consciousness of power. Above all, perhaps, they had been the partners of the American Revolution. They had seen Franklin fêted in the *salons* of Paris. They were told to admire the adventure of Lafayette. After some hesitation they came to believe that American ideas were the natural expression of a rational philosophy. "The American cause seemed to be our own," wrote a contemporary observer, "and we were proud of their victories." After the peace which recognized American independence there was an obvious increase in the demand for reform. The very title of the pamphlets, the articles in the newspapers, the popularity of Lafayette, the intense unpopularity of all effort at new taxation, all go to show that it could no longer be withstood. Ever since the time of Louis XIV the ancient bond between monarch and people had been broken. It was necessary to find a new basis for authority; and when the States-General was at long last summoned it took the right, which belongs to every people, to assume control over its own destiny.

II

DIDEROT

I

IT was said by Comte that Denis Diderot was the greatest genius of the eighteenth century, and by Goethe that a failure to appreciate him was the sure mark of a Philistine. Every age, indeed, is too complex to be embodied in a single figure; and the eighteenth century in France was both more and less than all that Diderot implied. Yet it is not untrue to say that he summarized supremely certain fundamental aspects of its spirit. Its infinite curiosity, its passion for omniscience, something of its endless talent for the making of systems, its faith in the destiny of man, its desire to end the needless infliction of pain, its confidence in the power of science to conquer the realm of nature, its happy certitude in the ability of man to overcome the need for the supernatural—all these are of its essence; and all of these are more certainly a part of Diderot than of any other thinker of the time. Compared to him, the hard clarity of Voltaire's mind partakes of the superficial; and even Rousseau seems only the most eloquent of mystic reactionaries. He is the leader of a mighty army in search of conquests which still elude our hopes. He is the high priest of a church none the less ecclesiastical because it marched to do battle with the self-styled armies of the Lord.

To appreciate what he was, we must remember when he did his work. The France of 1750 offered little prospect of good to ardent and inventive minds. Politically and economically bankrupt, it still disposed of a social system which made of birth the supreme test of personal merit. Religiously stagnant and theologically obscurantist, it was so morally degenerate that, as Voltaire said, vice had ceased to pay to virtue even the homage of hypocrisy. Its social life was built upon a theory of aristocratic privilege which surrendered to patronage the rights of intelligence; and to think fearlessly was still to court the risks of prison and exile. Not even the elegant minuet of the *salon* can obscure the price which humble men and women paid that their betters might enjoy ease and leisure. If there was Madame Geoffrin, there was the Chevalier de la Barre; if there was the brilliant tragi-comedy of Madame du Deffand, there was also the grim fate of Calas and his kindred. Wherever we turn in the eighteenth century, its brilliance, before the advent of the philosophers, is obscured by the ghastly shadows of the cost it involved. The *ancien régime* deprived men of half their humanity that a fragment of their kind might know something of the beauty of life.

In the thirty years before 1789 a revolution was effected in the mind and temper of the French people, the quality of which compares, for its intensity, with that of the Renaissance two hundred years before. New prospects opened before mankind. New hopes were kindled, new discoveries were made. The chains which fetter the human spirit lost something of their power to imprison and to impede. The hopes, perhaps, were hardly realized; the discoveries contained, in fact, less prospect than their makers had dared to dream. Yet no one can study the French literature of the last thirty years of the eighteenth century without the sense that real progress had been made. A blow was struck at obscurantist despotism, both in politics and religion, from which it has never recovered. The right of the common man to be master of his own fate was declared with an emphasis which no longer brooks permanent denial. The privilege of reason to follow its discoveries whithersoever thay may lead, the splendour of unlimited speculation for its own sake, these were laid down with a conviction that has left their opponents ever since upon the defensive. There is something of the exhilaration of spring in those thirty years. Mankind seems to have renewed its youth; after the dead inertia of winter it has once again the freshness of a new promise of growth.

II

In that revolution Diderot is a primary figure. Born in 1713 of prosperous working-class parents, he was, like so many distinguished radicals of his generation, a pupil of the Jesuits; and they were not without hope that their brilliant scholar would become an ornament of their order. But neither the Church nor the Law, to which his father apprenticed him, had any attractions for Diderot. Once he had tasted the charms of Paris life, its endless talk, its feverish exhilaration, its sense that one hovers perpetually upon the verge of great discovery, nothing that involved routine could hold him. For nearly twenty years he was a dweller in the upper reaches of Grub Street, different only from a thousand other natives of that dreary waste by his infinite resourcefulness and his inability to keep an enemy. Like a thousand others also, he married and repented of his bargain; like many another, he worked stoutly for the woman to whom he was unsuited and adored the daughter of the marriage. He had one mistress whose futility was equalled only by her folly, and another of whom little can be said save that his letters to her are perhaps the most valuable source of our knowledge of his character and ideas. We can see him in these early years doing any hack job that offered, from sermons for the Jesuit missionaries to the Portuguese colonies to a clever adaptation of Shaftesbury's essays. He seems to have torn the heart out of every book he read and never to have forgotten its substance. There was no limit to his interests. Philosophy, art, chemistry, anatomy, medicine, physics, literature, the drama, he had read about them all, made practical researches into most, could write about all

DIDEROT

of them well, and about some of them profoundly. We have glimpses of a man upon whom police and clergy kept a watchful eye, of suppers with Rousseau and Condillac, of a man glad to do service to any poor devil of an author, always working and always talking: the kind of man who is a legend to the Fleet Street of his generation, and forgotten within a week of his death.

And, indeed, had Diderot died in 1750 he would have remained practically unknown save as a superior hack of promise who lived as the publishers' slave. By then he had written two or three interesting philosophical tracts and a volume of clever stories. What made him the leader of a movement was the offer to edit an encyclopaedia upon the basis of an English work by one Chambers. He accepted the task, and for twenty years he made its portly folios the artillery of one of the greatest armies that have ever served the cause of freedom. It is, indeed, impossible to overestimate the qualities Diderot displayed as editor. Courage, patience, resolution, devotion, these he showed as they have rarely been shown. He braved the thunders of the Church, the threats of the State, desertion even by such friends as D'Alembert and Voltaire, the treachery of his publishers.

The enterprise converted him into an eminent man who was at the head and front of the European movement for intellectual enlightenment. Without ever being wealthy he became comfortable. He could write for his own pleasure, and cultivate his friends. He could go out to the Baron d'Holbach's, and at those famous dinners pour out that endless stream of ardent discourse which made Marmontel rightly say that no one knew Diderot who had met him merely in his writings. Men like Grimm and Voltaire, Helvétius and Montesquieu gave him their respect and friendship. He was courted by Frederic of Prussia and that Empress Catherine who so nobly esteemed the free play of intellect in all countries save her own. If he was seen rarely in the *salons*, whose elaborate etiquette embarrassed him, he was always, as Madame Necker's letters show, an honoured guest there. He tested the life about him to the full. He met everyone and examined everything. Save Rousseau, he never lost a friend; and he met no one of whom he did not become the friend. He had the power to be interested in all that is a part of human experience, and the genius to adapt himself to the Empress Catherine in her palace in St. Petersburg as well as to the workman who explained to him the machinery in some factory he was visiting. The man of books saw life around him about as completely as it has ever been given to man to see it. No one met him without attraction, and no one who was attracted but was influenced. He did not, indeed, like Voltaire, become the uncrowned king of the mind of his generation; nor did he, like Rousseau, give birth to a movement of European significance. But when he died, in 1784, it could be truly said of him that he was at the centre of every effort in his age which sought the betterment of its quality; that, if he did not plan the battle, it could not have been so fruitfully won if he had been absent when the essential decisions were made.

III

Diderot is one of the few seminal figures in the history of thought who never gave birth to a masterpiece and was incapable of building a system. To understand him we must grasp first the significance of the *Encyclopaedia*, and the richness of the hints he threw out upon almost every aspect of philosophy. He was not a great philosopher, but he made his impact there. He was not a great critic, but he has influenced both the novel and the theatre as well as the theory of art. Though he did no original work in theological criticism, the Church rightly regarded him as, after Voltaire, the most important of its enemies. His political ideas are for the most part the best commonplaces of his time; but they are notable for the eloquent clarity with which they are stated and a certain plebeian note in their substance which reveals that, with him and, more notably, with Rousseau, the Third Estate was at last beginning to emphasize its claims. There is hardly a whole work of Diderot's which is still worth reproduction in its entirety; yet so powerful was the range and force of his mind that one could make an anthology from his writings as outstanding in quality and insight as any in the history of the modern mind.

There had been encyclopaedias before that of Diderot's, notably the remarkable volumes in which Bayle foreshadowed the coming of the Enlightenment. There has been none, before or since, to which the same importance attaches as to his. It is not merely that there are valuable articles in its volumes, those of Quesnay, for example, which mark an epoch in economics, or of Turgot, which are decisive in the history of philology. It is not even that no one had ever previously thought of producing a work which should literally cover the whole range of human knowledge as it was then known. It is much more the temper in which the work is written to which its importance is due, together with a realization of reaches of human effort the social impact of which had escaped all previous inquiries. The *Encyclopaedia* is a manifesto of a party struggling to free itself from the trammels of a despotic State and an obscurantist Church. It is a claim for the unlimited right of free inquiry, and insistence that reason, not faith, intelligence and not dogma, are the tests by which truth is established. It has, of course, its faults. There are inaccuracies and to spare; there are compromises with truth that the censorship may be evaded; there are wholesale thefts from other and second-rate works. But no man can read its pages without a new sense of the dignity of the mind or a new ardour for the establishment of its rights. What it garnered was the outcome of that speculative revolution which in majestic progress from Descartes to Newton had replaced hypothesis by observation and conceived of the universe as capable of rational explanation without supernatural intervention. It transfers the centre of intellectual interest from the forces we cannot apprehend to those within our control. It makes knowledge the outcome not of mystic insight but of verified experience, not of dogmatic command but of consistent inquiry. The *Encyclopaedia* registers the triumph of the scientific spirit over its religious rival; and it was Diderot who dominated the organ of victory.

Not less important is the social spirit which pervades the *Encyclopaedia*. Here the novelty of temper is greater than may appear upon the surface. It is the first popular exposition of the Baconian thesis that the increase of scientific knowledge is the measure of man's power over his environment; the sense of science as an agent that must be left unfettered because of its capacity to increase the happiness of mankind. Notable throughout is the reformer's mood, the constant insistence that man must not only seek to assuage but act to prevent misery. There is the emphasis on this life as that with which men are concerned, the refusal to make eternity the keynote of effort. It is also striking that Diderot should have given such detailed and exact attention to the state of the industrial arts; here he was a genuine innovator who glimpsed the significance not only of the application of science to industry but also of the social value of the part played by productive effort in human good. Throughout also Diderot seeks the reform of an antiquated legal system; he has advanced, and even modern, views on economic organization; he attacks privilege and inequality with all the passion of 1789. The treatment of government is always upon the assumption that, in his own words, "the lot of the workingman is the end a good Government must keep in view; for if he is miserable, the nation is miserable." There is nothing left of feudalism after the devastating analysis to which, in a score of articles, it is submitted. The price which society has to pay for a rich and privileged sacerdotalism is as clear before the reader as the impossibility of the good life where the conscience is fettered. And the duty of the State to develop the education of its citizens may almost be termed the impalpable atmosphere in which the whole work is clothed.

It is improbable that any save the professional student now turns over the pages of these mountainous volumes; scholarship has not stood still in two hundred years. But the *Encyclopaedia* may claim without presumption to have established the liberal and critical spirit as part of the permanent inheritance of mankind. The thin flame which the Renaissance kindled, at which men like Rabelais, Montaigne, and Bayle had warmed their hands, became with Diderot a mighty furnace which consumed a dead forest through which men had been unable to plough their way. Its assumptions are all-important for ourselves, not least because its opponents accepted its publication as a challenge and failed to meet its power. The reality of progress, the self-sufficiency of the world about us, the inexpugnable claims of scientific method and, with them, the necessity of tolerance, the duty of men to bow before the demands of reason, disinterested inquiry as the only true source of happiness, with the corollary that wars of conquest are invariably a setback to mankind, the impossibility of accepting religious dogmas as the measure of truth—these are its fundamental assumptions. They are, for the most part, commonplaces to ourselves.

It is worth insisting that they are only commonplaces because Diderot, and others about him, were prepared to risk their liberty for their diffusion. He organized a great army to do battle for the right of intelligence to the profit of its victories. He gathered about him every man in his generation whose achievement we respect. It is not fanciful to compare the fellowship of the Encyclopaedists to an army upon the march; and to the general who directed its strategy belongs the credit for the victory.

IV

Had Diderot done no more than bring the *Encyclopaedia* to completion he would have an assured place in history. But it is, in fact, only a small part of his labours. In the evolution of philosophy he played an important part in three ways. Beginning as a deist in the English mode of the eighteenth century, he was rapidly converted, largely by his interest in physiological discovery, to an atheistic materialism which, whatever its defects, is a current of decisive importance in the great stream of metaphysics. Here, indeed, he is not an originator; both La Mettrie and D'Holbach played a more important part than he. But what he was striving to do was to extend the meaning of Newtonian physics into a system of all-embracing laws which should resume not less the animate than the inanimate universe. His attempt, with all its vigour and ingenuity, must be held to have failed very largely because it lacks a comprehensive theory of knowledge. But it was a challenge to alternative systems of inestimable value; and its search for a bridge between science and philosophy may be held, without injustice, to be the starting-point for all who seek a rational explanation of life.

Nor is this all. Diderot, with Rousseau, must be held to be one of the outstanding figures in the eighteenth-century effort to vindicate the right of human nature to respect. His considered rejection, for example, of Christian asceticism is built upon the insistence that a denial of the right of impulse to satisfaction disfigures the nature of man. He searched for principles of conduct which should at once satisfy the ultimate factors of our constitution and the limitations upon their expression which experience indicates as necessary. He refused to admit that an ethic can be true which starts, as Christianity starts, by assuming that man is in a state of sin. Much of this work is a brilliant exposition only of what was in the mental climate of his generation. Its value, as in the famous *Letter on the Blind*, lies less in what he said than in the way in which he related his positions to the orthodox positions of his day. He may claim, indeed, without injustice to have been the first French thinker who plainly understood the relativity of knowledge to our methods of perception, who was able, accordingly, to attack at its base the absolutism of his opponents and thereby to shatter the claim of Catholic dogma to contain an exhaustive theory of the universe. De Maistre saw the importance of Diderot's effort when he endeavoured to rehabilitate Catholicism after the Revolution by an attack upon the principle of relativity. But the work had been thoroughly done; and the essential result of Diderot's analysis was to show that a philosophy built upon science can make no terms with dogmatic theology.

One final point in this contest may be made. As early as 1754, in the *Interpretation of Nature*, and, a little later, in *D'Alembert's Dream*, Diderot had clearly seen that the inherent principle of biology was evolution. The root of this insight in him is the dominant one of explaining the operations of nature without the aid of supernatural hypotheses. His acceptance of the idea of evolution was not a chance glimpse of a great principle, but the considered adoption of what seemed to him the only possible way of explaining the relationship between the simple and the complex in nature in such fashion as to bring all its parts within the embrace of a single comprehensive law. It is the sense of matter as self-sufficient, the view of it as shaped at each step by the demands of environment. For him there must either be evolution or an acceptance of final causes, and the latter he rejects as inconsistent with the whole of scientific experience. Forty years before Lamarck, nearly a hundred years before the *Origin of Species*, Diderot had, by deliberate intellectual effort, found the one explanation of nature which makes possible the grasp of her complexities. That, assuredly, is not the least striking of his achievements.

Of Diderot the literary artist there is less to be said. None of his novels is a great achievement; one, at least, of them reminds us that if he was the contemporary of Montesquieu and Rousseau, he was also the contemporary of Crébillon *jeune* and the Abbé de Voisenon. Both as a novelist and a playwright he lacks the art of creating persons who live and the power to write dialogue which has psychological relation to the people who speak it. Yet, even here, there are noteworthy things. *The Nun* is a brilliant psychological study of what convent life does to a soul unsuited to it. There are pages of *Jacques the Fatalist* where the verve is not less remarkable than the capacity to create the illusion that we are sharing in the experiences of a living being. He can narrate amusingly, invent brilliantly, write dialogue in which things are said which are unforgettable. But, alike in his novels and his plays, what he shows is less the necessity of invention than its facility. He writes them because he can, not because he must. They are rather an episodic aspect of his range than an essential index to its character. *The Nun* apart, they are read more because they illuminate the mind of Diderot than because they are a permanent part of literature.

But Diderot the critic is a different matter. Here, with much wrong-headedness, he is of the first order in everything that he touches. Not seldom, indeed, the evolution of ideas has moved in a direction other than he desired; but almost always the influence of what he had to say is traceable in the debate. And this is the more remarkable since most of his critical work was, for himself, simply the by-product of an interest which could not brook denial. He cared passionately for the theatre; and anyone who reads his *Paradox upon the Player's Art* will see why Hazlitt could judge that no man has ever written better upon the actor's function. He hated the stilted and artificial conventions to which the classical drama of the Augustan age had reduced the theatre of his time. Deeply influenced by the turn Lillo had given to the English theatre of the eighteenth century, he desired a drama which should be in direct contact with nature itself, which should also deliberately seek to make itself a propagandist vehicle of great ideas. No one now accepts the methods by which he urged the attainment of this end; but it is not an exaggeration to claim that he would have recognized in Ibsen and Mr. Shaw the realization of his ambition. He was, moreover, an agency of great influence both in the development of literary naturalism and in making known to French readers the significance of English literature. His appreciation of Shakespeare stands out in remarkable contrast to the contempt of Voltaire; and his passionate eulogies of Richardson gave the latter his letters of credit in France and were no small factor in revolutionizing both the form and substance of the French novel. Diderot, indeed, could without injustice claim that he was the first writer of eminence to see literature as a genuine social function whose object is the criticism of life. For him the man of letters is the priest of great ideas who fails if he does not elevate the mind of his generation. He has nothing but indignation for the view of literature which makes it merely a source of rest from effort. Its quality is a measure of civilization; and it is untrue to its purpose unless it keeps that high ambition steadily in view.

Yet his service to aesthetic theory was perhaps even more important. Here, indeed, it would be sufficient to quote the remark of Lessing that, without Diderot's contribution, he could not have written the *Laokoön*, or to remember Goethe's exclamation that in this realm he had the quality which calls out the highest powers in others. Diderot's services to aesthetic theory are twofold. On the one hand, by the famous descriptions of the Paris *salons* which he contributed to Grimm's literary correspondence he may be said to have founded the literary criticism of painting; and even Carlyle could display what can only be called delight at the vivacity and brilliance of his descriptions. No man has ever equalled his power to make the reader see for himself what the painter has sought to achieve, or has surpassed his skill in making description a vehicle for the conveyance of principle. He would not, indeed, be Diderot if his *Salons* did not abound in glorious irrelevancies; but the moral reflections, the eloquent apostrophes, the inviting asides are all part of the charm one feels in contact with a first-rate mind taking its ease.

And, as in the theatre, so in the world of art, Diderot is the insistent advocate of the rights of nature. Realizing as he did that the painter is an expression of his social environment, he was the determined foe of academic convention. It is true, as Goethe said, that he did not sufficiently realize that art has its own rules which are not those of nature; but the man who said that he would give ten Watteaus for a single Teniers had got to the root of the matter. He saw, as few people have ever seen, the just relations of the arts to one another; why, for example, the poet should eschew detail which a painter can fearlessly represent. He saw, as no one before Lessing had seen, the meaning of the limits set upon the artist by the nature of his material; just as he was the first to grasp the social function which the artist performs. As always with Diderot, his aesthetic work, as he himself realized, is a superb torso rather than a finished effort, a rich series of hints scattered over the widest field. But where he so generously sowed, Lessing and Goethe reaped the harvest. That in itself is a sufficient title to our gratitude.

Diderot's versatility is such that any picture of its achievement would end only at the boundaries of knowledge. If his political ideas have no claim to originality, at least they are well expressed and representative of all that is most creative in the liberalism of his time. The writings on education are more important. They show not only his sense that the problem was urgent; there is a modernity of temper about them—especially in his preference for modern languages and science over the scholastic discipline of his day—which is noteworthy. On physiology, on the principles of legislation, on music and mathematics there are vast collections of memoranda, never, indeed, of the first importance, but rarely without point and distinction. All of it is conceived in what may be termed the Baconian spirit; in all of it there is that restless and exciting sense that, to use his own words, "we touch the moment of a great revolution in the sciences." All of it also is inspired by a large humanism before which it is difficult not to feel humble. They are fragments from a great man's workshop, the outpourings of a mind so full of ideas, so rich in invention, that he can hardly stay to hold the pen which should express the thoughts which crowd one another. And even in their incompleteness, they make one understand why the range of Diderot's inventiveness fertilized so much of what was best in the creation of his age.

V

Yet in the end the greatness of Diderot lies not in what he did but in what he was. No one can meet him, either in his own letters or in those of his friends, without acquiring affection for him. The great, hearty appetite of the man, his endless good nature, his splendid indiscretions, his devotion to his work, his courage, his insatiable curiosity—these are qualities which bind one to him inescapably. No doubt he lacked delicacy of mind and manner; no doubt also, as Rousseau was to experience, his imperatives in counsel were as excessive as that ebullience in talk which, as Voltaire drily said, made him incapable of dialogue. He always was a little over-emphatic, usually over-sanguine, often a little vulgar. He yielded too easily to instinct and rarely showed the capacity for second thoughts. He was passionately interested in himself, over-prone to interfere in the affairs of others, lacking in tact, turning to coarseness with the characteristic facility of his time. But, as Voltaire truly saw, there was something of Socrates in him. He brought to whatever he touched a genuinely daemonic quality. He really put truth in the first place; no man has ever had a profounder passion for knowledge. In whatever he touched he had to dig down to the foundations. He stimulated other men to their best effort in a degree that not half a dozen men have equalled during the history of thought. He found happiness everywhere in simple things and simple people; he respected in an ultimate way the dignity of his fellowmen. He hated deeply everything that made for cruelty, obscurantism, and ignorance. He helped the advance of knowledge to the full limit of his powers.

And wherever we meet him he exerts over us his irresistible fascination. This mass of energy, half-workman, half-intellectual, was at home in any company where the mind could work freely. It may be at the Baron d'Holbach's when the servants have withdrawn and, over the coffee, men dispute the existence of a first cause. Diderot proclaims his ardent atheism in a voice like the call of a trumpet, and the Abbé Galiani interjects one of those sparkling epigrams which were the delight of Paris. Then Diderot's great eyes flash fire, and with minatory forefinger he pours forth a stream of ideas before the sheer brilliance of which his listeners sit in silent rapture, until the guttural voice of the Baron interrupts to point out that the sun is already peeping through the curtains. We see him, in his beloved dressing-gown, on the fifth floor of the little apartment in the Rue Taranne; there comes to him a down-at-heel journalist who hopes to obtain money by suppressing a libellous attack he has written against Diderot. But the latter has a better way. He urges the journalist to publish it with a dedication to a nobleman who hates the Encyclopaedists and will pay for patronage. After his manuscript has been corrected, the young man leaves but hesitates on the threshold; he is nervous of writing a suitable dedication. So the good Diderot sets to work and produces a suitable inscription which sends the journalist off rejoicing. Can one help loving such a man?

And he is the same everywhere. Whether he is in the factory, learning from workmen the secret of their technique; or in the *salon* of Madame Necker at the famous dinner where it was decided to erect the statue to Voltaire; or, again, in the antechamber of the Empress Catherine where his argument is so vigorous that the need for emphasis compels him to strike Her Majesty ardently upon the knee; or in his native town of Langres where he and his father, so different in hopes and ideas, yet weep with joy at meeting; or, finally, in his prison at Vincennes where he is visited by Rousseau and develops, in a perspiration of excitement, the theme of the latter's *First Discourse*—here, as always, he is Denis Diderot, hungry for life, ardent only for ideas, incapable of malice, full of generosity, the embodiment of Bacon's saying that "the nobler a soul is, the more objects of compassion it hath." Those who met him for the first time must have felt the same kind of enchantment that Socrates exercised over the youth of Athens.

Diderot is one of the first men of letters in French history who were proud of the class to which they belonged and did not seek to exalt themselves above it. He had, to the end, the qualities of the *petite bourgeoisie* from which he sprang. He advanced by the great virtue of endless hard work. He never sought to separate himself from his original *milieu*. He judged social systems, to the end, by their effect upon the lives of the class of which he was a part. In large outline, indeed, the whole atmosphere of his philosophy is shaped by the needs of that class; and the victory of his principles meant nothing so much as the certainty of response to their needs.

The suppression of privilege, toleration, civil liberty, representative government, the application of science to practical life, freedom of contract, a patriotism which put peace before war, and low taxation before monarchical splendour, who can fail to see in the social doctrines that he preached the wants he must have heard discussed half-fearfully many a night in his father's house at Langres! Because, of course, he was an extraordinary man, he saw them with exceptional clarity; and because, again, he had extraordinary knowledge, he stated them with exceptional power. But just as Rousseau made articulate the unconscious hopes of the proletariat, so Diderot expressed and justified the half-articulate ambitions of the little property owner, always hard-working, never rich, and, as every good Frenchman must be, a little inclined to play the Frondeur. They came to power after the Revolution; and Diderot might claim with justice that he played his full part in laying the philosophic foundations of the middle-class industrial state.

There are books, the *Institute* of Calvin, the *War and Peace* of Grotius, the *Social Contract*, the *Wealth of Nations* which rank in the record as great historical acts; Diderot cannot claim to have written any such book. There are men who by sheer beauty of style have kept the attention of posterity long after their ideas are obsolete and their causes forgotten; Diderot's style had none of this magic. There are others, again, Descartes, Newton, Darwin, whose ideas are so seminal that they seem to remake the foundations of knowledge; no such discovery is connected with Diderot's name. He lives partly because, on its own showing, he fertilizes the whole mind of his generation by his remarkable fecundity, partly because his rich and vigorous personality made him an outstanding leader in one of the half-dozen essential battles for freedom of which the modern historian must take account.

He had few of the material rewards which come to successful men. The Academy honoured him only by excluding him from election; and he was never until his last years without the need to work hard for his daily bread. But he moved always amid the play of great ideas and he kept, without compulsion, the affection of his friends. Above all, he had the joy he accounted so high, of fighting consciously in what Heine called the "Liberation War of Humanity." What haunted him in life was the longing for that immortality which comes with the recognition by a later generation that one of the forerunners has served it well. "Even if this were but the sweetness of a lovely dream," he wrote to a friend, ". . . it lasts as long as my life and holds me in perpetual intoxication." But for Diderot that yearning has not been vain; the praise of posterity, "that lovely concert" he strained in life to hear, in death still echoes its music.

III

THE SOCIALIST TRADITION IN THE
FRENCH REVOLUTION

I

ALL Revolutions centre around the relation of political authority to the distribution of economic power; for, as Madison long ago insisted, the only durable source of faction is property. Anyone who examines the history of French social thought in the eighteenth century realizes at once that its very essence is a changing conception of the place of property in the State. In a sense, indeed, the main work of the Revolution was simply the translation of that change from the realm of ideas into the realm of fact. From Fénelon to the outbreak of catastrophe there were few thinkers who were not impressed by two things: the indefensible character of privilege, upon the one hand, and the immense disparity between rich and poor, with its attendant and inherent dangers, upon the other. Not merely the systematic philosopher and the professional pamphleteer, but the novelist, the playwright, even the theologian, find it difficult to defend the actual distribution of economic satisfactions. They seek consistently for a remedy for this condition. They are widely aware that its continuance must inevitably mean the disruption of the State.

The consequence is the presence, throughout the eighteenth century, of an attitude to the rights of property which is profoundly critical in character. In a sense, it is even a socialist attitude, in that, not seldom, it is altogether sceptical of the *régime* in which individuals possess the means of production. But I hesitate to call it definitely socialist for three reasons. In the first place, it is a purely moral criticism; outside the Abbé Meslier there is no writer of repute who seriously considered the means of redressing the balance of social good. It is, moreover, hardly aware of the relationship of an economic system to the power of the State; even in Rousseau, this defect is noteworthy. It is, in the third place, diagnostic rather than reconstructive; Mably and Morelly, Diderot and Rousseau, Sébastien Mercier and Rétif de la Bretonne are all in an essential sense socialist; but for all of them the mechanism of transition to an egalitarian order is always by the conversion of men's hearts to better ways.

Rousseau and those I have named are, properly speaking, merely the extreme wing of a wider attack upon the notion that property can be a legal or moral right independently of the social consequences it involves. Attack upon the contemporary social order proceeded from the most various angles. Some of it came from a bitter revival of the sixteenth-century discussion of usury. Some of it was the outcome of that curious controversy over luxury of which Mandeville's too famous *Fable of the Bees* is, through Voltaire's *Mondain*, the real parent. Not a little can be traced to that grim defence of Conservatism by Linguet, in which he anticipated so many of the theses of Karl Marx for almost antithetic ends. Part of it can be traced to the makers of imaginary Utopias where private property is unknown, or, related to this, to the reports of travellers of places like America, in which a Utopia of fact has come to birth. The creation, moreover, with Quesnay and the Physiocrats, of an economic philosophy upon something like scientific foundations was important. Administrative chaos, economic confusion, religious bankruptcy, all contributed their lesson to the torrent of criticism. When the States-General was summoned, the mind of France had been widely prepared for large economic innovation.

II

I understand by Socialism the deliberate intervention of the State in the process of production and distribution in order to secure an access to their benefits upon a consistently wider scale. From this angle, it is clear that no theories are entitled to be regarded as socialist which are not distinguished by at least two features. They must admit the right, and duty, of the State to subordinate individual claim to social need, not as an occasional incident of its operation but as a permanent characteristic of its nature; and they must, in the second place, seek the deliberate and continuous reconstruction of social institutions to the end of satisfying social demand upon the largest possible scale. It is in terms of these definitions that I propose to approach the difficult and complex years from 1789 until the failure of Babeuf, in 1796. I shall consider, first, how far a genuine socialism is discoverable in the cahiers and pamphlets which accompanied the summons of the States-General. Then I shall analyse the period until the advent of the Directory to see what of Socialism there is in both the literature and the legislation of the time. I shall seek, above all, to show that the effort of Babeuf and his fellow-conspirators was the one genuine socialist movement in this epoch with a definite programme and an equally definite method of moving towards its realization. Finally, I shall seek to estimate what of significance there was in the socialist experience of this epoch and how far it has given any specific character to the socialist movement of a later time.

Let me begin with a simple affirmation. Neither in the cahiers nor in the pamphlets which resulted from the summons of the States-General is there any important or general socialist doctrine. That does not mean that it was non-existent; for, as Chassin has pointed out,[1] what we are

---

[1] *Génie de la Révolution* (1862), i. 334.

dealing with here are the wants, at the most, of six million Frenchmen, and the needs of at least as many may have gone unexpressed. But when this type of literature is examined neither the grievance expressed nor the claims put forward are socialistic in any serious sense. There is bitterness, indignation, protest; but if these are the inevitable accompaniment of socialism, they are not of its inner substance. Taken as a whole, what do the cahiers demand? Fiscal reform, especially in the matter of equal taxation, judicial reform, administrative reorganization. There is profound hostility to feudal rights. There is some criticism, not seldom urgent, of ecclesiastical property. There are occasional attacks on the greed of rich landowners. There is protest against the erosion, by aristocratic usurpation, of communal property. There is some demand for taxation in terms of ability to pay, a tendency to desire limitation of testamentary disposition. A careful search will discover scattered demands for the restriction of inheritance, occasional schemes for public granaries, the fixation of prices, the limitation of usury. No one, I think, can honestly go through the cahiers upon any considerable scale without the impression that they represent not a theory of social reconstruction but the keen expression of practical experience. They are what the solid merchant, the comfortable peasant, the thinking and social-minded *curé*, would naturally set down as the lessons of the *ancien régime*.

Nor is this all. Throughout the cahiers there is a universal sense of the respect that is due to private property. The main complaint, indeed, against the past age is that the capriciousness of its system prevented the wholesale expression of that respect. "The object of the laws," said the Third Estate of Paris, "is to secure liberty and property." That note is omnipresent. Men seem unable sufficiently to emphasize the fact that property is sacred and inviolable, that no one can be deprived of property save for public purposes and with adequate compensation. District after district emphasizes the right of all property to respect, save where its possession entails abuse; and, to my own knowledge invariably, abuse only means the justly hated privileges of feudalism. There is no objection that I can discover to unequal property. There is dislike of luxury, a demand for special treatment of the needy and the orphan, a sense that the proletariat should be lightly taxed or even free from all imposts. One discovers suspicion of the financier, a claim that the poor man should be able as surely to live by his labour as the rich to be secure in his property. There is the well-known plea from Paris for the creation of public workshops. There are various suggestions for the more humane treatment of the poor and the mendicant, and the improvement of hospitals. No one can look at demands like these and call them specifically socialist unless socialism is a mere synonym for humanitarianism. For the most part, they are the obvious dictates of common sense; and they are far less radical in temper than much of the social criticism of the eighteenth-century *philosophes*. Those who drew up the cahiers of 1789 were entitled, like Clive, to be astounded at their own moderation.

The pamphlets of 1789 cannot, I think, be put upon quite the same footing as the cahiers; they announce certain principles which it is difficult not to describe as socialistic. But before I summarize some of their ideas I would venture upon a word of caution. It is necessary, I suggest, to distinguish between declamatory denunciation and definite plan. It is easy to find the first; it is difficult to find the second. We are no more entitled to call denunciations of inequality and misery socialistic than we can justifiably term Southey and Carlyle and Ruskin socialists because they were indignant with the horrors of factory civilization. There are innumerable pamphlets which insist that the right to property is a social creation, which society can abolish as it pleases; there are literally hundreds which establish the principle of the right to work as inherent in the structure of the State. But most of the first group insist equally on the immense danger of disturbing established expectation; and few, if any, of the second group leave the right as more than an empty declaration to which no concrete scheme is annexed. Even Marat, in his *Project of a Declaration of the Rights of Man*, while he begins by insisting that the law must prevent excessive inequality of fortunes, and that a wise redistribution of wealth is necessary, ends by saying that the best thing that could have happened to France would have been for Montesquieu or Rousseau to have drawn up its constitution. But no one would have expected either to construct a socialist State.

We must, then, distinguish between declamation and positive plan. Of the first there is abundance and to spare. There is passionate denunciation of those rich who "eat in a single meal what would suffice for ten families in a year"[1]; there is the warning that unless the people is fed and the right to work assured, insurrection is certain and justified. There is the bitter plea of men like Devérité that the worker is like an army mule who breaks beneath his burden; but the only remedy of which he can think is the suppression of machinery as the root-cause of low wages. One writer, Dufourny de Villiers, points out with acuteness that the real poor are not represented in the States-General, and argues that they are entitled to compensation for the property they lack; but his cure for the evil he vividly depicts is merely "a new moral foundation for a better-organized society." Another writer, after a piteous description of the sufferings of the workers, is satisfied to urge that public workshops are the logical consequence of the right to work; yet he tells us nothing of how they are to be organized or what they are to produce.

We are nearer to socialistic ideas with Gosselin,[2] whose

[1] *La Colère du Père Duchêne.*
[2] *Réflexions d'un Citoyen* (1787); on Gosselin, see A. Lichtenberger, *Le Socialisme Utopique* (1898), p. 132.

views are very akin to the agrarian socialists of the Cromwellian Revolution. After a trenchant exposure of the injustice of the existing social order, and an emphatic note that conditions would justify such a socialization of land as existed in Sparta, he agrees that the remedy would be worse than the disease. But he urges the desirability of four measures in order to obtain equality. Uncultivated land should be given to the poor, as the Romans formerly settled soldiers on the soil. The clerical demesne should similarly be used, the recipients paying a small rent to the State and its former possessors; and each year the Government is to set aside a sum for buying up the estates of large landowners and distributing them in the same way. Finally, he suggests a progressive capital tax on private fortunes to extinguish the public debt. In a brief time, he thinks, these measures will establish a "happy equality," if the land so divided is declared indivisible and inalienable. The worst features of luxury will disappear; and the engagement of a vast majority of citizens in agricultural pursuits will make commercial fortunes of insignificant importance. Sufficiency will mean an instructed people. Population will increase; and emigrants will take this new model to happier climes. Gosselin has no doubt of the practicability of his scheme, and he offers it to the king with a simple faith of which no one can deny the charm.

Two other schemes of socialistic tendency deserve a word. Seven years before the Revolution Rétif de la Bretonne, in his *Andrographe*, had published a complete Utopia upon a rigorously communist foundation. But, like Plato with the *Republic*, he had realized that it was meat too strong for human digestion; only complete agreement could achieve it, and for this it was hopeless to look. In 1789, therefore, he published a revised version of his plan in the *Thesmographe*, which might, he thought, be capable of realization. While private property is to remain, its possession is to be limited and difficult. Prices are to be controlled by local authorities and failure to cultivate as Government prescribes is to result in forfeiture. At the back of the whole scheme is the principle that private property is a mere legal convention made by the State, and subject at any moment to its power of eminent domain.

Rétif's ideas, clearly, have no more than a paper value, for he had no vision at all of how to bring them into being. If Babeuf's Utopia is not less visionary, it is more important, because it shows how constant was his devotion to the principle of equality. The son of a former tutor of Joseph II, after a grim and starved childhood he became an agent to a nobleman, and acquired there that practical acquaintance with feudal privileges which played so large a part in the shaping of his life. In 1787 he began to correspond with the secretary of a provincial academy, to whom he put questions which make evident his preoccupation with equality as the key to social good. It is to inequality that he traces the pride of the rich and the excessive humility of the poor; and he urges upon his friend that it is the cause of all the evils of our social condition. The correspondence reveals him as a man profoundly influenced by Rousseau, passionate, and bitterly antagonized by the inequalities of the *ancien régime*.

In 1789, in conjunction with the mathematician Audiffred, he submitted his views to the National Assembly in something like coherent form. The *Cadastre perpétuel* does not yet envisage the need for revolution, but something at least of the spirit which, seven years later, was to take him to the scaffold is already there. No man, he says, who has sufficiency can be regarded as other than an exploiter if he seeks to obtain more than this. Men are by nature and right equal, and it is the business of the law to keep them so. Yet, as the law works, the very opposite is the case. The rich are the masters of society. The poor grow in numbers and their wages continually decrease. This is an impossible position. The land, "the common mother of us all," must be divided equally so that each citizen has an assured patrimony which he cannot lose. Instruction must become general lest the wise oppress the ignorant. Unless this is done, the rich will cut the throats of the poor; and the latter are entitled to property, as a ward may, when he attains his majority, recover his rights from a defaulting trustee. But the first step on the road to reform is education. Equality in knowledge is the keystone of the arch of social reconstruction.

Babeuf's plans, doubtless, did not reach more than a handful; the Assembly was occupied with more immediate questions. What I wish only to emphasize again is the presence of a socialist ideal among the pamphlets of 1789, while noting that it is extraordinarily rare. Where there is an attack on the existing order, that is not socialism. It is nothing more than the final deposit of that sense of waste and injustice common, for instance, to all reformers of the age of Louis XIV. There is a good deal of Utopia-making, not a little violent paradox. But what there is of revolutionary destructiveness comes from sources which, as with Mably or Rousseau or Montesquieu, we cannot call genuinely socialist in the sense in which I have defined that term. Men feel vaguely that a new age has come, big with possibilities. There is a spirit of optimism abroad. But reform, and not revolution, is the essential tenor of men's minds in the first hours of the new dawn. What socialism there is is small in volume and insignificant in expression. It needed the realization that civil equality and the reform of politics did not mean an end of suffering before a widespread change was possible.

III

By the early months of 1790 the ultimate character of the Revolution had been fixed. Feudal privileges had been abolished; the monarchy had been put in fetters; the Church had been overthrown. The Declaration of Rights contemplated a middle-class liberal State. If it was an exaggeration to say with Loustalot, that "everything tends to substitute an aristocracy of wealth for an aristocracy of birth," the proletariat had not seriously benefited by the changes made. Phrases had been used in the Assembly, even by men so conservative as Mirabeau and Malouet, which implied a belief in equality, but the social legislation of the next few years showed clearly that they meant nothing. Already property was afraid; and the warnings of Edmund Burke had fallen upon ready ears. By 1790 the main preoccupation of the leaders was to stabilize and make effective the results of the first enthusiasm of the Revolution, while assuaging the sufferings of the common people. Few were able to see the effect of foreign war upon social policy, or to guess, as Burke so marvellously foresaw, that a successful general would emerge as the dictator of the State.

Anyone who analyses the literature and the legislation from 1790 until the fall of Robespierre has, above all, to be careful not to discover too much in what he reads. He must remember that he is dealing with a peasantry which was hungry for the indisputable possession of the land, and angrily suspicious of its former masters; where, therefore, he sees peasant riots he must not assume that they are grounded in socialist principle. He must remember, too, that in these years bad harvests were general, and unemployment widespread. The problem of feeding the towns and finding work for the proletariat was a difficult one, intensified by the timidity of the rich and their anxiety to put a term to experiment in social policy. Every revolutionary leader treads the edge of an abyss; and in the effort to satisfy a hungry and indignant constituency he uses phrases and threatens measures which are meant as denunciation rather than argument. The period, therefore, is full of declamation which has a socialist character. Rights are asserted, pledges are made, which suggest much more than they in fact mean.

The political figures of the time cannot, in my judgment, be called in any case socialist; nor were they dealing with a public which, in any serious degree, expected socialist measures. What rather we are confronted with is a people full of misery to whom attacks upon the wealthy as the source of their misfortune might be expected to appeal. The Girondins, certainly, had no sort of sympathy with socialism; Danton, as I think, had no sort of social principles at all, and Brissot, differently from his earlier views, was the defender of the small proprietor rather than anything else. There is socialism among the Jacobins, as there is also among the *enragés*; but I regard it less as a body of consistent and systematic principle than as a series of extraordinary ideas meant to cope with an extraordinary situation. It is not until the Conspiracy of Babeuf that we meet with socialism in a serious and effective form. In a word, until Babeuf there are socialist ideas, but there is no socialism.

So to regard the character of this period is, I know, to run counter to a famous thesis of Taine. But I think his view is built upon a complete misunderstanding of the evidence. Undoubtedly there were attacks on property, hatred of the rich, revolutionary risings, a good deal of pillage and confiscation. But these are the inevitable accompaniments of any revolution where there is a hungry mob, a bewildered government, foreign and civil war. Socialism, as I have said, is a theory of social reconstruction and a methodology; it is not an angry crowd attacking a speculator or burning the documents of its ancient servitude. It is not even a Jacobin deputy preaching the agrarian law, or Marat insisting that, in time of crisis, each commune can take measures without limit to help its poor; nor is it Robespierre arguing that excess of property is only justifiable where there is general sufficiency. Broadly speaking, the temper we confront is one which insists that, in a period of scarcity, the rich man who does not put his surplus at the disposal of the community is an enemy of society. It is a hatred of greed, of speculation, a suspicion that great wealth implies counter-revolutionary sentiment, that we meet almost everywhere. But this attitude cannot be described as socialism any more than its Russian analogue means an acceptance of the principles of Lenin.

The true approach lies, I believe, along quite different lines. The Revolution inherited from the *philosophes* a rigorous criticism of property as an absolute right, an ethical defence of communism, and a profound sense that, because the privileges of aristocracy are indefensible, the State might be made to serve the people creatively. These notions had to be applied in a time of crisis, without time to think either of their philosophic significance or their administrative possibility. They had to be applied when there was civil war at the centre of national life, and foreign war at its circumference. Measures which are suitable to an extremity are rarely the expression of a considered philosophy. They represent merely the response to immediate exigency, and their very authors are, often enough, the first to deny that they have permanent significance. Certainly there could not have been any widespread socialism in a revolution which began in enthusiastic loyalty to Louis XVI and ended in a loyalty at least superficially enthusiastic to Napoleon. Girondins who anathematized the agrarian law, Jacobins who hissed the leading *enragés* out of the Paris clubs, do not sound like the apostles of socialist principle. Effectively, I should argue, there would have been no socialism at all if the economic condition had not been acute. What men were prepared for was the abrogation of what was restrictive in the *ancien régime*. Crisis drove many to heroic words and measures which they felt to be suited to an heroic time; but when the situation, after the death of Robespierre, became administratively manageable, what emerges as stable is the bourgeois liberalism which drove Babeuf to revolt. And the very memory of how property had been in danger was so driven into men's minds that, after 1796, it was in process of becoming the very absolute against which the eighteenth century had made its magistral protest.

This, at least, is how I read the evidence. It does not exclude the fact that there were socialist ideas; it does deny that there were either many to put them forward or a wide public conscious of their meaning and anxious for their application. It is worth while to consider the expression of those ideas in some little detail, and to note their affiliations with orthodox Jacobinism on the one hand and the Conspiracy of 1796 upon the other. I begin by noting one general point: all parties in the State agreed upon the undesirability of excessive differences of fortune. Mirabeau, Malouet, Vergniaud, Brissot, Condorcet all spoke in this sense; and there was a fairly widespread tendency to approve the simple life and a progressive income-tax. These are, of course, views which the eloquence of Rousseau had made almost platitudes. They were things which everyone had to say who did not wish to be regarded as reactionary. The first person worth mention who went at all far in a socialist direction was the Abbé Fauchet, who founded in 1790 a discussion circle, and was himself, later, a Girondin deputy. His views undoubtedly influenced a wide circle, though the fact that, as Camille Desmoulins tells us, he could be hissed in his own section for support of the agrarian law shows that men were rather interested in than moved to accept his ideas.

His views are obviously founded upon Rousseau. His journal—the *Bouche de Fer*—preaches the original goodness of man, and his right to an equal share of the earth. When he enters the State he surrenders all his rights which are then possessed by Government for the general welfare. By this is meant that all men have something, and no man has too much. What must be prevented is extreme poverty and wealth and, above all, social parasitism. He recommends the establishment of national factories, the limitation of land-holding, a rigorous control of inheritance, and such a regulation of the marriage laws as would prevent the union of large family fortunes. It is noteworthy that even these moderate views were bitterly attacked, not only by Conservatives like Mallet du Pan, but also by Radicals like Desmoulins. Fauchet himself continually softened whatever of rigour they may possess; and he put them forward rather as an ultimate than as an immediate programme. He was less a doctrinal socialist than a Christian mystic imbued with the importance of equality by his desire for a change in the heart of mankind.

Among the Girondins, I think, there was no one who was socialist in any real sense of the term. Brissot was an exponent of Jeffersonian democracy, Condorcet was a Radical much of the school of Thomas Paine, Sébastien Mercier shares the horror which, as he tells us, Rousseau would have felt at the ideas of Babeuf; and Rétif abandoned his *Thesmographe*, being content, amid wild denunciation of Jacobins and *sansculottes*, to insist that equality in land or in incomes below fifty thousand francs is both impossible and criminal. The only important Girondin who shows signs of more radical views is the one-time pastor Rabaut Saint-Étienne; though he may be said less to embrace Socialism than to fringe its boundaries. Equality, he tells us, is the soul of a republic; unequal wealth divides classes and ruins equality in politics. But it cannot be established by force, and the best we can hope for is to reduce inequality by law. How this is to be done he does not tell us in detail. A maximum fortune can be fixed, the State taking the remainder, whether by gift or force, for foundations of public utility or unforeseen State expenditure. National workshops should be created, and inheritance and testamentary disposition should be controlled. But, even more, Rabaut Saint-Étienne would desire the State to encourage those moral habits in the people which are favourable to the atmosphere of equality.

These can hardly be called extreme views; though it is worth pointing out that they, and their like, excited the wildest alarm among conservative thinkers. Equality and an agrarian law seemed to a charitable worker named Lambert "a violation of all the laws of nature." Men like La Harpe exhausted themselves in expressions of horror at the extreme and dangerous attacks upon the foundations of social order. Their very demand to have done with experiment naturally provoked the antithesis of their caution. To have accepted their attitude would have meant simple futility before the grave economic problems—how grave M. Mathiez has recently shown[1]—which confronted the State. The conservatism of the Right did not appeal to the Girondins. But the latter, to whom disorder was hateful, and whose fear of the proletariat was omnipresent, shrank from a policy which seemed to jeopardize the property of the middle classes. They were naturally overthrown by the Jacobins, whose policy of centralization and experiment provided the only hope the masses could see for assuaging their misfortunes. Brissot might join hands with Mallet du Pan and Barruel to accuse them of subverting the foundations of social order; to themselves, and, in general, I think, quite honestly, they merely appeared as men prepared to utilize the authority of the State for the preservation of the Revolution.

I do not mean to imply that there was not a definitely socialist background to Jacobin policy. Certainly there was; though, to understand it, we must remember that its sources are complex. Partly, it was born of immediate necessity, partly of the fact that their leaders, Marat and Robespierre in particular, were deeply read in those earlier thinkers, especially Rousseau and Mably, who had insisted that the right to property is a social concept made by, and limited by, the will of the State. They never had a new theory of a

[1] *Robespierre et la vie chère* (Paris, 1927).

different social order. For the most part they were the *petite bourgeoisie* to whom Montesquieu and Rousseau were a gospel to which they were prepared to sacrifice much. And the sacrifices they were prepared to make were such as the poorer classes welcomed, especially when these saw in hostility to the Jacobins the privileged of the old *régime* and the rich men of the new. What they said and did no more made them deliberately and consciously socialist than did the programme unfolded by Mr. Lloyd George in 1909 make him a member of the Socialist Party. They would attack the rich, but they would not have the agrarian law. They would demand sacrifices—Mr. Chamberlain's doctrine of "ransom"—but they would do nothing to injure the idea of individual property itself. Danton, for example, was merely a democrat who wished that the rich should bear their full share of the common burden, and that men should be recognized to have an equal right to happiness. Marat, as I have noted, was a moderate Liberal in 1789. Experience made him more violent in declamation. But no journalist who merely thinks from one day to the next, especially if he is gambling for his head, has a considered philosophy. If he regarded economic equality as desirable, it was for some distant future he need not discuss. What he was above all concerned to maintain was the sovereign right of the State to take whatever measures it might think fit to prevent disaster. Reasonable wages, prices within the reach of the poor, local control of food supply—these were the things he emphasized day by day in the *Ami du Peuple*. But no one can read his articles without seeing that he is merely inventing remedies for a crisis. He has no thought of permanent principles.

With Robespierre it is different; from his writings and speeches one can, I think, piece together a coherent doctrine which has clearly socialist affinities. Property for him is simply a social institution; it is the citizen's right to enjoy as he will the goods guaranteed to him by the State. The latter can, therefore, limit its rights, punish speculators, and control inheritance. But absolute equality is a chimera impossible of realization in civil society. To preach it is to invite a detestable anarchy. There is an excessive inequality which the State should control. It leads to the domination of the community by a few wealthy men, and their vices contaminate society. The State owes to the poor, the source of moderation and civic virtue, the right to work or maintenance; to procure this for them is a more sacred task than to protect the wealth of the rich. Fixation of prices in their interest is essential, and no punishment is too strong for speculators in food. A severe and progressive income-tax is justified; in an ideal State no one would have more than an income of three thousand livres. All this, clearly enough, is the mind of a man nourished on Rousseau and Mably, the partisan of a simple and equal society, the enemy of the rich whom he feels to stand in the way of its achievement. He speaks the language of bitterness and hate; for, to him, the rich are the enemies of the republic. But if Robespierre's ideal is anything, it is that of the small town radical rather than the socialist. It is the excess of wealth, not property itself, to which he takes objection.

Much the same might be said of Saint-Just, whose *Institutions Républicaines* shows us pretty fully the direction of his mind. A nation of small farmers, general equality, a compulsion upon all to work, a rigorous control of inheritance to the direct line, a national system of education, and the endowment of young married couples, are the chief proposals he makes. The Saint-Just of the Convention is less Utopian and more bitter; but loathing of the rich apart, there is nothing positively extreme in what he has to say. And this is, in general, the temper of his colleagues. The right of the poor to property, the danger of excessive wealth, the duty of the State to confiscate that excess for the general benefit, these are the themes of a thousand speeches. Violent class-war is, of course, widely preached, especially by some of the representatives on mission. Lecomte Saint-Michel's phrase that the rich are "the mortal enemies of the Republic" is typical of innumerable others. Billaud-Varenne calls them "the bane of ordered states"; but it is significant that he should add that property is "unfortunately the necessary foundation of civil society." But when, with them, or such journalists and pamphleteers as Prudhomme, Harmand, Desgrouas, we have exhausted the terminology of vituperation, we come back inevitably to a positive theory on the lines of Robespierre's doctrine. When Boissy d'Anglas, in his exposition of the Constitution of the Year III, said that "un pays gouverné par les propriétaires est dans l'ordre social," he was not far from the Jacobin ideal; the owner must not be rich and all must be owners. That is the distinguishing feature of Jacobin theory.

I would emphasize again the fact that all this is not socialistic innovation, but the inheritance of the criticism of property made by the eighteenth century. Political equality, it had taught, is nothing without economic equality; men like Turgot, Sieyès, and Condorcet had said so incessantly. "Equality in fact," said Condorcet, "is the final aim of social technique, since inequality in riches, inequality of condition, and inequality of education, are the main cause of all evils." And alongside this notion was the full realization that a State composed of the two nations of rich and poor is bound to conflict. "There has never been, nor will there be," says a pamphlet of 1789, "any but two really distinct classes of citizens, the owners of property and those who have none; the first have everything, the second nothing." Jacobinism is simply these ideas applied to a critical period in which danger sharpened the antagonism between classes, and made the idea of equality and simplicity seem a definite measure of public safety. It was neither a theory nor a method of thoroughgoing social transformation. Rather was it a demand that the surplus of the rich be deliberately used by the State for the mitigation of popular suffering.

IV

Before I turn to Babeuf and his conspiracy, it is worth while to spend a little time on one or two of his precursors. It is probable that ideas which may vaguely be termed communist began as early as 1789; for we are told by Baudot that the "acrimony and bitterness" of the Girondins was due to "fear of seeing the ideas of the Communists predominate." The sense continually grew that any society in which men, as Billaud-Varenne said, "existed upon a direct but not mutual dependence upon some other human being," was in fact in a condition of slavery. In 1793 and 1794 there were among the sections, and notably in the Club des Cordeliers, men to whom Jacobin doctrine seemed needlessly conservative. We get hints of secret societies, suggestions of plans like the credit schemes of Proudhon, demands that the profits of banking revert to the State. In men like Jacques Roux, Varlet, Dolivier, Boissel, Lange, there is a clear stream of doctrine looking towards a communist solution of social problems.

Thermidor destroyed whatever hopes and prospects these men may have cherished; after it there came signs of what a police-spy, one hopes ironically, called "a profound and universal peace." But these men had their dreams, and it is worth while to note their substance. For they show how, even in their gravest moments of the Revolution, the incurable optimism of men was still prepared to make all things new. They had no clear idea of how their views could be realized; and I think it probable that they had no sort of sympathy with the methods Babeuf was later to propose. They saw all the fallacies of *laissez-faire*, and their desire was to realize that equality of fact of which I have spoken. We know, alas, too little of most of them; one would give much, for instance, for a detailed biography of Rose Lacombe, who must be very nearly the first woman communist. But what we do know suggests simple-minded and honest men, honoured by the masses for the high character of their ideals.

Among them, perhaps, Jacques Roux is worthy of particular mention. He had been a priest, and was, perhaps, one of those who had been freed by the Revolution from that burning indignation which still lives for us in the bitter pages of the Abbé Meslier. He was always poor, and we have a picture of a lonely figure, whose sole companion was a dog, preaching a simple communism in the working-class quarters of Paris. There is Chalier, of Lyons, a mystic, whom Michelet has noted as an extraordinary man, and Lange, in some sort the precursor of Fourier. Important, too, is Varlet, a Parisian workman, about whom our ignorance is complete, and the *curé* of Mauchamp, Pierre Dolivier, whose book was published for him by his fellow-citizens of the commune of Anvers. All of them are typical of an outlook not without wide support in those days of agony. They desire the limitation of land-holding, forced loans to feed the people, the confiscation of all property due to speculation, national workshops, and the public control of the food-supply. They differ from the Jacobins in that they do not pay regard to the rights of property. They consider the urgency of the position too great for measures of conciliation to be desirable. They see quite definitely in the rich and the comfortable the deliberate enemies of the poor, who will not hesitate to take advantage of public misery for private profit. They are mostly, again differently from the Jacobins, in favour of the agrarian law, though with definite leanings to a national control of its operation. Thermidor left them exasperated, largely because they saw, in the disappearance of Robespierre, the failure of their hope for drastic economic legislation. But they could not go so far as Babeuf, because they definitely respected a democratic system. "Dictatorship," said Roux, "is the annihilation of liberty"; and there is in most of them, especially in Dolivier, a marked trend towards anarchism.

Their ideas, on the whole, are seen most clearly in the pamphlet, published in 1789, by Boissel, a Jacobin of the extreme left who was active throughout the Revolution.[1] Bitterly attacked in the Assembly, it seems to have exercised some influence, especially after 1793, and it is certainly an interesting link between ideas like those of Mably before 1789, and of Babeuf afterwards. It begins with a passionate attack on organized society as the nurse of all evil. It examines, and rejects, property, marriage and religion as the expressions of the worst impulses of men. Property is simply an instrument of oppression, and the root of a discord which the invention of money merely increases. The business of society is to respond to our true instincts, which are naturally good. This can be done if we recognize that God is the only true owner, and that we have the right to nothing save in terms of need. We must reform education, nationalize industry, and train men in the spirit of a collective ownership with a view to the introduction of complete communism. Here, clearly, his trust is in an educational system which will one day make men ready for the new order. By 1793 he was insisting to the Jacobins that the fruits of the earth belong to the poor by natural right and may be taken by force, for property is an usurpation of the inalienable right of man to subsistence. But beyond that vague sense of the duty to use the law, Boissel, like his fellows, has no clear notion of how the change he desires may be definitely effected. With him, as with Dolivier,[2] a society can be reconstructed on the principles of a communism somewhat like that of the Russian *mir* and the right of each man to the

[1] *Le Catéchisme du Genre humain.* [2] *Essai sur la justice primitive.*

whole product of his labour. And much of their outlook is determined by the clear perception that the real result of the Revolution has been to establish the farmer and the merchant in the seat of power. They realize that the aristocrat has been dethroned in the interest of the middle classes. They insist that anything short of communism must mean of necessity the retention of a class-structure in society.

But they do not really know how communism is to be attained. I agree with Kropotkin that an analysis of this early philosophy anticipates much of the principles of 1848, that little of what was elaborated by Fourier and Owen and Proudhon cannot be found in pamphlets and speeches and local decrees of the period. They had an ideal but not a method. The importance of Babeuf and his colleagues lies in the fact that not only did they envisage this ideal with some particularity, but they had quite definite notions of how to seize power for its attainment. It is probable enough that few of the two or three thousand people who seem definitely to have been influenced by the conspiracy knew or shared in their views with any precision; they may have known the battle-cries without thinking through the programme. That is not, I think, particularly important. All revolutions are the act of a minority; they depend for their success on sympathy for their general end rather than for their bill of particulars. Babeuf and his fellows knew how they proposed to proceed; and the strategy they invented has provided ever since the methodology of revolutionary socialism at least in its large outline.

I have already noted that Babeuf was a communist from the outset of the Revolution. I need not here detail his later career. Though his *Système de Dépopulation* shows that, at one time, he was both anti-terrorist and anti-egalitarian, he was one of those who saw in the fall of Robespierre the end of what was beneficent in the Revolution. Always in want, often in prison, rash, enthusiastic, self-confident, single-minded, he was just the man to lead a desperate attempt upon the conquest of power. The Conspiracy seems to have been formed during one of his terms of prison. A few fellow prisoners were initiated into his ideas; the group grew steadily, and became the Society of the Pantheon, which the Government did not fail to watch and proclaim. It had two wings: at the very centre were the real communists, and, closely affiliated, but remote from the heart of the affair, a number of ancient Jacobins to whom the abrogation of Robespierre's constitution was a bitter memory. The scheme was linked together by a secret committee of direction, to which its publications were almost certainly due. Among them were some extraordinary men, Darthe, Sylvain Maréchal, Germain, and Buonarroti, who was to survive them all and to be their historian. They had contacts with some former members of the Convention, with the army and the police, even with the underworld. I need not add that from their early days they were honeycombed with spies, one of whom was, unknown to them, introduced by Buonarroti and Darthe to the very heart of the affair. They never had any real chance of success. Their plans were known, almost from their inception, to the Directory; it needed less honest and zealous men than they to elude the cold-blooded machinations of Barras. Everyone, moreover, was tired of bloodshed and misery; the police reports and the diplomatic correspondence show clearly that the revolutionary spirit was exhausted. The leaders were arrested and tried by a special tribunal. Babeuf and Darthe, after a vain attempt at suicide, were executed; other important conspirators, including Buonarroti, were imprisoned or deported. Those who lived on became the depositaries of a tradition which, after 1830, they found the new generation eager to cherish.

I shall discuss, first, the programme of Babeuf, and then his strategy. Neither is a very easy thing to do, partly because some of the evidence, being produced by spies at the trial, is suspect, and partly because not a little of what we have is clearly not in its final redaction. Yet the literature, checked by the narrative of Buonarroti, and, even more, by the valuable discoveries of Advielle, enables us to see pretty clearly what was involved. And this can, I think, be put in a single sentence. There is no real innovation in doctrine, which is the eighteenth-century tradition, clarified and made precise by the profound experience of seven revolutionary years; there is a definite innovation in method, which opens an epoch of decisive importance in the history of socialism.

Let us start with two significant sentences used by Babeuf in his trial. "My companions and I," he told his judges, "have groaned over the unhappy results of the Revolution . . . it has merely replaced a band of ancient scoundrels by a band of new ones." For the object of society is the realization of the common happiness. That is impossible without the rule of equality, which is the clear implication of natural law. This does not mean the agrarian law, which is not equality at all. All men have a permanent right to a continuous share in the social product. To recognize private property and differences of fortune is to admit theft to the heart of society. Inheritance is unjust, respect for the superiority of talent is dangerous. All work has the same value, and all capacity should be equally rewarded. Communism is the only way by which this can be realized. It means the common ownership of land. It means the socialization of industry and universal and compulsory labour. Education, too, should be equal and common. The theory differs from what has gone before in that earlier thinkers demanded relative equality. The Babouvistes insist that this is more difficult to achieve and to maintain than equality in the full sense of the term. Any society in which less than this exists is built upon civil war and is bound to mean the exploitation of the poor, of, that is, the mass of the community. There can be no justice unless the only recognized differences in the State are those of age and sex. To put the whole wealth of society at the disposition of the people is to assure the maximum of virtue, justice, and happiness. Envy and hate disappear. Each can recognize that his well-being is intimately related to that of his neighbour. To serve society in such an order is to serve oneself. The reign of equality will be the last revolution necessary to the well-being of man.

This body of doctrine was developed in the most diverse and ingenious ways; in the art of literary propaganda the Babouvistes had certainly nothing to learn from their generation. Careful doctrinal analyses, as in the famous *Analyse de la doctrine de Babeuf*, a brilliant short programme, as in the *Manifeste des Égaux*, drawn up by Sylvain Maréchal, songs, poems, newspapers, special literature for the army and the police, placards, memoranda, slogans, invective, all the typical devices of modern publicity are there. It is easy to see how their eloquent denunciation of existing conditions would appeal to the unemployed, for they set out with simplicity the experience through which the working-classes had passed. It is even probable that their emphasis upon the failure of the Revolution, their attacks upon the rich, their hatred of the Directory, their impassioned defence of the honesty and greatness of Robespierre, commanded wide sympathy. The programme, clearly, as Babeuf himself would have recognized, is simply a careful restatement of Rousseau and Mably, of Diderot and Morelly. It is both bolder and more precise than its predecessors. It has none of their faith in the possibility of changing men's hearts in an individualist society. It is much more bitter against the rich, much more insistent that they are "brigands," for whose destruction all patriots must hope. The Babouvistes are more optimistic than their predecessors, in that they think the essential revolution is capable of immediate achievement. But in the general contour of their objective there is nothing essential to distinguish them from a half-score of thinkers in the pre-revolutionary epoch.

That is not, as I have said, the case with their strategy, where there is genuine and important novelty. This can best be analysed in two ways. On the one hand, there are the definite steps they took in the organization of their conspiracy up to the time of their arrest; on the other, there is the theory of what was to be its conduct after they had seized political power. At the head of the affairs was the small Central Committee, with Babeuf at its head. This was the brains of the whole conspiracy. It met in secret, practically every night, always alone, and not seldom changing its headquarters to avoid any possible suspicion. It dealt with day-to-day business, the actual conditions under which the insurrection was to take place, the legislative measures to be taken on the morrow of the insurrection, and the future institutions of the new republic. It was responsible not only for the overt propaganda, but also for stimulating the activities of its local agents, to whom the personnel of the Committee remained unknown. Its individual members had relations with the agents, but rather as themselves officers of liaison than as chiefs. The agents, most of whom were chosen with great care, were of the essence of the plan. Tried revolutionaries, they were the contact between the Central Committee and the masses. They reported on the feeling of the population, its grievances and aspirations. They supplied, therefore, that knowledge upon which the leaders could build successful propaganda and action. Linked with them were local committees in the district of Paris, who made their impress upon the workers, put up placards and distributed leaflets, addressed meetings in the workmen's clubs, talked in cafés and factories, and spread as widely as possible the volume of discontent, the hope that one final effort might make all things new. Women, also, played their part, and it was hoped, particularly, to employ the services of the *demi-monde* to neutralize any hostility in the Army.

To the latter special attention was paid. The leaders had carefully chosen military agents, to each of whom a definite task was allotted. General Fyon was in charge of the Invalides; Germain took care of the police; Massey controlled the detachments at Saint-Denis; Vanneck was given the task of infecting the remaining troops in Paris. Agents were obtained in each barracks to work on the minds of the soldiers; others, sometimes women, frequented their cafés. Sophie Lapierre, whose beauty was well known in Paris, declaimed the proclamations of the Central Committee and sang its songs. The evidence at the trial suggests that no mean success attended these efforts. They were paralleled by similar attention to the police. Information was also obtained about *agents provocateurs* from sympathizers in the force; and in several cases the head of a police section was in close contact with the conspirators.

Through these means every sort of step was taken which might injure the Government and create the expectation of some great impending event. Every rumour likely to injure the Directory was widely spread. Complaints were broadcast, meetings held, sympathizers from the provinces brought to Paris to create the illusion of a national movement, assemblies of street-mobs were organized. The Laws of the 27 and 28 Germinal, by which the Government took power to dissolve all political meetings, show that the importance of the movement was realized. Insubordination among the troops, the punishment of which revealed unrest in the police, is further proof that the danger was real. But the fact that Barras actually negotiated, probably dishonestly, an attempt at an alliance with Germain of the secret committee, shows both that the Directory was alarmed, and that it was, probably throughout, cognisant of the plan. When the Committee, after discussions of military plans, was waiting for the critical moment, the Directory swooped upon them. It was estimated at that time that, the masses apart, the Insurrectionists could count upon 17,000 men, of whom 9,500 were regular troops. These were to march upon the arsenals and the seat of Government, while others were to hold the streets of Paris and repulse all hostile attack. The plan was never put into action, as Barras was the first to strike his blow; but it is, I think, evidence of the hold the conspirators had obtained that some seven hundred men should have marched to Grenelle and sought to excite the troops there to revolt and rescue their leaders. They were only dispersed by military attack and numerous arrests. After that, the conspiracy was at an end.

Clearly enough, as a piece of organization, the plans of the Babouvistes were remarkably conceived. Not less interesting was their conception of the methods to be used in the event of success. Here their views were built upon the theory of class war. Society, for them, was divided into rich and poor, and neither had any interest in common with the other. The rich depended for their position upon their power to keep the poor in subordination; the latter could conquer their rights only by the dethronement of the rich. In a society in which overt civil war was the main feature, it was unthinkable that power could be conquered by the poor, save by violent means, for the rich would never abandon their privileges without fighting for them. This, they felt, was the real lesson of 1789; it was the lesson of 1793; it was the lesson implicit in the experience of Thermidor. It meant that when the political State had been captured, a period of rigorous dictatorship would be necessary as the prelude to communist democracy. Only in this way could the people be withdrawn from influences hostile to equality, and given that unity of will essential to the adoption of republican ideas. "It was evident," wrote Buonarroti thirty years later, "that the inherent necessity of things, even the success itself of our enterprise, meant an interval between the fall of aristocratic power and the final establishment of popular democracy." An assembly was impossible since it left the success achieved to the hazard of a popular vote. The revolution had not been made merely to change the form of administration; its object was to change the nature of society itself. This could not be left to the people who had been trained to habits which ignored the natural order of things. The revolutionary Government must therefore act on behalf of the people. It must, as Buonarroti wrote, "snatch from the natural enemies of equality the means of deceit and fear and division." What was required was "an extraordinary and necessary authority which would restore its liberty to the nation, despite the corruption which was the consequence of its ancient slavery, and, despite the attacks of those enemies, within and without, sworn to its destruction." It is the doctrine of permanent revolution by dictatorship in the name of the proletariat.

To seize power is, therefore, only the first step; it does not end the revolution. Parliamentarism and democracy are impossible because they risk the whole purpose of the insurrection; the people is not yet fit to be entrusted with a power which counter-revolutionaries might seize from them again. "What was necessary," wrote Babeuf, "was men whose doctrines and manners, whose whole life was in full harmony with the spirit of the institutions which they were called to create." Liberty must be denied at the outset lest it be lost for ever. What was to be done was in accord with natural law. It was what the people would itself desire when it came to understand the egalitarian State. The Dictatorship was thus, in effect, the general will of the proletariat. It lost its freedom only the more fully to find it.

The institutions and measures this Dictatorship would create are extraordinarily significant in the light of our recent experience. The Central Committee had at first considered the idea of appointing a single person as dictator; but this idea was rejected in favour of the government of the Committee itself, advised by an assembly composed of one democrat chosen by each of the departments from a list of suitable persons submitted to them. This had, however, to be modified after discussion with their Jacobin allies; and the final form of assembly was to consist of some sixty former members of the Convention and a hundred other democrats nominated by the people from safe candidates. The Committee retained the right to initiate legislation, together with full executive powers. Beneath it there was to be created commissars in each department, with great authority. Their business was to speed the successful revolution. They were to make propaganda for its ideas, create local societies for its completion, deal with counter-revolutionaries, and assist all active democrats in the provinces. Before appointment they were to declare their financial position, and a special tribunal was created to examine their accomplishment of their task. Further, to strengthen the new order, there was to be created a kind of revolutionary academy, a *séminaire normal*, "where citizens from each department would be sent, in a predetermined order, to learn the principles of the new revolution, and to be imbued with the spirit of the reformers." To complete the structure of the Dictatorship, the Babouvistes decided to recreate all local institutions, including the revolutionary commissions, as they existed before the fall of Robespierre in Thermidor.

I cannot even attempt here to analyse in detail the actual measures by which the Central Committee proposed to accomplish its task. But it is, I think, worth while briefly to indicate the principles upon which those measures were based. All healthy persons were to work, and no idle person was to possess political rights. The homeless and the poor were to be housed in the houses of all who had conspired, or might conspire, against the Revolution. The people were to be armed, and all "parasites" were to be disarmed. The Press was to be controlled to prevent the spread of false news or attack. Special taxes were to be levied on all not sympathetic to the new *régime* with a right, at need, of complete confiscation. The old defenders of the Revolution and the unfortunate were to be given the use of new possessions. Anyone who had emigrated or rebelled was to lose his property; and confiscation was also visited upon the negligent farmer, the public servant enriched by the exercise of his office, and any who were judicially condemned. The sale of national property was suspended; and, inheritance being abolished, all private estates, on death, were to revert to the State. Machinery was to be developed, and uncultivated land brought into use; to this end State-shops were to be opened in each commune, and an economic council, representing the different professions, was to aid the local authorities in the provision and organization of work. Education, with the necessary vocational bias, was to be common to all, and so developed that the average man might hope to play his full part in the life of the State. Foreign trade was to be a State-monopoly, while money and wages were abolished for internal purposes. There was to be assistance for the old, and free medical service for the sick; and the treatment of criminals was to be entirely reformed. Whatever its weakness as a practical scheme, it is obvious that Babeuf and his colleagues had arrived at a clear perception of the programme they wished to achieve.

V

The modern theory of social revolution is naturally the outcome of a profounder study of historic conditions than it was open to Babeuf and his colleagues to make. Yet anyone who compares their analysis with the *Communist Manifesto*, on the one hand, or the writings of Lenin and Trotsky upon the other, can hardly doubt the original source of their inspiration. The line of affiliation, indeed, is a direct one; for Buonarroti was the master of that generation whose words and acts were the basis of Marxian strategy. The class-war, the failure of reform, the necessity of dictatorship, the insistence on a social revolution, the ultimate significance of the economic question, the realization that insurrection is an art, the careful preparation of the measure it is to entail, the insistence on the proletariat as the sole revolutionary class, the perception of the importance of education and propaganda, the sense that intellectual theories are born of the methods of economic production, all these the Babouvistes clearly understood. All these, also, became part of the essential socialist tradition of the nineteenth century. "It is nearly forty years since Babeuf died," wrote Charles Nodier, in 1836, "and his party is still living... he recognized truths which no Government has designed to accept, truths which can never die." Of the Socialism of the Revolution, indeed, Babouvisme is the one element destined to permanent influence. Voyer d'Argenson, Teste, Raspail, Louis Blanc, Leroux and Blanqui in France, Belhasse and Potter in Belgium, Bronterre O'Brien in England, have all borne testimony to the part it played in their lives through contact with Buonarroti. Weitling's work in the Canton de Vaud brought him into direct contact with it also; and it is worth remembering the part that the League of the Just played as an instrument of early Marxism. And it is worth remembering also that one of the Communards of 1870 was the grandson of that Clémence who had sat with Babeuf in the Central Committee. It was with reason that Count Albert de Mun should, in 1896, in the Chamber of Deputies, have accused the French socialists of being the descendants of Babeuf. That is, in fact, their real and effective origin.

We must not, indeed, exaggerate their insight into the technique the modern Marxian has developed. They had practically no conception of Socialism as an international force; it needed the impact of the Industrial Revolution to emphasize the limits of nationalism in revolutionary strategy. There was not enough realization of successful revolution as grounded in a set of objective economic conditions, and not merely born of determined organization at a premature moment. There were many of those elements in the theory of Babeuf which, in 1847, Marx stigmatized as "Utopian Socialism"—the belief in an ultimate natural law, the conception of an original endowment of human impulse which was definitely good and merely obscured by evil institutions, something, at least, of the acceptance of insurrection for its own sake, upon the dangers of which Lenin has written so brilliantly. The latter's phrase, indeed, that "Babeuf was a Jacobin who leaned on the working-classes" has a real truth in it; for he never sufficiently perceived the danger of the alliances he was prepared to make for the end he had in view. Nor did he realize at all how much in advance of effective possibility was his programme. A social revolution cannot be successful on the falling tide of a political revolution Babouvisme was doomed to failure before it got under way.

Yet, it must be emphasized, the depth of its insight is remarkable. Anyone who reads its voluminous literature with attention, and compares the habits it postulates with the operations of Bolshevism, cannot help being impressed by the resemblance. Elsewhere I have pointed out[1] that the strength of Communism lies in its effort to effect a complete transvaluation of values in terms of a great ideal passionately cherished. I have pointed out the strength given by faith in that ideal to its adherents, their profound sense of its exclusive truth, their willingness to sacrifice themselves to its principles, their insistence that the end is so great that the means adopted to it are, whatever their cost, justified. The detailed resemblances between the programme of

[1] *Communism* (1927), p. 138 f.

Babeuf and that of the Russian communist are remarkable enough; but even more remarkable is the similarity of ultimate temper which runs through the two movements. There is the same exhilaration of spirit, the same bitterly drawn distinction between friend and foe, the same urgency that all things be made new, the same power relentlessly to dissect the weaknesses of contemporary society, the same capacity for self-confident optimism, the same genius for propaganda and invective. Lenin, so to say, is the Babouvistes writ large; and the architect of the November Revolution was greatly indebted to men who, if they saw less clearly than he, envisaged a civilization upon the same pattern he sought to build.

VI

What results from this analysis? The French Revolution, in a narrow perspective, must, I think, be regarded as primarily individualist in character; the real expression of its effective outcome is the Civil Code, in no sense a socialist document. Its real result was to transfer power from the aristocracy to the peasant and middle classes. The impress made upon them by the socialist tendencies of the period, especially by their extreme translation in the Conspiracy of Babeuf, was to make the idea of private property more sacred, and less susceptible to attack, than it was held to be at any time in the eighteenth century. If it attacked the property of the old *régime*, it consolidated that of the new upon a wider basis; and the era of change and confiscation only made men more eager to suppress the possibility that titles could be called into question. We must not forget that the abolition of feudal rights and corporate privilege was made in the name of the individual; that, where confiscation took place, it was done in the name of public safety and could thus be regarded as essentially a transitory measure. Most of the attacks upon the rights of property which did take place were rather the inevitable accompaniment of civil war than an expression of any wide desire for social transformation. Given political liberty, a constitutional state, and equality before the law, and most men were content to abstain from speculative innovation. A state was created which lay at the service of the hard-working peasant and the active *entrepreneur*. No condition is more favourable to classes whose power is a function of the property they possess.

On a longer view, however, the French Revolution is a capital event in the history of Socialism. It is so, I suggest, for four reasons. Before 1789 there was not, in the modern sense, any social problem. Men asked how the poor were to be relieved, not, as afterwards, what part they were to play in the State. The Revolution began that awakening of a social consciousness in the proletariat of which universal suffrage is merely a partial, and by no means the ultimate, consequence. Every radical party thenceforward has found that it must reckon with the wants, indistinct, indeed, and but half-formulated, of the poor; and every State has discovered that the growth of economic organization sooner or later transforms the incoherent mass of the poor into a movement ultimately capable of organization upon the classic lines of party conflict.

This birth of the social question has a special importance for another reason. Before 1789 socialist ideas were simply moral theories which lived in a vacuum and had no chance of effective realization. After 1789 they were in a different position. Men had seen the deliberate introduction of proposals the purpose of which was to legislate for equality. The fixation of maximum prices, the abolition of feudal privilege, the confiscation of Church property and the possessions of those hostile to the Revolution, the attempts at progressive taxation and the control of inheritance, these, as experiments, have an importance it is impossible to overestimate. Doubtless they usually failed; doubtless, also, they were often suggested without conviction and, more often still, applied without sincerity. This is less significant than the fact that men became accustomed to the perception that the State might be made the tactical instrument of those who possessed its machinery. It is less significant, also, than the fact that the Jacobins, not least their representatives on mission, schooled the masses to the understanding that distinctions of wealth are legislative creations, and that, where crisis demands it, egalitarian innovation may be deliberately attempted.

A third reason is outstanding in the impact it has made upon subsequent history. Before 1789 society was divided into privileged and unprivileged; since 1789 it has been divided into rich and poor. The distinction is a notable one. The pre-revolutionary division was the expression of an age-long tradition rooted in the psychology of habit and custom; its landmarks were as mentally familiar to men as the house into which they were born. To the new division the sanction of tradition was no longer attached. Men could see change before their eyes. They could see that the attainment of riches meant food and shelter, clothing and security; they knew that its absence meant hunger and suffering. They learned not only that law could make and unmake the wealthy; they learned also that these opposed such changes in the law as involved sacrifice upon their part. They grew to think of the division as an antagonism of interest, a necessary hostility which could only be bridged by an attack upon the rights of property. From 1793 the life of the Republic was, until the execution of Babeuf, something not unlike a war against the rich in the interest of the poor. The Jacobins waged it, no doubt, for the preservation of the Republic. The poor who supported them did so, no doubt as well, because they were miserable and hungry, and not because they were socialists. But it was waged, also, with the idea in the background that equality is an ideal, and that the rich are the enemies of equality. The notion permanently remains therefore that great riches are always illegitimate; and, with the class-conscious worker, the more general view that the weaknesses of society are the outcome of class privilege. This feeling bit the more deeply because of wide disappointment with the results of the Revolution. After the fall of Robespierre the sense was widespread that the Revolution which was to benefit the whole community had, in fact, merely aided the *bourgeoisie* to the detriment of the worker. The latter's revolution, it was felt, was still to come; it was inherent in the nature of things. In this sense, as the principles of 1789 begin to impregnate the consequences of the factory system, revolutionary socialism became an inevitable part of nineteenth-century ideology.

The final outcome was the definition, with invincible clarity, of the problem of equality in all its aspects. Can barriers be erected, of any permanent value, against the advent of universal suffrage? Is the existence of a privileged aristocracy compatible, over any considerable period of time, with the achievement of a common good within the State? Can we maintain a society marked by grave economic inequalities unless we can convince the poor that these inequalities are themselves bound up with their own well-being? I shall not venture to rely upon my own diagnosis in dealing with these questions. I am content to point out only some implications they involve. If a people seeks to improve its situation by the alteration of political institutions, and is dissatisfied, either with the result itself, or the slowness with which its benefits accumulate, it is unlikely to remain inactive in the economic sphere. It will ask itself, as Tocqueville suggested, whether the privileges of property are not the main obstacle to equality among men and assert that they are neither necessary nor desirable. Once it asks the question, it seems almost bound to experiment with the possibility of response; and it may well be that a new Napoleon will be demanded to put a term to its enquiries.

To examine these possibilities would take me far beyond the boundaries of the French Revolution. It must suffice here to say that these issues have been raised and that the happiness of mankind depends upon the way in which we seek to meet the grave problems they involve.

IV

THE PROBLEM OF A SECOND CHAMBER[1]

I

IT is sixty years since Bagehot made his "severe but friendly critic" of our English institutions remark that the only cure for an admiration of the House of Lords was to go and look at it. In the period that has passed since he wrote no new grounds of eulogy have appeared; and the large number of attempts at its reform in the last half-century are evidence that a term has been set to its present structure.

It lacks, indeed, some of the merits to which it could once lay claim. Sixty years ago it was a Chamber of the old and great families, the men who, almost by inheritance, were charged with the governance of England. To-day it is a Chamber woefully out of tune with all its traditions. One-quarter of its membership has been added in the last three decades. The average peer has gone down into the city; and a list of the positions occupied there by its members would read like a footnote to the list of securities upon the Stock Exchange. It has shown no signs of renewal of spirit. Its debates are as badly attended as when Lord Chatham sarcastically termed it a "tapestry." It is still overwhelmingly Conservative. It is active, that is to say, only when the Tory Party is out of office. Since its adventures with the Liberal Government of 1909 it can no longer touch Money Bills; and even ordinary legislation it can, under the Parliament Act of 1911, only delay without the power to destroy. But it remains the protective armament of vested interests. It is certain to spring into new life once a Labour majority in the House of Commons seeks, as it will have to

[1] (1925).

seek, to revise the foundations of the State. For the handful of Labour peers could not, even with Liberal support, hope to pass there any drastic measures about which deep feeling was aroused. For two years, at any rate, the House of Lords could delay them by using its temporary veto; and that would mean, in all probability, the wastage of the first half of the Parliament in which Labour, for the first time, had the opportunity of creative legislation. No one can confront that danger with equanimity.

A new situation, however, has come into existence. A Tory Government is in office with the largest majority that party has enjoyed since the Reform Act of 1832. It is being pressed, not unintelligibly, to reform the House of Lords before the next general election, so that any possible Labour Government in the future shall be confronted with a strong Second Chamber capable of opposing a stout front to what are called dangerous innovations. We do not, of course, know what scheme the Baldwin Government is likely to adopt. We know only that its purpose will be to strengthen the Upper House against the power of the Commons. We can imagine, from the Curzon Resolutions of July 19, 1922, that its basis will be a combination of (*a*) Peers of the Royal Blood, Lords Spiritual, and Law Lords; (*b*) Members elected from outside, perhaps directly, perhaps indirectly; (*c*) Hereditary Peers elected from among themselves; (*d*) Members nominated by the Crown. The House, so constituted, will probably be smaller than at present; and those elected under (*b*) and (*c*) will probably sit only for a term of years, though they will be re-eligible. Occasion will be taken, while retaining the supremacy of the House of Commons in finance, to restore the full veto of the House of Lords in other matters. What would be the effect of such changes?

They would undoubtedly make the problems of a Labour Government with a majority even more difficult to solve than they would be with the present House of Lords. For the latter dare not tamper with any measures which have the considered support of the electorate behind them; and, if it did, it could always be compelled to submit by the creation of enough new peers to alter its complexion favourably to Labour. But a revised Chamber would have a fixed composition, unalterable save with its own consent; and it is important to realize what that composition would be. Let us take each section of its probable membership separately. (*a*) Peers of the Royal Blood are innocuous and unimportant since, by tradition, they do not vote. The Lords Spiritual are, with rare exceptions, wedded firmly to the *status quo*; and there is hardly a Law Lord to-day, and but few conceivable Law Lords, whose opinions are likely to be progressive in temper. (*b*) The elected members will have a character which depends largely on the nature of the constituency adopted. If this is geographical and direct, as now, they will probably be Conservative, since the larger size of the constituency, the problems of publicity consequently involved, favour the candidates with more money to spend on making themselves known; for you cannot address one or two hundred thousand electors cheaply. If the basis is indirect, and such bodies as the municipal and county councils are allowed to choose them, they are, again, especially in the counties, likely to be Conservative; and since indirect election is, as American experience with the Senate has strikingly shown, the nurse of corruption, they will probably, in the towns, represent the big interests, and, in the counties, the landowners and farmers. If the basis is professional, and an attempt is made to secure an occupational franchise, the power of Capital and Labour will, at best, be equally balanced; and this, with the other sections of the Chamber, will be sufficient to place Labour in a permanent minority. (*c*) The hereditary peers will clearly be Conservative; there are only seven or eight

THE PROBLEM OF A SECOND CHAMBER 107

Labour peers in the House of Lords, and even the Liberals represent less than one-sixth of the whole peerage. It should, moreover, be noted that the term of office of these selected members under (*b*) and (*c*) is likely to be some such considerable period as seven or ten years. For it will be argued that this ensures continuity and stability in the Second Chamber, and prevents it from being the prey of temporary passion in the electorate. But it is the plain lesson of all electoral history that one Chamber is bound to quarrel with another if they are chosen at different times by the people. It was that difference of electoral period which, in 1918, wrecked the programme and ideals of President Wilson.

There remain the members who are to be nominated by the Crown. Obviously, some technique of qualification will have to be adopted. What is it likely to be? Certain obvious categories of nomination suggest themselves. We shall be given pro-consuls and retired ambassadors, men like the late Lord Cromer and the late Lord Bertie; retired politicians who have grown too old to stand the heat and stress of the House of Commons; one or two distinguished clergymen from the Nonconformist Churches, together with, perhaps, a Roman Catholic Archbishop and the Chief Rabbi; some representative scientist like the President of the Royal Society; a half-dozen retired generals and admirals; great business men like the Governor of the Bank of England, and the President of the Federation of British Industries; some outstanding figure in the Trade Union world; some such notability in local government as the Chairman of the County Councils Association; and, it may even be, a representative of the Livery Companies of London. However, in fact, these categories are determined, they are almost inevitably bound, with the single exception of the Trade Union representative, to be hostile to Labour. And it must be remembered, further, that these Crown nominees would be chosen by a Conservative Prime Minister;

and that, if they served for a term of years only, their successors would, in all probability, be chosen also by a Conservative. Any such reform as this scheme involves, therefore, means a Second Chamber vaccinated against Labour ideas, and with authority to reject all measures other than financial Bills greater than the House of Lords has possessed since 1832.

That way, frankly, lies disaster. For it would be useless to reform the House of Lords unless the new body were intended to be active; and if such a Chamber as this were active, it would come immediately into active collision with the first Labour Government which took office with a majority. It would reject such measures as Mr. Wheatley's Bill against profiteering in building materials; such Bills as attempted to set up a legal minimum wage, or the nationalization of mines. It would contain practically no hostile voices to attack its predominant temper, and it would leave accordingly the impression that the whole impact of propertied interests was arrayed against the popular will. Such an impression is bound to create a revolutionary temper. It suggests that property is, of set purpose, entitled to a predominant interest in the State. That view is directly antithetic to the position Labour occupies; for Labour is, as a democratic party, bound to insist that the State is built upon the rights of persons regarded as equally entitled to share in the gain and toil of living. If, therefore, its view of what constitutes an equal share is deliberately obstructed by constitutional reaction, it will have no alternative but to seek its end along different paths.

II

But it is important to discuss in general the theory of a Second Chamber, before we can arrive at any view of its functions and composition. It is usually argued that it is

THE PROBLEM OF A SECOND CHAMBER 109

necessary for three purposes: (*a*) to check the rashness of the Lower House, its tendency, that is, to leap at unwonted and unwise measures in the passionate aftermath of an election, (*b*) to revise the measures of the Lower House in order to correct errors of drafting and to draw attention to points and principles that have been overlooked in the primary debates, (*c*) to bring into public life types of character and experience that are not likely to be selected for such service by the ordinary electoral process.

Let us take each of these arguments separately. The theory that a single Chamber is normally precipitate is unsupported by any serious evidence in English history. The movement for the reform of the Franchise is usually dated from 1769; the first Reform Act is 1832. Each subsequent Act took, on the average, thirty years to reach the Statute Book. It took half a century of political conflict to realize the principle of Home Rule for Ireland. The Combination Acts were repealed in 1824; but it was fifty years before Disraeli gave the Trade Unions a recognized status in English law. A proper system of national education was demanded during the Napoleonic Wars; but the ideal was not achieved, and then in but a partial fashion, until the Forster Act of 1870. Or, in another field, we may take the main items in the programme of the Labour Party. Practically all of them have been the subject of public discussion for a generation; and their failure to achieve the form of a Government project has been due, not to the absence of debate, but to the fact that no party representative of Labour has, until 1924, attained political office. Or, again, we may take a third test. It is the English habit, when some problem is ripe for solution, to appoint a Royal Commission to make recommendations upon it; and, on the average, it takes some fifteen years to persuade a Government to legislate upon the subject of its reference. The observer, indeed, of the House of Commons will be tempted to accuse it, on its record, not of precipitancy but of amazing slowness in the disposal of great issues.

Sometimes the argument against rashness takes another form. Great changes, it is said, ought to be supported by a clear majority in the House of Commons; but unless we have a Second Chamber with at least the power of delay, they might well be passed by a single vote. Or there are measures brought in by a Government, and supported by the power of its majority, to which public opinion is decisively opposed, measures, for instance, of moment passed by a House of Commons on the verge of dissolution, or in a sudden burst of fear or temper. A Government may definitely conspire against the power of the people and, like the younger Pitt or Lord Sidmouth, use the mechanisms of the House of Commons to achieve that end. So, for example, Mussolini used the processes of Italian parliamentarism to pass his recent and vicious scheme of proportional representation. Such a House of Commons, unless a check existed upon its power, might well vote to prolong its own life indefinitely; and short of revolution there would be no means of terminating its usurpation of popular authority.

But abstractions of this kind are hardly related to reality. No Government is likely to attempt great changes unless it is fairly certain to command general support for them; to carry, for instance, a Bill for the nationalization of mines by a single vote would so diminish the prestige of a Ministry as almost certainly to involve its downfall. The sudden fit of fear or temper is, historically, much more prone to effect a Conservative Government than any other. It is men like the Duke of Northumberland who ask for panic measures; and a Second Chamber composed, as it would normally be composed, of solid and middle-aged men is exactly the type of assembly to be swept off its feet by evidence produced to prove the need of "panic" legislation. Men like Lord Danesfort and Lord Sydenham are the ideal assistants to a Government which seeks the curtailment of liberty. And if this is the object a Second Chamber is intended to prevent, it is much more simply achieved by a written constitution in which the abrogation of such statutes as Habeas Corpus is made especially difficult of attainment by any Government. So, also, no Government, under such a scheme, could be permitted to prolong the life of the House of Commons.

The second argument is decisively contradicted by all that we know of legislative assemblies the world over. The technical amendment of Bills, the niceties of drafting, the realization of probable result, are all of them highly expert matters. They are much more likely to be done effectively by half a dozen people meeting privately than under the full panoply of a legislative debate. The need to make Bills adequate to their principle is ground for the prior consultation (*a*) of the interests likely to be affected by them, and (*b*) of men like the late Lord Thring, or Sir H. Jenkyns, who had a definite genius for giving form to measures. But it is difficult to treat seriously the belief that the Archbishop of Canterbury, or an ex-Viceroy of India, or the President of the Federation of British Industries, has anything of value to contribute in so expert and delicate a realm as this. Amendment and debate in a Chamber, as distinct from a committee, always involve the crudity it is the purpose of this revision to avoid.

Nor is the third argument at all attractive. It is the primary thesis of democratic government that those by whom the people are ruled shall be directly chosen by themselves. If a man is unwilling or unfit to submit to the mechanisms of popular choice, he ought not to be imposed as a governor upon the people. There are many methods whereby any special competence that he possesses can be made available to a Government which desires to use it. And it is noteworthy that, with the single exception of Lord

Rosebery, every member of the House of Lords who has attained eminence in the House of Lords during the last half-century had already distinguished himself in the House of Commons. That is true of Lord Beaconsfield, Lord Salisbury, and Lord Balfour on the Conservative side; it is true of Lord Courtney, Lord Morley, and Lord Bryce on the Liberal. In a democratic society no one is entitled to the palm without the dust; yet that is exactly what is involved in this proposal. If men of great intellectual distinction desire a place in public life, they will always be able to find it; and if they are permanently rejected by the electorate they are not entitled to creep into it by a door over which the citizen-body cannot stand on guard.

So much for the supposed special advantages a Second Chamber affords. But we must not neglect the difficulties of finding an authoritative Second Chamber that does not raise far greater difficulties than it solves. Let us take the possible methods of choice and consider the difficulties to which they give rise. (1) If the Second Chamber is nominated by the Government it will, as the Canadian Senate has made plain, be simply a partisan body to which no authority attaches. If it is nominated by outside bodies, whether territorial or vocational in character, it will certainly be narrow, and possibly corrupt. And selection upon a vocational basis would raise the insoluble issue of finding suitable units of choice. Anyone who considers the history of the German Economic Council will discover that no such vocational body can ever be entrusted with more than advisory powers. For any unit selected is not only a *pis aller*, but it lacks that simplicity and directness which are the first necessities in a legislative system.

Nor is election in better case. If it is direct, it may either be simultaneously with that of the House of Commons, in which case its composition will be, in all probability, similar to that of the latter; and it will then, for party reasons, pass the legislation which comes before it without much difficulty. If it is elected at a different time, it will probably have a different composition; and in that event it will mainly tend to wreck the legislation of a Government to which it is hostile. It is a general truth that if a Second Chamber agrees with the First, it is superfluous; while if it disagrees, it is obnoxious. For, in the first case, it merely involves the wearisome reiteration of argument already sufficiently ventilated; and, in the second, it transfers the volume of discussion away from the substance of the problem involved to matters of constitutional form, and hinders that primary function of an executive which consists in driving an ample legislative programme to the Statute Book. This truth has been made elementary, not only by the relations between the Senate and the House of Representatives in the United States, but also by colonial experience, particularly in Australia. And everyone will remember how the controversy with the House of Lords, after 1909, completely wrecked the social programme of the Liberal Government. A directly elected Second Chamber, it may be added, would have so much more authority than one built upon nomination, that we may expect rather an addition to, than a subtraction from, the difficulties it creates.

It might, however, as with the Senate of the United States before 1913, be chosen by indirect election. We might, for instance, group together the local authorities of this country into electoral units returning some suitable quota of representatives. But this will not obviate the difficulty of securing a Chamber likely to work with the House of Commons; for since the local authorities are elected for a fixed term of office, their complexion will bear no relation to the mood of the people in judging general political issues at a dissolution. Such an electorate, moreover, would be too small to provide a sufficient basis of authority for an assembly with effective power. It would, from its very nature, tend to parochialism; and its relationship to the legislative assembly would introduce undesirable and unreal issues into the politics of local government. Anyone, moreover, who realizes how intensely our local bodies, especially by reason of the fact that service upon them is unpaid, are weighted in the interest of the wealthy ratepayer, will be able to measure the degree to which they would handicap the choice of more progressive representatives for the Second Chamber. And if indirect elections were built upon occupation as distinct from neighbourhood there would be the two problems (*a*) of finding suitable units of representation and (*b*) balancing the interests of capital and labour. The first, I have urged, is insoluble; and the second, if the principle of equality were adopted, would clearly destroy the effectiveness of the Assembly.

I have already discussed the idea of a Second Chamber built upon some fusion of these principles. It is clear that Labour cannot accept the principle of representation built upon the hereditary peerage in any shape or form. Because a man (or woman) has been careful in the selection of his parents is no ground for giving him an especial authority in the legislative power of the State. Nomination, as I have pointed out, will inevitably result in partizan choice; and, especially in a capitalist society, it affords no categories of qualification that do not involve a permanent weighting of the scales against those with little or no property. A small infusion of elected persons raises all the difficulties of suitable constituencies, and, in any case, would not balance the defects of nomination and of election by and from the peerage.

III

These difficulties, however, are small compared with the problem of powers. What is a Second Chamber to be able to do? It is universally agreed that it cannot have powers superior to those of the House of Commons; and it is generally admitted that it ought not to be able to amend or defeat those measures which the Speaker agrees, under the Parliament Act, to certify as financial. Anyone, indeed, who considers the relationship of equality between the Senate and the House of Representatives in America upon financial measures will realize why this is the case. The result is to allow every petty interest to magnify its opportunity of corrupt influence; and where the Second Chamber is small, this opportunity is at a maximum.

The relationship, therefore, finance apart, between the two Houses may be one either of equality or of inferiority. The first creates insuperable difficulties. It cannot, in the first place, be maintained; for to any assembly with the taxing power there is bound to gravitate both the interest of the electorate and the prestige of authority. But, this apart, equality is bound to mean deadlock whenever great issues are in debate. Deadlock, in its turn, means, ultimately, either dissolution or conference. The latter is unsatisfactory because there are too many issues on which compromise—the real purpose of conference—is impossible; a Government, for instance, which had brought in a Bill for the nationalization of the mines could not accept amendments from the Second Chamber intended to transform it into a scheme like that advocated by Sir Arthur Duckham. The power absolutely to reject is inevitably the power to dissolve; for a Government which cannot get its programme through must inevitably seek a new lease of authority. But no Government can be expected to live a creative life with such a sword of Damocles suspended over its head. It exists essentially to legislate on the basis of principle; and if the principle it adopts is to be found unsatisfactory, the only body morally entitled to say so is the electorate as a whole. The problem of equal powers, moreover, raises the question of the relationship of the executive to the Second Chamber, and especially that of the Prime Minister. Every legislative assembly is jealous of its dignity and its honour. Equality would mean a demand for the presence in debate of those primarily responsible for measures; and, under the pressure of modern parliamentary conditions that would involve an intolerable strain upon members of the Cabinet. It is the subordination of the House of Lords that enables Ministers to devote themselves to the Commons.

The Second Chamber must, therefore, be inferior in power to the First. What does inferiority imply? It involves, I suggest, the possession of four powers: (*a*) There must be the power to ask for information, including the right to demand papers and to appoint committees of investigation. (*b*) There must be the power to pass resolutions, it being remembered, as Lord Mansfield said, that the resolution of a Single Chamber, while it "looks like a legislative act, has yet no force nor effect as law." (*c*) There must be a power to attempt the amendment of Bills. (*d*) There must be a power to delay the passage of legislation for some period.

Obviously, only the third and fourth of these powers raise any problems of importance. Amendments may be either of detail or of substance. If they are of the first type, it will surely not be difficult to persuade a Government either to accept them or to effect some suitable arrangement. If they are of the second type, their fate must be dependent, clearly, upon the will of the House of Commons. That will, in its turn, depends upon the decision of the Government, at least in the normal instance; and it therefore seems to follow that rejection of amendments of substance must be final. For, otherwise, insistence on either side produces a deadlock; and it is the hypothesis of inferiority that no deadlock is admissible.

The power to delay is a far more complex matter. It raises a multiplicity of questions, none of which can be answered in a direct way. What, for example, are to be the conditions of delay? Is the belief that a Bill is a bad Bill ground for its rejection by the Second Chamber? Or because the latter body believes that public opinion is hostile to it? Or because, at the last General Election, the Government obtained no mandate for such a measure? But, in the first case, the House of Commons feels differently, and it is, from its nature, a more authoritative assembly. Merely on the ground that it dislikes the Bill, a Second Chamber cannot legitimately reject any more than the Supreme Court of the United States can reject legislation because it believes it to be unwise. In the second case, further, there is no reason to assume that the Second Chamber is more likely to be sensitive to the demands of public opinion than the House of Commons. The members of the latter body will pay more dearly for errors of judgment. They are more likely to be informed of the total popular view. They are certain, upon grounds I have already pointed out, to be more closely in touch with the opinion of the working class. And an estimate of public opinion is not, after all, an easy matter. Does it mean opinion that appears in the Press? Or what is received from such organized bodies as the Chamber of Commerce? No act, clearly enough, is more subtle or more delicate than that of gleaning the mind of the public; and no Second Chamber is so likely here to be right as to make its view worth more than that of the House of Commons. So, also, with the mandate. For it is, firstly, always difficult to pick out the issues upon which a party has been victorious at the polls; and it is, secondly, clear that every Government will have, in the intervals between election, to deal with unforeseen problems, and to guess at the solution acceptable to its constituents. That is the case in the event of war—as formidable a solution as can be attempted. The social environment does not remain static; and the theory of a mandate is, in general, only a means whereby the forces hostile to some particular legislation seek to prejudice its merits in the eyes of the nation.

There is, also, the problem of over how long the power to delay is to extend. Under the Parliament Act, for instance, if a Bill is rejected by the House of Lords, it does not become law until it has again been passed by the Commons in two further successive sessions. That means, in practice, a delay of practically two years. It means, also, in practice, a power to uproot the foundations of a Government's programme for that period; for the life of any Government is built upon its control of the time-table. Most people would, I think, feel that such a power is too great. But what is the alternative? Mr. Lees-Smith suggests a single session, with the proviso that the Speaker should prevent the illegitimate use of the closure in the second discussion of the Bill by the Commons; but he is assuming a Second Chamber which reproduces the proportionate composition of the First, and is therefore unlikely to reject a Government measure of the first importance.[1] We are faced, in other words, by the dilemma that if the period of delay is more than a year it disrupts the programme of the Government, while if it is less than a year it is hardly worth the expenditure of time and effort involved. The measure, moreover, may be passed by the House of Commons in the last year of its life; in which case the Second Chamber is given the power to destroy measures which the Government will not, quite possibly, have the power to introduce a second time. And if it is said that a Government which feels strongly about a defeated Bill can always, by a dissolution, attempt to get a mandate for its passage, as Mr. Asquith did twice in 1910, the plain answer is, I suggest, that of all constitutional instruments a Second Chamber not built upon popular election is the most unsuitable to possess the power of compelling reference to the people.

[1] *Second Chambers in Theory and Practice*, p. 249.

IV

I suggest, therefore, that whether from the angle of its composition or of its powers, it is, in fact, impossible to discover a satisfactory Second Chamber in any way able to check the authority of the House of Commons. Where a control is desirable, it can best be attained by limiting the power of the Lower House to pass constitutional measures unless a specified majority, which might be as high as two-thirds of its membership, voted in its favour. Outside that narrow realm, the power to control ought to lie in the common sense of the party in office, on the one hand, and the ultimate judgment of the electorate, upon the other.

I believe, therefore, that Single-Chamber government provides much the best solution of the problem. That is, of course, to traverse the generally accepted judgment of experience: a bicameral assembly is usually assumed to be the basic dogma of political science. But it is only such a dogma because, as Tocqueville warned us, we confound our wonted institutions with the necessary foundations of society. We have bicameral government because, for historical reasons, the English Parliament finally became a legislature with two Chambers; and most constitutions have been founded upon that example. The English Parliament, however, developed into its present form only by a series of accidents; and anyone who examines the nature and history of Second Chambers in general will discover that their main purpose is at least to delay, and, if possible, to prevent, the disturbance of the *status quo*. They are, in fact, part of the general tactic of conservatism. They enable the propertied interests in a State to interpose a barrier in the way of Radical legislation. No one has ever heard of great progressive measures being insisted upon by the House of Lords or the Canadian Senate or those of Italy or

France. No one doubts that great changes ought not to be rashly made; but few, I take it, will doubt either that they ought not to be opposed merely because they are hostile to the interests of a small section of the community.

And while the accidental history of the English Parliament has built the canon of political theory, it should also be remembered that those States with a Single-Chamber government have suffered no disaster on that account. Bulgaria may have had a Single Chamber; but pre-war Serbia had two. Costa Rica may have had a Single Chamber; but the old Austria-Hungary enjoyed the benefits of bicameralism. "Nowhere in the colonies," writes Mr. Temperley,[1] "is the Upper Chamber really imposing, in few is it actually powerful, and in many it is regarded as a rather tedious relic of a bygone age." Ontario has suffered no harm from its disappearance; in New Zealand, in New South Wales and Queensland, it has merely served to fortify the interests of property against the struggle of the poor towards power. Its existence, indeed, in the British Colonies and Dominions is mainly the result of that autocratic dread of the multitude so characteristic of the Whig Party in the middle part of the nineteenth century; and it is worth remembering that the protagonist of the bicameral principle, the third Earl Grey, was persuaded by the difficulty of finding a suitable form for the Second Chamber. "I now consider it to be very doubtful, at least," he wrote in 1853,[2] "whether the Single legislature ought not under any circumstances to be preferred."

It is worth while, moreover, to remember that there exists in the literature of political science a very respectable body of opinion in favour of Single-Chamber government. Certainly no one could reject without discussion a

[1] H. W. V. Temperley, *Senates and Upper Chambers* (1910), p. 47.
[2] See his *Colonial Policy of Lord John Russell's Administration*, vol. ii. p. 96.

view upheld by Franklin, Samuel Adams, and Tom Paine in America, and by Turgot, Sieyès, and Condorcet in France. It is noteworthy, also, that there is widespread discontent with the Australian Senate which, when the Constitution was made, was accepted as an axiomatic necessity. It was stoutly opposed in the Convention which constructed the Constitution of South Africa, and accepted there only upon the condition that it would be revised after ten years; if it has remained in the revision of 1920 that is rather because it has proved impotent in practice either to delay or to revise. Indeed, it might be urged with justice that even in a Federal State no real necessity for a Second Chamber exists; certainly the binding force of party has, in the American Senate, proved more than able to transcend effectively the limits of State boundaries. A Democratic Senator from Florida does not vote in any noticeably different way from a Democratic Senator from Massachusetts on any important issue. Every purpose the Senate is supposed to protect can, in a Federal as in a Unitary State, be protected by other means.

V

Tradition, of course, dies hard; and it is improbable that we shall abolish the House of Lords directly without an attempt at some intermediate experiment. It is, therefore, worth while to inquire what form, given the nature of the problem, that experiment could most suitably take.

The best form, in all probability, is a modification of that which obtains in Norway. After the election of the Storthing the members of that body choose one-fourth of their own number to form the Upper Chamber—the Lagsthing—the remaining three-fourths constituting the Lower Chamber. The Norwegian Parliament acts as a bicameral body only in dealing with ordinary measures. It cannot initiate legislation, though it may revise or reject it. If its amendments are rejected, the two Houses will meet as one, and a two-thirds majority overrides the view of the Upper Chamber. So, also, with cases where Bills are definitely rejected. And, clearly, since the Storthing as a whole elects the Upper Chamber, its composition naturally reflects that of the party or parties in power. The system has been in operation for over a century, and it has worked, thus far, quite admirably. The Lagsthing can only delay for three days, and the difference between the two Houses can therefore be settled at once. As a rule, disagreement occurs on matters of detail rather than of principle. The type of member chosen is, of course, broadly an accurate sample of the membership of the Storthing as a whole. It is, moreover, worth while to note that this principle of election of the Upper House by the Lower was excepted as one of its constitutive principles by the Bryce Report, and that it has been partially adopted, also, in the new Senate of the South African Union.

With minor changes, such a method could easily be applied to the Second Chamber in this country. Each new House of Commons, as it met, might choose for its own lifetime a body of some hundred persons in proportion to the strength of the parties in its own composition. It would be better, I think, that they should be elected from outside the Commons than from inside, since, otherwise, the fact of popular choice would give the new body an undesirably large authority. This new House should not have the power either to initiate legislation, or to touch financial measures. It should be able to ask questions, and to revise or reject all other Bills. But refusal on the part of the House of Commons to accept its amendments should lead to their failure if that refusal is supported by a majority of one-tenth of the Commons; and, in the event of rejection, a second passage of the Bill, one month after rejection, should override the will of the Second Chamber. The new House could be given, as now, a Secretary of State and an Under-

THE PROBLEM OF A SECOND CHAMBER 123

Secretary to represent the Government of the day there in debates.

What would be the effect of such a scheme? We should have a Second Chamber amenable to the will of the popularly elected Assembly. It could not control or defeat the purposes of the latter. But it could make known criticisms and objections; it could delay, for a short time, measures that it thought fatally unwise, or definitely counter to public opinion The real onus of decision would rest, as it ought to rest, with the House of Commons; and the penalty for error could be inflicted, as it ought to be inflicted, by the electorate. The small size of the House would tend, as it tends in the Committees of the Commons, to make discussion concrete and practical, and there would be less danger than there is in an assembly as large as that foreshadowed in the Curzon Resolutions of eloquence as such being important. Every type of experience it is desired to utilize in a Second Chamber might find a place there—the distinguished lawyer, the retired civil servant, the trade union leader, the great educationist with a gift for affairs. It might be a useful way of using the authority of men defeated at the General Election whose absence would be a loss to public life, and it would give them a suitable platform of continuous influence until they returned to the House of Commons. It would be a Chamber with prestige, but without power. It could influence, but it could not determine. It could oppose a Government without embarrassing a Government; it could criticize without the opportunity to destroy. Above all, there would be no danger of its functioning as the safeguard of privilege. If a Conservative Government was in office, its predominant complexion would be Conservative, if a Labour Government was in office it would be, predominantly, a Labour Chamber. Those who regard its functions as insignificant, may be reminded that they will be larger than those now exercised by the electorate; and those who consider that the predominance of the House of Commons would be overwhelming, may well remember Bagehot's admirable remark—even truer to-day than when he made it sixty years ago—that the national attention to politics is too incessant to make possible in the House of Commons "a steady opposition to a formed public opinion." Here, of course, as elsewhere, it is urgent that a formed public opinion should exist. For, ultimately, the only true safeguard against legislative error lies in the quality of the national mind.

V

THE STATE IN THE NEW SOCIAL ORDER

THE English political scene has always changed its perspective after a crisis in the national fortunes. The civil wars of the fifteenth century produced the centralized despotism of the Tudors. The sense of national confidence gained from the victory over Spain led the Puritans to resist the Stuart attempt at further usurpation; and the ultimate result of the Great Rebellion was to put the Crown in fetters. War always transforms the foundations of national thought, and the scale of our last experiment has been vast enough to leave no institution or doctrine untouched. It is clear already that its onset marked a new and pronounced epoch in our affairs. Just as the Napoleonic struggle freed the commercial classes from the last remnants of aristocratic control, so, in the long run, it is probable that the main result of the recent conflict will be to bring the working classes to a new position in the State.

The emergence, indeed, of the Labour Party as the main Parliamentary Opposition is not the least important index to the new temper. It means that the Third Estate has ceased to associate the idea of government with the ownership of property. Exactly as the main consequence of the Reform Act of 1832 was the destruction of those political privileges which separated the middle classes from the seat of power, so, it may be suggested, the result of the Reform Act of 1918 will, in the background of war experience, be the slow destruction of those economic privileges which prevent the access of the workers to the moral assets of the State. It is not, of course, likely that the process will be either logical or straightforward. The English people is not accustomed to make a direct highroad to its intellectual goal. The national method is rather to mitigate the evils we have than fly to obvious benefits of which doctrine can demonstrate the substance. But, based upon the reforms of 1832, the ultimate character of nineteenth-century legislation in England was to make a world in which the profits of business men were economically possible and legally secure. So upon the basis of the reforms of 1918 it will be the tendency of legislation in our own day to make a world in which men who have no commodity to sell save their labour will share in a fuller way in the riches that civilization can offer.

The directions in which that effort will be made are already becoming clear. There is abroad, however half-heartedly, a new sense of the significance of education. If the democracy is to be master in its own house, it must be adequately equipped for its task. Control of the sources of knowledge is the one sure road to power; and it is evidence of high import that the workers themselves are foremost in demanding an educational system which gives them access to that control. Hardly less urgent is the feeling that basic monopolies, coal, power, transport, land, must be directly managed by the people themselves. Nationalization is a word that has manifold interpretations; but nationalization, in some form, of the obvious basic monopolies is an inevitable corollary of democratic government. Not less certain, as the future expands, will be the conference upon the workers of definite institutional security against the tragedy of unemployment. That the resources of the State must be used to safeguard its citizens against the hazards of trade is already a commonplace; and since the principle was admitted in the Insurance Act of 1911, it is rather with its administrative application than its legislative substance that the next age will be concerned.

Second only in importance to education, and in large part dependent upon it, is the growth of industrial self-government. It has become intolerable that the mass of

THE STATE IN THE NEW SOCIAL ORDER

men should be the mechanical recipients of orders they are compelled to execute without scrutiny. It has become finally clear that the release of individuality—after all, the ultimate purpose of the State—is utterly impossible so long as the control of industry is confided to a small number of men whose decisions need not take account of the wills of those who work under them. It may be admitted that the transformation of industrial control presents immense difficulties. The mass of the workers has not been trained to work that is instinct with responsibility. The capitalist *régime* has sought not the men who think but the men who obey. It has subordinated to the acquisitive impulse whatever spirit there is of service and creativeness in those who are subject to its dominion. It has obscured the processes by which it governs. It has so divorced the actual work of production from the business of direction as to leave the industrial pattern unintelligible to those whose lives are dependent upon its right arrangement. So complex have its mechanisms become that no single formula—guild socialism, consumers' co-operation, the multiplication of small peasant proprietorship—has any but a limited application. In the discovery, therefore, of institutions which enable the industrial worker to be something more than a tender of machines it is inevitable that there should be hazardous experiment; and the corollary of experiment is failure. But that feeling of unfreedom which Lord Sankey discovered among the miners, which interferes with the quantity and quality of their work, is typical of labour as a whole. It demands, as is now recognized, channels of response which will minimize its intensity.

These are, of course, predominant currents of effort in their largest outline. There is no aspect of our social life which remains unaffected by the impact of new desires. The Industrial Revolution turned urban England into a slum, and since Mr. Sartorius, ably seconded by Sir Alfred Mond, shows no sign of abdication, he is destined, sooner or later, to be supplanted by a community at last awakened to its responsibilities. Housing is the bedrock upon which the health of the nation depends. Parallel with its improvement there is certain to be a realization that the development of the medical services is a vital public concern. What are now half-casual and half-starved amenities, the public libraries for instance, are bound, as education develops, to be regarded as charges upon the public income not less fundamental to the general well-being than the Army and Navy. Nor can such amenities be adequately enjoyed unless the working day is adjusted to meet their claims. The worker cannot respect the obligations of citizenship if he is simply and solely an unreflecting unit in the productive system. It is, moreover, becoming probable that the centre of importance for most men in the future will be the period of leisure rather than the period of work. In that aspect, the limitation of the hours of labour is fraught with deep consequence to them at a vital point. Nor can the substance of our civilization remain unaffected by the changing prospects of women. Marriage for most has meant a position akin to that of a trusted servant in an upper-class family, with the added right to frequent the sitting-room, in the rare cases where there is one, when the day's work is done. But women have not only invaded industry in wholesale fashion; they have also come to see that they may make of marriage a career as significant as the Bar or the Church. They have thus come to regard it in a sense very difficult either from the faded spinsters of Cranford or the genteel harpies of Jane Austen. What influence their views will have upon our social economy we cannot yet tell; it is clear only that it will be profound and decisive.

Nothing of all this implies either that such changes are immediately impending, or that their path will be easy and straightforward. Their consequences go too deep into the fabric of the State for most of them to be welcome. They involve an assault upon tradition which will invoke the resistance of all the forces of conservatism and inertia. They imply a change in the property relation so vast as to alter in their implication the very purpose of the State. They will have to proceed piece by piece, advancing here, there suffering defeat, until most of them become in turn traditions. Then, perhaps, in typical English fashion, because they have become institutions to which we have grown accustomed, we shall regard them as the necessary foundations of society. They will, in part, be dependent upon the possibility that we can avoid revolution, on the one hand, and foreign warfare upon the other. If we recognize sufficiently the inevitable basic infirmity in all human institutions so as to be convinced that with all its slowness the path of reason is preferable to the path of violence, that the inadequate good of peace may be preferable to the cost of ideal good attempted by war, an atmosphere of constructiveness may emerge from the present reaction. But only upon the condition of peace. For it is clear that the resources now at the command of conflict may, if utilized, destroy any possibility of civilization. If force should triumph over reason in the next age, ideas such as these may well pass into dim memories; and, as in Mr. Wells' dramatic picture, some ancient survivor of the struggle may seek to explain them to grandchildren who do not understand even the primary notions of civilized life.

But if we may count—it is a large assumption—upon a peace as long and as extensive as that given to England in the Victorian age, we may be confident that social theory will undergo a radical transformation. A new world will arise from the ashes of the old; and a new political science will be necessary to the statement of its meaning. Already, it is possible to discern some at least of the elements that will go to its making. It is likely, in the first place, to be far more complex than the old. The sanction of our institutions will not be Divine right, as with the Royalists of the seventeenth century, or fear, as with Hobbes, or the facile simplicity of direct and omnipresent consent, as with Rousseau. It is likely to come from the slow development of a social psychology based upon inductions about human nature far wider than in any previous time. It will take account of the magistral demonstration by Marx that political power is the handmaid of economic power; and it will therefore insist as integral that the existence of great wealth and widespread poverty in the same State are incompatible with the attainment of social good. It will seek to discover the largest way commensurate with national efficiency of associating the creative energies of men with the actual business of government. It will realize that the main reason why social systems have decayed in the past is their inability to make adequate response to the primary impulses of men. For the onset of revolution does not mean the existence of a will to wrong in the people. It is they who always, and most deeply, are the sufferers from disorder. Revolution never comes from the effort of chance conspirators or malevolent ideas. It is the outcome always of wrongs that have become too intolerable to be borne; and the moral judgment it involves is decisive against the Government which has failed to see in reform the only real safeguard against it.

The coming of the democracy to power involves a change in the purpose of the State. It means placing the riches of civilization at the disposal of that democracy. But, still more, it means a change in the methods by which that effort is made. In the aftermath of the Industrial Revolution it was believed that the conflict of private interests would result in a well-ordered commonwealth. The duties of government were the duties of a police force. The atmosphere of the courts—always the surest index to the temper of the governing class—was mainly an insistence that in nothing was the public welfare so essentially protected as in the safeguarding of industrial private rights; and the classic case of *Mogul Steamship Co.* v. *McGregor*[1] was evidence that restraint upon freedom of action in the name of public policy was regarded as a definite evil. It was somehow assumed that since every person is, in the main, the best judge of his own happiness, the larger the boundaries of freedom of contract, the greater would be the happiness of the nation. It was not understood that there is a difference between judging what is for one's happiness and having the means to effect it. Freedom of contract only begins, as Mr. Justice Holmes has said, where equality of bargaining power begins; and there is no real equality of bargaining power, so far as the means of adequate subsistence are concerned, unless there is approximate equality of property. When Bentham and his disciples set an individualistic perspective to the theory of the State, what in reality they did was simply to put that State at the disposal of the owners of political and economic power. The second half of the nineteenth century was mainly occupied with the effort to relax the rigours of an individualistic *régime*, while retaining an active and profound faith in its main assumptions. Such measures as Factory Acts, Employers' Liability Acts, Housing Acts, were, at bottom, concessions made to humanitarian sentiment which shuddered at the cost of *laissez-faire*. They did not involve a belief that it is the business of the State to see that the citizen realizes the full power of moral development which is in him.

Until, roughly, 1870, Benthamism held practically unmitigated sway over the English mind. From then onwards, T. H. Green and the Oxford idealists wrought something akin to revolution in the English theory of the State. Trained in a Platonism sharpened by contact with Hegel, they recognized that the Benthamite opposition between

[1] (1888) 21 Q.B.D. 544; [1892] A.C. 25.

State and individual was at once artificial and dangerous. The individual was a citizen, and he therefore had no meaning apart from his citizenship. Unless, then, the State could guarantee to each man the powers without which he could not realize himself, it became devoid of ethical content. The State was, for them, an instrument through which and in which its citizens realized themselves; and it was thus its main function to secure to each such rights as would achieve his full moral development. There can be no doubt of the high service rendered by the idealist philosophy in destroying the notion that State intervention is, in its nature, an evil thing. Unfortunately the failure of idealism lay in its inability to differentiate between State and Government. It did not with any sharpness disentangle the acts of principal and agent, with the result that it confused the temporary acts of the latter with the permanent purpose of the former.

The idealist philosophy of the State so highly exalted its power that individuals and societies obtained their meaning, and therefore their rights, only by its permission. It was so occupied with the theoretic purpose of the abstract State that it hardly, T. H. Green apart, regarded the actual achievement of concrete States. It did not see that a purpose abstractly noble may, in the hands of human agents, be stripped of every whit of moral splendour. By insisting that every institution was the incarnation of a spiritual principle idealism failed to develop a theory of moral values, and was therefore unable to distinguish between degrees of right. It thus provided no solution for the situation where social obligations conflict. It so confounded the actual motives of social agents with the ideal purpose by which they ought to have been informed that it detected the existence of benevolent progress where none, in fact, existed. It beatified Imperialism, for example; and the noble picture of the white man's burden blinded the eyes of its devotees to the natives who were in fact bearing it. It did not help a miner called upon to choose between his union and the Prime Minister to be told that the latter represented an institution whose abstract end was good. It afforded no real direction to a Quaker who believed in the moral wrong of war to be informed that war might be exalted when the State undertook it. Idealism, in short, tended to beatify things as they are. It was too occupied with abstract ends to be sufficiently critical either about the time-factor in the process of their achievement, or the methods by which they were effected. It asserted, and with justice, that right and truth ought to prevail; but its actual result, in the hands of its chief exponents, was to identify right and truth merely with the decisions of the governmental authority legally competent to make them. It did not penetrate beyond those decisions to the sources from which they were derived.

It was possible, in the years before the War, to see that idealism as a political creed was rapidly losing ground. It had become a commonplace that the authority of the State, neither in its forms nor in its achievement, justified the allegiance it demanded. Socialism came in its varied guises to offer proof that the State did not secure either the freedom or the happiness of its members. Churchmen like Figgis came to see that its assumed pre-eminence might deprive voluntary organizations of powers necessary to the fulfilment of aims not less noble than its own. Lawyers like Maitland urged that the State was merely one form of human association, and that it could make no moral claim to sovereignty other than that which it could prove on the ground of moral achievement. The survival of its power, especially in the background of European revolution, has become dependent, in part upon the national inertia of men, in part also upon its ability to respond to new wills and new demands that had, before the War, been hardly organized or articulate. It is true, of course, as Mr. Barker has said, that the State being with us, we must make the best of it. But what has moved into the hinterland of doubt are the motives which underlie its institutions and the forms they use for their expression.

The society in which we live is organized upon the basis of property. Ownership confers rights, and rights are legally unrelated to the performance of service. The society towards which we are moving will be organized upon the basis of functions, and the rights it will confer will be dependent upon the functions we perform. For it is obvious to anyone who scrutinizes the present social order that the one thing it has secured is a continuously larger production. It has not regarded equity in the distribution of the product. It has not achieved even a minimum level of decent existence for the mass of the producers. It has never, above all, sought to stimulate at their highest level the creative energies of men. But the test of social institutions is the extent to which they develop those creative energies for social ends. If we assume a moral ideal that is capable of being aimed at by the State, each individual is clearly entitled to those rights which enable him to contribute to its attainment; he must be enabled, that is to say, to fulfil his moral vocation as a man. But the outstanding feature of the present society is that most men have, substantially, no rights at all, while those who do possess them are not bound to the service that they ought to involve.

The consequence may be seen in the absence of a common purpose binding men together in the State. There is, of course, common dependence in the sense that if an employer secures orders, his men secure work; and that he, in turn, depends upon their labour for the fulfilment of his contract. But the absence of any principle in the method of distribution leaves the partition of the product simply to the pressure of opposing forces, and the result is what is called the class-war. So long as that social disharmony persists, the currents of social activity can never so flow together as to converge into a single channel. Nor can any institution which is touched by that disharmony really attract the motives which promote civilization. For the absence of principle at the root is bound to affect the upper branches of the tree. If we start, not from the assumption that property has rights because it is property, but that socially valuable functions require rights in order that the individuals fulfilling those functions may achieve their end, in proportion as those ends are realized, the foundation of disharmony disappears. We then move to the conception of a minimum basis of civilization secured to each individual in order that his citizenship may be possible. Beyond that, because the interest of the State in the happiness of its members is equal, we attempt the maximization of equal opportunity. We do not, that is to say, associate opportunity with a status that is mainly economic, but with the mere fact that the individual, as a member of the State, must be given the fullest chance to prove his worth.

It is perhaps worth while insisting that this is not an effort after identity. Equality of opportunity is simply the admission that unless each citizen has an equal access to the heritage of the State, the persistence of disharmony, with the internecine warfare it entails, is certain. It is, moreover, clear that men will very variously avail themselves of the equal opportunities conferred. Their tastes are not the same. Some are by nature leaders; to others, the temptation to inert acceptance of direction is irresistible. In particular, it does not seem probable that the increase of interest in politics will be as intense as is usually supposed. The social nature of men must always be carefully distinguished from the political nature of some few. The average Member of Parliament, even, is not there because he has a love of State-building. He is there, like Lord Banbury, to defend an economic interest threatened from within, or, as in the case of many retired business men, between the House of Commons is an avenue towards certain social distinctions that are prized by their class. Equality of opportunity will undoubtedly multiply the number of citizens fit for political function. But the two important possibilities it opens are, first, that the State becomes informed by a common purpose, and, second, that it is enabled to utilize the reservoir of talent that, with the present disparity, is bound to remain largely undiscovered.

Nor does this doctrine involve the abolition of property as such. It simply limits the rights of ownership by insisting that they shall be conditioned by the performance of service. It must, of course, further limit those rights by organizing social institutions in such a fashion that they leave each citizen who desires the sense of freedom in their working to perform, where he has the capacity, responsible functions. It involves, that is to say, the democratization of industrial control and the decentralization of political control. It means for the mines such a form of organization as that, for instance, which Lord Sankey has depicted. There, at least, in pit, in district, and in the industry as a whole, the abolition of private ownership would remove barriers which now stand in the path of service and achievement. The miner who could convince his fellows that he was competent to direct their labours could test his powers in an increasingly wider field. So, too, in another sphere, with local government. At present, the amenities the latter can secure are limited by parliamentary enactments devised at every point in the interest of ratepayers and ground-landlords. If, apart from the need of general reorganization, a compulsory minimum were fixed centrally, and the degree of effort beyond that minimum left to the local authority, many of the shadows that now lie across the face of English life would disappear. For the truth is that, in the eyes of property owners, extravagance is not the sin of Poplar, but the desire of its councillors to make the lives of their constituents less empty of the aids to well-being that Belgravia can afford. It is the notion of using the national resources for the purpose of promoting equality against which the defenders of the present system are adamant. Yet, whether in industry or politics, democratization tempered by *expertise* is the only path to creativeness.

In any philosophy which seeks the grounds of national co-operation, a thorough grasp of the significance of such equality is fundamental. The miners who went on strike in 1921 knew not less well than other citizens that they imperilled by so doing the foundations of the economic security afforded by the present system. But because that system was unequal in its operation they had the less interest in the maintenance of its stability than those who, owning it, denounced them. Just as, during the War, the system of rationing produced better health in the nation because the food consumed, though less in quantity and quality, was more fairly distributed, so in the general organization of social life, men who feel that the product is equally available in return for equal service will be willing to serve gratefully and in full measure. Let it be added, too, that equality implies a higher standard of knowledge and effort than can now be secured. Democracy, it is obvious, has as much need to test the standards of its performance as the chemist to test the accuracy of his balance. Equality must always be conditioned by the establishment of criteria of qualification for the performance of functions. But these criteria will not be resented where they bear equally upon all. Where they are destructive of social solidarity is in their inequality of operation. The son who inherits his father's business because he is the accident of an accident, the nobleman who becomes a company director, the judge's son who becomes clerk of assize, are examples of the acquisition of status without qualification which imperil the co-ordination of effort. The average working-man does not begrudge the standards of entrance to the Civil Service; but he rightly resents the inequalities of an educational system which, practically speaking, prevents his children from being able to attain that standard. The absence of an equal interest in the assets of the State inevitably begets an inferior interest in the maintenance of its foundations; and it is the obvious lesson of our experience that the inferior interest of the many is the active hatred of the few. No State can long survive in which a group of citizens aim, through profound moral conviction, at its overthrow. That is why the movement towards equality is the one sure safeguard against revolution.

It is doubtful, indeed, if ends such as these can in any full measure be attained through the classical institutions of representative government. We have evolved the great society without any real effort to see that our political methods keep pace with the changes in social and economic structure. No one who examines the large outlines of the English governmental system can point to any capital discovery in the past fifty years. The emergence of the Labour Party has altered the general perspective of their effort. The transference of the centre of importance from the House of Commons to the Cabinet, the consolidation of that pre-eminence given by Mr. Gladstone's long career to the office of Prime Minister, a superb improvement in the quality of the Civil Service—these, and things like these, have an importance beyond denial. But the normal assumptions which, for example, Bentham had in mind in the prophecies he made for the future of the representative system have ceased to work. The private member is a pale ghost of his former self. Debate has become utterly unreal; and divisions merely register mechanically decisions the real grounds of which are rarely determined in the House of Commons. The old system of party government has lost its mainspring; and the suspicious inertia of those who are not active in the machine itself is a commonplace. Nor is all

THE STATE IN THE NEW SOCIAL ORDER

this true of England alone. In France, in Italy, and in the United States, the same disharmony between political method and the social process may be detected. The legislative assembly is not merely overburdened by the pressure of its work; it is, in its classic form, unfitted to carry out the functions for which it exists.

It is, of course, possible to improve the actual machinery we have. Members of Parliament could be given direct contact with the business of administration by the creation of committees to watch the work of each department. They might be in part organs of consultation, and in part an effective and necessary liaison between the bureaucrat and the House of Commons. The transformation of the present committee-stage of Bills into a process akin to the working of committees upon municipal bodies would not only destroy much deliberate obstruction, but it would also ensure to the private member a more real understanding of the measures upon which he votes, and a more real consideration than he now receives. A reduction in the size of the Cabinet has become clearly essential to the vital habit of corporate decision; and it is at least equally clear that there does not exist in the civil government any body whose business it is to undertake the investigation and research that are necessary to the proper working of policy. Nor are the functions of the different departments allocated upon any coherent principle. Until each department has before it a properly organized field of activity, there is bound to be waste and confusion. At present, there is overlapping and cross-division to a degree that makes officials surrender to contests for control with other officials time that should be given to creative work. No one can doubt that the serious consideration of political institutions could result in inventions for their improvement of capital importance.

Yet even if these and similar changes were effected the modern legislative system would be inadequate to its task.

That there are many functions, the provision of law and justice, the maintenance of the national health, the provision of public education, defence and foreign policy, which require an undivided communal organ for their general direction, is clear enough. But when we pass from functions such as these, which concern men as citizens rather than men as producers, analysis makes it obvious that the simple formulae of representative government do not apply. What we need, then, is to take the services that have to be performed and devise institutions for their government. We have so to devise them that we may secure to each function the rights without which citizenship is impossible, and, within the boundaries of that limiting principle, to free the general legislative assembly from the task of intimate and incessant supervision. It is not, in any case, fit for such a task; for, as Mill long ago pointed out, a popular assembly is in its nature unfitted to administer or dictate to those who control administration. Here it becomes necessary to depart from the narrowly geographical habit of our political thinking. We must learn to think of railways and mines, cotton and agriculture, as areas of government just as real as London and Lancashire. They are relatively unified functions which need, just as much as geographical units, organs of administration. Clearly, of course, it is easier to give a simple form of institutionalism to an industry like mining, which is susceptible of immediate nationalization, than to an industry like cotton-spinning, in which the formulae of nationalization are far more dubious. But, granted the conference of powers to a representative assembly for the cotton industry, granted, also, the principles of citizenship within which it must work, it is not difficult to imagine mechanisms through which a constitutional system of government might work there. As with the mines, it is necessary to give representation in such a functional assembly to interests which need special protection—

the consumer, the technician, allied industries in a special sense related to cotton. It is necessary, also, to use such associations as the trade unions and the employers' federations as the basis upon which selections of personnel must be made. Nor should any barriers be put in the way of joint consultation between industry and industry. Whether a national economic council is implied in such a scheme as this it is very difficult to say. The problem of its constitution is extraordinarily complex; and the solution of general industrial questions is, as a rule, really the solution of problems of citizenship which come within the scope of Parliament. Their administration is always a special problem of a particular function, and is better left to the function for settlement. When the German Economic Council has had a longer life we shall be better able to judge the possibilities it involves.

It may be useful at this stage to indicate the institutional pattern implied in a social philosophy of this kind. We visualize a Parliament with the taxing power, which lays down fundamental rules, and administers, through the Cabinet, the matters of general citizenship. Below it would be territorial and functional institutions. The one would be concerned with the normal subject-matter of local government; and, under the revised areas of control, they would possess that greater complex of powers characteristic of the first-class German municipality, rather than the narrow delegation inherent in the British system. Each industry would possess an industrial council in which management and labour, technicians and the representatives of allied industries, together with the representatives of the public, would take their place. Such a council would have as its business the application to the industry it controlled of the minimum basis of civilization we have suggested as now fundamental. It would consider all questions affecting industrial relations within its scope of reference. It would issue decrees, perhaps of the nature of provisional orders, where it was desired to go beyond the principles of the national minimum. It would undertake research; and it would have a special costings and audit department of which the task would be to secure complete publicity upon the details of the business process within the trade. It is possible, also, that a National Industrial Council would be required; but it is doubtful whether it is possible to build it, and uncertain whether the questions it would seek to resolve are not, in fact, problems with which the ordinary Parliament is better able to deal.

At the back of all this lies an implied insistence upon education as the main channel of hope in our ultimate relief. For if the object of the State is to enrich the social heritage through the enlargement of individual personality, then individual personality must be given that power of adequate expression which comes through knowledge to make its needs known. At bottom, therefore, the problem is the instruction of individual wills, and the building, as in our institutional pattern, of channels through which those wills can flow. It is not suggested that wills can or should function equally, since abilities are unequal. But it is suggested that the general environment in which these wills function must be at a certain minimum level. It follows, therefore, that the charges of maintaining and raising that level are the first national burden to be borne; and the whole concept of property must undergo a radical change to that end. For, ultimately, the real implication of a national minimum is the replacement of the spirit of acquisitiveness by the spirit of service. That may not mean destroying the legal notion of property; but it does mean spiking its guns.

If we approach in this way the central problem of the State we make it, as Plato made it, that notion of justice which is the right ordering of human relationships. It involves the view that each citizen has an equal claim on the common good in respect of equal needs; and the corollary is therein implied that differences in response to claims are differences that the common good itself requires. This would, in all likelihood, rule out any rigorous scheme of communism on the ground that it leaves no room for the recognition of the social importance of individual differences; though we must ceaselessly remember that the tribute paid to those differences has its marginal utility. It would also allow the payment of a monopoly-rent to ability only when we can be certain that a social need can be satisfied in no other fashion. Broadly, then, justice implies equality where human beings are equal in their needs. But justice must function in that psychological atmosphere in which we get the best out of our ablest men. The principle of the payment for service, the standard, therefore, by which property can be justified, is a measure of remuneration which harmonizes individual interest with the common good. It ought here to be emphasized that the importance of profit-making as a motive has been greatly exaggerated, and that experiment with its replacement could not effect other than benefit. The State owes to each of us the opportunity of useful service; but it does not owe us the occasion to spend the substance of other men's lives.

We are seeking to visualize a State in which the individual citizen is entitled to an effective voice in collective decisions. Admittedly, of course, the power he can have is limited by the inherent needs of large-scale organization. But it ought still to mean that the ordinary man can help to select his rulers and to get himself elected if he can. It ought to mean his right to unfettered criticism. It should involve the right to be informed of all important decisions and the consequent opportunity to revoke, in concert with his fellows, the mandate to government. So, in the economic sphere, every capable individual must have a right to work, with, of course, the corollary that it is his duty to work well. Within the limits of social requirement, he ought to have the opportunity, as few now have, to choose and to vary his occupation. If he has merit, he ought to be able to advance by it. If he has initiative, he ought to be able to exercise it through the structure of his function. He should be able by his work to purchase a reward of service that meets all material needs; and from the accidents of unemployment and sickness, as from the cares of old age, he should be protected. This, at least, is what the State in substance means; and if its institutions have so far failed to give content to that meaning, it seems to follow that they stand in need of change.

The political science of the next generation will be mainly occupied, if it is to be fruitful, with the explorations of channels through which this end may be attained. It will seek to discover ways in which the individual may be made significant. It will have to remember that he is not absorbed by the State; within the mind of every man there are reserves into which organization does not, and ought not to, enter. Society is the harmony of a system of selves, not a harmony over and above them. It is the *milieu* in which they live; it is not itself the life. Control is social because individuals act directly upon each other, and it is necessary, therefore, to have criteria of right action. Here, we have argued that control must not lie in any vocation, or area, or rank, but in the citizen-body as a whole. For, otherwise, the lives of the many lie at the disposal of the few; and they are used, as history makes evident, not for the common good but a perversion of it. Our business is to give to the common man that access to his inheritance of which he has hitherto been deprived. Of that inheritance he has become aware; and the future most largely depends upon the response we make to his awareness. Our complex civilization is being tested by men who do not judge it by the thought and effort that have gone in its making, but by the happiness it brings to ordinary men and women. It is only by endeavouring to meet their desires that we shall be able to await their judgment with confidence.

VI

THE POLITICAL PHILOSOPHY OF MR. JUSTICE HOLMES

I

JUDGES, as a rule, must approach political problems interstitially, for they do not choose the subjects upon which they are to pronounce. It is rare, therefore, for a judge to exhibit a philosophy of politics which implies more than a series of half-conscious assumptions from which the ingenious student may hope to extract inferences of a general kind. The judge, moreover, is rarely, either by nature or training, a systematic philosopher. His life has been passed in minute attention to the particular; his practical value to the community depends at least as much upon his deliberate avoidance of the universal as upon his search for its attainment. We can hazard a view about the way in which Chief Justice Marshall or Lord Eldon, Sir Edward Coke or Mansfield would have approached the political scheme of things entire; for the circumstances of their period bound them to diverse exposition in varied fields of effort. But, for the most part, the political philosophy of judges is a series of half-articulate hints which men like Montesquieu or Bentham or Savigny must mould into a system.

To this general rule, Mr. Justice Holmes is no exception. We know, in fairly rigorous outline, the manner of his approach to political problems; but fate has made the connection between philosophic background and detailed principle inevitably fragmentary in character. The things we might wish to know, his views, for instance, upon the merits and weaknesses of democratic government, his theory of the ultimate nature of the State, his attitude as to the proper limits, if any, of collectivist action, these are not issues susceptible of exhaustive analysis from the Bench. He has had to work within the framework of a constitution which shaped the permissive boundaries of his possible speculations, and upon the legitimacy of statutes of which the social desirability was, for the most part, beyond his competence as a judge. And the attempt to construct a general framework is, in his case, the more difficult because his work has been singularly free from the habit, not uncommon among his colleagues of the last half-century, of erecting private prejudice into legal principle. His decisions probably contain fewer *obiter dicta* which seek a definite measure of the expediency of legislation than those of any judge of the Supreme Court in modern times. With a self-abnegation which is remarkable, he has used the principles of the American Constitution as a method of analysis and not a scale of judgment, a pathway to, not a barrier against, an end which must remain permanently undefined.

Nor is this all. It is an essential characteristic of Mr. Justice Holmes' judicial work that it is inherently sceptical and relativist in temper. In a sense, perhaps, the category of time has been for him the penumbra which gives validity to all exercise of judgment. Nothing in his decisions exhibits the confident dogmatism of Field or Brewer or Peckham. He has been much more concerned with the ways of attaining ends than with the ends themselves. Himself a consistent experimentalist in outlook, he has not conceived that the Constitution debars men from attempting experiments which he himself has obviously thought dubious or unwise. He has always had a profound sense of the possible varieties of social opinion, the uncertainty, accordingly, whether any or all of them are finally adequate; and this has meant, for him, a view of the judicial function which limits its competence to checking obvious infractions of fundamental rules, instead of so extending it as to make the judiciary the ultimate arbiter of the national destiny.

Yet, back of it all, there has lain a fairly consistent vision. The analyst cannot pin him down to a detailed code of beliefs; but he can at least exhibit the temper in which he has approached their making. He can see, above all, the influence upon him of that historical school of thought in which he has himself been so eminent a figure; with the interesting difference that whereas, with all save Maitland, historical learning has tended to make most lawyers conservative and averse from deliberate experiment, with Mr. Justice Holmes, awareness of the inevitability of change has made him accept the innovation of others, even where he has doubted its wisdom, as part of the necessary social process. It has made him, in a word, the spectator of law in a sense that has enabled him to see, as few judges have seen, what Montesquieu really meant by his definition of its substance. There has thus entered into him something of that power to see things *sub specie aeternitatis* which mainly assures the power to make a permanent contribution to the development of political thought.

II

The keynote of Mr. Justice Holmes' political outlook is a rejection of absolutist concepts. All principles are true in merely a relative way. The individual is not a subject of rights which the State is not entitled to invade. Men are social animals; and what they are entitled to do is a matter of degree, born of experience in some particular time and place. Man may be an end to himself; to society he is but a means likely enough to be used for purposes he may passionately deny. We are not entitled to formulae of any kind for the simple reason that the things we cannot help believing to be true are not necessarily the inescapable laws of the universe. Our code of behaviour, for him, is simply "a body of imperfect social generalizations expressed in terms of emotion," adequate only as they are capable of quantitative tactical confirmation.[1] There is never in any society a single body of agreed desires, but always conflicting purposes usually attainable only by inconsistent means. At the bottom of social life there lies always this inescapable battle of human wills; and the decision is reached by the power which one set of men uses to vindicate its superiority over another set. There is, in short, in Mr. Justice Holmes a Spinoza proclaiming that might gives to right its letters of credit; and that realism refuses the admission of ultimates as attainable in political philosophy.

So he rejects the idea of natural law.[2] It is no more than man's restless craving for the superlative, and, at bottom, it means no more than the system which has become so fully a part of our intellectual climate that we cannot work our institutions successfully except upon its assumptions. And with the idea of natural law there goes also the idea of rights which, a little scornfully perhaps, he has defined as the "hypostasis of a prophecy." Rights, for him, are claims of which the validity is proved by their capacity to realize themselves. They state our desires; they leave behind them no more than what he has called "the fighting will of the subject to maintain them."[3] He rejects, accordingly, any attempt at *a priorism*. Rights are not the postulates of a pre-existing framework within which law must work. They are the product of law, maintained as the possession of citizens because that part of the community which has the power to maintain them is prepared to fight to that end. Law, therefore, becomes the expression of the will of the stronger part of society; and the State is the organization of the institutions which give form and coherence to the expression so maintained.

It is, in part, the creed of a soldier, and, in part, also, the

[1] Holmes, *Collected Legal Papers* (1921), p. 306.
[2] *Ibid.*, pp. 310 ff.   [3] *Ibid.*, p. 313.

realism of one who feels intensely the limits of human knowledge. What he has called the cosmic plan of campaign remains for him unrevealed. All we can do in matters of social constitution is to seek the realization of our desires. If we are wise, we shall scrutinize the facts about us and seek so to adjust our will as to make it accord with the possible; "personally," he has written, "I like to know what the bill is going to be before I order a luxury."[1] To feel it possible that one may be wrong; to doubt the wisdom of all panaceas; to subject the claim of the individual to the inevitable criterion of social welfare; to recognize how inescapably one's ideals are bound up with a finite system of experience, how little, therefore, they are entitled to pose as universal; to interpret the historic process as the outcome, not of a victory for necessary truth, but as the record of what men were prepared to die for rather than surrender; these are the contours of Mr. Justice Holmes' political faith. It is, in a sense, a Stoic's philosophy, a refusal to accept optimistic illusion as against the sense of the facts that *die Weltgeschichte* has indeed been *das Weltgericht*. There is, too, a certain note of sadness in it, as in all Stoic philosophy. But, with him, as with Spinoza once more, the sadness is modified by its permeation with the sense that what men claim carries with it a contingent validity by the fact that it is already a claim. For those who become, by their demands, the plaintiffs against tradition may start as a minority. They yet work in the prospect that the force of the future may be on their side.

That attitude is the root of what has not seldom been interpreted as Mr. Justice Holmes' radicalism. In truth, the interpretation is a wholly mistaken one. A famous speech makes it evident that the basis of his economic faith would have been rejected neither by Adam Smith nor Ricardo; that, where property is concerned, he is satisfied to consider

[1] Holmes, *Collected Legal Papers* (1921), p. 307.

POLITICAL PHILOSOPHY OF JUSTICE HOLMES 151

wise administration as the justification of ownership.[1] What has been called his radicalism is, in fact, no more than the inevitable result of his sceptical outlook. To regard tradition as invariably upon the defence is necessarily to allow the other man the maximum opportunity to discard its teaching. Within, therefore, the limits that the preservation of order permits, he has not been willing to deny effort of which he disapproved.

This explains his liberalism in relation to tenets which his more conservative colleagues have rejected. It explains, for example, the famous dissent in the *Abrams* case;[2] that is not, as has often been supposed, the consecration of freedom of speech, but the announcement that in his judgment for Mr. Abrams to differ from the Government of the United States was not a direct incitement to immediate disorder. It explains, again, a view he has often taken, as in *Lochner* v. *New York*,[3] of the limits to social experiment. If, he says in effect, a body of my fellow-countrymen choose to take the view that certain legislation is wise, their failure to conform to previous canons of wisdom does not inherently upset their right to their opinion. The test of legitimate purpose in State action is not the wisdom of our ancestors, but whether reasonable men could, upon the facts before them, have drawn the inferences which a particular legislature has chosen to draw. Here, once more, the very foundation of his outlook is the vivid sense of the relativity of tradition.

It is almost inherent in this philosophy that Mr. Justice Holmes should have been the forerunner of the sociological interpretation of law. He sees law, no doubt, as the sovereign's fiat, valid, in essence, because the authority of the State will go to its enforcement. He states it, also, in terms of an irresponsible and unlimited will such as Hobbes himself

---

[1] Holmes, *Collected Legal Papers* (1921), pp. 279 ff.
[2] *Abrams* v. *United States*, 250 U.S. 616, 40 Sup. Ct. 17 (1919).
[3] 198 U.S. 45, 25 Sup. Ct. 539 (1905).

would have strongly approved.[1] But he sees always behind the act of sovereignty that mysterious congeries of impalpable forces which made John Chapman Gray say in despair that the real rulers of a society are undiscoverable.[2] It is this, also, which makes him separate with some sharpness law and morals.[3] Law is simply the body of rules of behaviour which a particular society at a particular time is prepared to enforce. To say that they are right means for him only that the particular society is at that particular time prepared to enforce them. The content of its will is always born of a special experience which circumstances may change.

And this, again, has made him wary of exaggerating the place of logic in social arrangements. Many years before Professor Graham Wallas had written his epoch-making *Human Nature in Politics*, Mr. Justice Holmes, in a classic paper,[4] had written with brilliant insight into what he called "the fallacy of logical form." He had seen for how much tradition and imitation count in our acceptance of rules of which the substance has long since been obsolete. He had refused to agree that "a given system . . . can be worked out like mathematics from some general maxims of conduct."[5] The facts count; and the facts are aggregate experience and the relative power behind its different elements can alone determine which group of them will prevail. This, once more, has led him to see how much the driving power of emotion counts in the shaping of social forces; and I should not, I think, unduly misrepresent his view of social good if I defined it, in William James' phrase, as the response to demand on the largest possible scale. The Spinoza in him makes him admit that it is good for a man to get what he wants if, other things being equal, he is successful in its attainment. That is why he has described the justification

[1] *Kawananakoa* v. *Polyblank*, 205 U.S. 349, 27 Sup. Ct. 526 (1907).
[2] Gray, *The Nature and Sources of the Law* (2nd ed., 1921), p. 77.
[3] Holmes, *Collected Legal Papers* (1921), p. 179.
[4] "The Path of the Law," *ibid.*, p. 167.   [5] *Ibid.*, p. 180.

of a statute as consisting "in some help which the law brings towards reaching a social end which the governing power of the community has made up its mind that it wants."[1]

That last sentence is, perhaps, the key to the whole political outlook of Mr. Justice Holmes. For him, as for Spinoza, the right of a Government over its subjects is in reality its power to command their obedience. He does not postulate ideal rights; he infers actual rights from the empirical behaviour of men. He states Spinoza's theory in fairly unqualified terms, and then, like Spinoza himself, sets out the grim qualifications of fact to which its actual exercise is subject in daily life.[2] He would, I think echo Spinoza's famous remark that "freedom and strength of mind are virtues in private men, but the virtue of governments is safety." For that reason, also, the psychology which underlies his principles is, as is essential to the judge's task, a human nature as the courts encounter it in the system that he knows, rather than one as it might be upon different assumptions of social value. He has a profound sense of both the variety of human wants and the scarcity which characterizes our power to satisfy them; from this is born his constant insistence upon conflict as the root of social change. And he infers from that conflict the need of law to regulate the expression of will in terms of principle—the impossibility, therefore, of more than a limited freedom for the citizen. He would add, I think, with Spinoza, that the reasonableness of a State is the measure of its strength, and that reasonableness is, for the most part, the outcome of a Government's willingness to show in its activities a decent respect for the public opinion of its citizens.[3]

It is this latter attitude which forms the basis for much

---

[1] " The Path of the Law," *Collected Legal Papers*, p. 225.
[2] *Kawananakoa* v. *Polyblank, ut supra*, p. 152, note 1. *Cf.* 3 Spinoza, *Tractatus Politicus*, pp. 5–9. [3] Spinoza, *op. cit., supra*, note 3, at 7.

of his supposed radicalism. He may admit that, logically, the sovereign can do no wrong simply because it is the sovereign; but he is too impressed by the fallibility of its human agents not to acquiesce in limitations in practice upon its power. He has insisted therefore on the value of those safeguards which, collectively, we call freedom; and he has been at pains to magnify the prospect of their maintenance. A constant faith that the other man may be right has made him vigilant about autocratic pretension; and this has made him seek ways of attaining that maximum self-expression in the citizen which is consistent with the maintenance of order. Clearly enough, he dislikes extremism, partly because he distrusts all certitude, and partly because his sense of history makes him think it wise to acquiesce in any government which is tolerably well administered. Once more, I believe, it is the ideal Spinoza envisaged; and one can assume that he would echo the famous words of the fifth chapter of the *Tractatus* where the great Dutch thinker tells us that "a government is best under which men lead a peaceable life, by which I mean that life of man which consisteth not only in the circulation of the blood and other properties common to all animals, but whose chief part is reason and the true life and excellence of the mind."[1]

III

So much in general background. Upon the peculiar problems of American politics, a foreigner must summarize with trepidation;[2] nor can he venture to concern himself with niceties of technical detail. Any general survey of Mr. Justice Holmes' work upon the Supreme Court, I think, must begin by noting the realism of his approach. He has sought to

[1] *Cf.* Holmes, *Collected Legal Papers* (1921), pp. 246, 251, 296, 305, etc.
[2] I draw attention to Professor Frankfurter's well-known article, "Mr. Justice Holmes and the Constitution" (1927), 41 *Harvard Law Review*, p. 121, for an admirable approach to this aspect.

interpret the Constitution not as a framework of immutable doctrine which scrutinizes with jealousy all social innovation, but as a system of limits capable of expansion in terms of new experience. It is, as I have noted, the outcome of a sense that, in politics, the category of time is all-important; "history," he has written, "sets us free and enables us to make up our minds dispassionately whether the survival we are enforcing answers any new purpose when it has ceased to answer the old."[1] Because of this, also, he has been what may be termed a liberal constructionist; whether it is congressional or State legislation that he is considering, his effort has been to find room for the expression of a power unless it runs decisively against the obvious intent of the supreme instrument. The result, for him, has been a conscious effort to limit, where possible, the competence of the Bench to substitute judicial for legislative view of desirable policy. All experiment seems to him legitimate that is not clearly forbidden.

Illustrations of this attitude abound. The American Constitution is, for him, federal in that special sense which does not deny the luxury of dubious experiment to the constituent parts. *Noble State Bank* v. *Haskell*[2] is an admirable warning against the temptation to centralize control in the interests of superior knowledge. So, also, the classical dissents in the *Lochner*[3] and *Adair*[4] cases are a memorable insistence on the right of social experiment wherever the weight of evidence would justify the holding of a particular view by a reasonable man. Neither the Fifth nor the Fourteenth Amendment constitutes for him the consecration of a particular economic theory; they are not a gate but a road. "A constitution," he wrote in the former case, ". . . is made for people of fundamentally differing views, and the accident

[1] Holmes, *Collected Legal Papers* (1921), p. 225.
[2] 219 U.S. 104, 31 Sup. Ct. 186 (1911).
[3] *Lochner* v. *New York*, 198 U.S. 45, 25 Sup. Ct. 539 (1905).
[4] *Adair* v. *United States*, 208 U.S. 161, 28 Sup. Ct. 277 (1908).

of our finding certain opinions natural and familiar or novel and even shocking ought not to conclude our judgment upon the question whether statutes embodying them conflict with the Constitution of the United States." So liberty of contract cannot be held to exclude the establishment by Congress of a minimum wage for women,[1] or of the regulation of the hours of labour,[2] or of the prohibition against dismissal of men because they are members of a labour union.[3] He has insisted that the Constitution is always perverted when it limits the victory of a dominant opinion for whose sanity a solid body of evidence may be arrayed in proof.

And as with the power of the States, so, also, with the authority of Congress. Granted that the Supreme Court was intended to pass upon the constitutionality of federal legislation, "I suppose that we all agree that to do so is the gravest and most delicate duty that this Court is called upon to perform."[4] It is legitimate, for example, for Congress to prohibit the movement in inter-State commerce of goods manufactured by child labour; the power to regulate may reasonably include even an indirect power to prohibit that of which the direct control has been given to the States.[5] And he has so interpreted congressional power as to argue that it is the business of the Court, if it reasonably can, so to interpret the statute as to save the Act, an attitude of which his dissent in the *Employers' Liability Cases*[6] is a good example. Nor is this all. He is not prepared to force upon Congress the duty of a mechanical uniformity in its legislation unless, as in the eighth section of the First Article of the Constitution, uniformity is specifically enjoined;

[1] *Adkins* v. *Children's Hospital*, 261 U.S 525, 43 Sup. Ct. 394 (1923).
[2] *Lochner* v. *New York, supra*, p. 155, note 3; and *cf. Ellis* v. *United States*, 206 U.S. 246, 27 Sup. Ct. 600 (1907).
[3] *Coppage* v. *Kansas*, 236 U.S. 1, 35 Sup. Ct. 240 (1915).
[4] *Blodgett* v. *Holden*, 275 U.S. 142, 147, 48 Sup. Ct. 105, 107 (1927).
[5] *Hammer* v. *Dagenhart*, 247 U.S. 251, 277, 38 Sup. Ct. 529, 533 (1918).
[6] 207 U.S. 463, 541, 28 Sup. Ct. 141, 163 (1908); *cf.* the explicit declaration of this view in *Tyson* v. *Banton*, 273 U.S. 418, 47 Sup. Ct. 426 (1927).

"I cannot doubt," he has written, "that in matters with which Congress is empowered to deal it may make different arrangements for widely different localities with perhaps widely different needs."[1]

On all this, and its implication, I venture with temerity to make one comment. It seems to me that Mr. Justice Holmes' way of approaching the nature of American federalism has enabled him to render to its interpretation a service comparable in magnitude with that of Marshall over a century ago. Exactly as the latter preserved the Constitution from the vice of a narrow particularism, so Mr. Justice Holmes has saved it from becoming the prisoner of a narrow individualism. He has done so by recognizing that what he has called the "inarticulate major premise"[2] of the judge is not entitled to set limits to possible and reasonable conceptions of social welfare. Again a foreigner must speak with hesitation; but I hazard the judgment that, in this regard, his opinions have been a major factor in the last generation in maintaining popular respect for the Supreme Court at a high level.

One foundation for this attitude lies, I think, in his conception of the nature of judicial power. American judges have too often taken the theory of the separation of powers as though by some divine prescription it enabled the Bench to declare the law without making it. Mr. Justice Holmes has seen deeper. "I recognize without hesitation," he has written, "that judges do and must legislate."[3] But, because the legislative aspect of their task is "confined from molar to molecular motions," they are not entitled to replace legislative decision by their own. The legislature is not to be hampered by judicial control unless the limitation proceeds

[1] *Knickerbocker Ice Co.* v. *Stewart*, 253 U.S. 149, 169, 40 Sup. Ct. 438, 443 (1920).   [2] In the *Lochner* case, *supra*, p. 155, note 3.
[3] *Southern Pacific* v. *Jensen*, 244 U.S. 205, 221, 37 Sup. Ct. 524, 530 (1917); *cf. Springer* v. *Government of Philippines*, 277 U.S. 189, 209, 48 Sup. Ct. 480, 485 (1928).

from the plain words of the Constitution.[1] Indeed, so far is he prepared to go in this view that, as far as congressional legislation is concerned, he has declared his doubt whether "the United States would come to an end" if the judicial veto were abolished.[2] He has been deeply concerned by legal ignorance of political economy, and the tendency of some courts to read into Constitutions "acceptance of the economic doctrines which prevailed about fifty years ago, and a wholesale prohibition of what a tribunal of lawyers does not think about right."[3] So he has preached to his judicial brethren what may perhaps be best termed the duty of intellectual humility, the obligation not to identify constitutionalism with social theories which happen to coincide with their own scheme of preferences. And it is worth while pointing out that this realist view of the judicial function is perhaps more true to what the theory of the separation of powers was in fact intended to secure than others which are less candid in their insight. For, the court whose prohibitions control the acts of a legislature accumulates in its hands those varied powers which Madison insisted became the very definition of tyranny.

What I have called his intellectual humility can be shown in many ways. It lies at the base of his conception of the police power, particularly in its relation to the Fourteenth Amendment. "There is nothing I more deprecate," he has said, "than the use of the Fourteenth Amendment beyond the absolute compulsion of its words to prevent the making of social experiments that an important part of the community desires, in the insulated chambers afforded by the several States, even though the experiments may seem futile or even noxious to me and to those whose judgment I most respect."[4] It is seen, again, in his continuous effort

[1] *Louisville & Nashville R. R.* v. *Barber Asphalt Paving Co.*, 197 U.S. 430, 25 Sup. Ct. 466 (1905).
[2] Holmes, *Collected Legal Papers* (1921), p. 295.   [3] *Ibid.*, p. 184.
[4] *Truax* v. *Corrigan*, 257 U.S. 312, 344, 42 Sup. Ct.142, 134 (1921).

towards a quantitative approach to the limitations imposed by the Constitution. We are not to search for mathematical precision in these matters; the lines of politics, as Burke said, are broad and deep as well as long.[1]

A word is necessary upon the manner in which Mr. Justice Holmes has approached the interpretation of the Bill of Rights under the Constitution. Again, his method of analysis has been quantitative in character. He has refused to regard it as a list of absolute prohibitions. Membership in the State, for him, involves the surrender of the absolute in politics. For, in the first place, extraordinary situations may demand extraordinary remedies; "when it comes," he has written, "to a decision by the head of the State upon a matter involving its life, the ordinary rights of individuals must yield to what he deems the necessities of the moment. Public danger warrants the substitution of executive process for judicial process."[2] And, in the second, the exercise of any right is always subject to the limitation that it shall not provoke those circumstances out of which an immediate and direct threat to public safety may arise; "the most stringent protection of free speech," he has argued, "would not protect a man in falsely shouting fire in a theatre and causing a panic."[3] But, subject to such margins, Mr. Justice Holmes has always favoured, as the very notable dissent in the *Abrams* case[4] makes plain, a narrow construction of safeguards intended to protect the interests of personality in their civic expression. For, as he has said, though persecution for opinion may be logical, "the best test of truth is the power of the thought to get itself accepted in the competition of the market."[5] So, also, he has argued against any

[1] *Cf.*, e.g., *Weaver* v. *Palmer Bros.*, 270 U.S. 402, 415, 46 Sup. Ct. 320, 323 (1926); *Frost & Frost* v. *Railroad Commission of California*, 271 U.S. 583, 600, 46 Sup. Ct. 605, 609 (1926). It is a constantly recurring idea.
[2] *Moyer* v. *Peabody*, 212 U.S. 78, 85, 29 Sup. Ct. 235, 237 (1909).
[3] *Schenck* v. *United States*, 249 U.S. 47, 54, 39 Sup. Ct. 247, 249 (1919).
[4] *Abrams* v. *United States*, 250 U.S. 616, 40 Sup. Ct. 17 (1919).
[5] *Ibid.*, 630, 40 Sup. Ct. at 22.

broad interpretation of the Postmaster-General's authority to control the freedom of the Press by the refusal of the mailing privilege.[1] So, once more, in the *Frank* case, he could not concur in the denial of a fair trial even when the forms of jury procedure had been superficially satisfied.[2]

In this realm, I think, there is a marked resemblance between the ideas of Bentham and those of Mr. Justice Holmes.[3] For both, the need for security is paramount; and the enjoyment of individual rights is secondary in every case to that major end. But, with him as with Bentham, once the major end is safe, the protection of the individual from arbitrary control is a sacred obligation. Rights may be born of the law; but their plain intent is to curb the authority of Government, and it is therefore peculiarly incumbent upon the judiciary to watch with special care their active exercise.

One final aspect of his attitude may be noticed. I have already observed that in matters of economic constitution the leanings of Mr. Justice Holmes are towards the classic doctrines of the nineteenth century; some, indeed, of his pronouncements upon socialism have about them a note of acid scorn.[4] But that has not meant with him, as it has not seldom meant in decisions of the Supreme Court, an effort to exalt the rights of property into a place of special privilege in the State. So long as a Government treats the owner of an acquired title with fairness, he is "infected with the original weakness of dependence upon the will of the State."[5] It is impossible to hold that "all property owners in a State have a vested right that no general proposition of law shall be reversed, changed or modified by the courts if the conse-

---

[1] *United States* v. *Burleson*, 255 U.S. 407, 436, 41 Sup. Ct. 352, 363 (1921).
[2] *Frank* v. *Magnum*, 237 U.S. 309, 345, 35 Sup. Ct. 582, 594 (1915).
[3] *Cf.* Bentham, *Principles of Morals and Legislation* (Oxford ed., 1907), p. 224 and note 1.
[4] Holmes, *Collected Legal Papers* (1921), pp. 279, 306.
[5] *Western Union* v. *Kansas*, 216 U.S. 1, 55, 30 Sup. Ct. 190, 209 (1910).

quence to them will be more or less pecuniary loss."[1] A State cannot be prevented from discouraging particular forms of economic activity by special methods of taxation.[2] Property may not be taken without compensation, "but with the help of a phrase (the police power), some property may be taken or destroyed for public use without paying for it, if you do not take too much. When we come to the fundamental distinctions, it is still more obvious that they must be received with a certain latitude or our Government could not go on."[3] He has protested on many occasions against an effort to make the Fourteenth Amendment a method for specially protecting the rights of property by reading into it a "delusive exactness" which is, in sober fact, contrary to its nature. "By calling a business 'property,'" he has urged, "you make it seem like land, and lead up to the conclusion that a statute cannot substantially cut down the advantages of ownership existing before the statute was passed.... It is a course of conduct, and like other conduct is subject to substantial modification according to time and circumstances both in itself and in regard to what shall justify doing it a harm.... Legislation may begin where an evil begins."[4]

The last sentence is the key to the whole. The inherent power of the State to meet its problems as they may arise is, for him, the unassailable and primordial postulate of political science. To that end it possesses sovereignty; and the limitations upon the exercise of its power are, in his conception, what may be termed limitations of manner rather than of substance. Judicial prohibitions, therefore, must be aimed not at the object sought for, but at the

[1] *Muhlker v. New York & Harlem R. R.*, 197 U.S. 544, 574, 25 Sup. Ct. 522, 529 (1905).
[2] *Quaker City Cab Co. v. Pennsylvania*, 277 U.S. 389, 403, 48 Sup. Ct. 553, 555 (1928).
[3] *Springer v. Government of Philippines, supra,* p. 157, note 3, at 210, 48 Sup. Ct. at 485.
[4] *Truax v. Corrigan, supra,* p. 158, note 4, at 342, 42 Sup. Ct. at 133.

way in which the object is sought. Admittedly, manner and substance shade off inextricably the one into the other; "the ordinances of the Constitution do not establish and divide fields of black and white."[1] But it is in the recognition that mathematical exactitude is not attainable in social legislation, that, accordingly, unless the individual right is gravely invaded the social interest must prevail, that the criterion of constitutionality must be found. It is difficult not to feel that Mr. Justice Holmes' long emphasis upon this attitude has humanized the jurisprudence of the United States.

IV

In the proud preface to Montesquieu's last work there are certain words than which none are more fitting to Mr. Justice Holmes' labours. "When I have seen," wrote Montesquieu, "what so many great men in France, England and Germany have written before me, I have been lost in admiration, but without losing my courage; I, too, am a painter, I have said with Correggio." That, as I think, has been the secret of Mr. Justice Holmes' pre-eminence in his time. It is not only that he has had the scholar's breadth of knowledge. It is not merely, either, that he has realized how the facts call the judge, and especially, perhaps, the American judge, to the tasks of statesmanship. Both these qualities he has had in full measure. But, above all, he has had the great artist's power of penetrating with the vision of genius to the essential, of making the bridge between the little fact of daily life and the sweeping generalization by which a State rises to the consciousness of its purpose. He has done it with singular felicity of expression, and with unvarying integrity of mind. We can only be humbly grateful in the presence of so rare and so distinguished an achievement.

---

[1] *Springer* v. *Government of Philippines, supra,* p. 157, note 3, at 209, 48 Sup. Ct. at 485.

VII

THE TECHNIQUE OF JUDICIAL APPOINTMENT

It is difficult to overestimate the significance of the judiciary in the modern State. The work of the executive has become so vast, the powers delegated to it by the legislature are so wide, that judges are, perhaps more than at any previous time, the real safeguard of personal liberty. It is only necessary to recall cases like *Coppage* v. *Kansas*,[1] or *R.* v. *Halliday*,[2] to realize how nearly judicial activity goes to the very heart of freedom. That is, of course, even more the case when, as with America, the constitution of the State is written, and the judges are its appointed interpreters. For they are then, inevitably, the masters of the constitution. Few written constitutions are easy to amend; and the ambit of legislative policy is not seldom defined by the knowledge of judicial decision. The fact that a court may regard a minimum wage law as a denial of freedom of contract,[3] the belief that it looks upon the secondary boycott as a combination in restraint of trade,[4] may well be decisive of what acts a legislature will place upon the statute book.

Obviously, therefore, the method by which judges are appointed, the kind of men, further, it is customary to choose, these questions become a matter of the first importance. The tasks entrusted to them are not the less delicate and fundamental because they are rarely dramatic. If their business is, at first appearance, merely the resolution of complaint, the nature of such complaint may, in fact, determine the quality of civic life. Too little attention has been paid in political science to the problem to which their

---

[1] 236 U.S. 1. [2] [1917] A.C. 226.
[3] *Adkins* v. *Children's Hospital*, 261 U.S. 525.
[4] *Duplex Printing Co.* v. *Deering*, 254 U.S. 443.

functions give rise. Here I propose to discuss only in general the various ways in which they may be chosen; and to illustrate one of those ways by an analysis of certain phases of the English system.

There are three general methods by which a judge may be chosen. His appointment may be hereditary, as in the France of the *ancien régime*; he may be selected by a person or persons competent for that purpose; or he may be elected by a direct popular or legislative vote. No one now urges that the first method has any validity. It did, undoubtedly, produce remarkable men in a few instances; but the memoirs of the seventeenth and eighteenth centuries make it clear that, in general, it was the nurse of corruption and incompetence. Since, moreover, the thesis upon which Western civilization is increasingly built is a denial of hereditary right, it is not worth while to examine this form in any detail.

The method of election by direct or legislative vote is more popular and needs much more careful examination. In the United States, thirty-eight of the constituent States elect their judges by a direct popular vote; in four others they are elected by the legislature. The term of election varies enormously; in Vermont it is for so short a period as two years, while the judges of the highest court in New York hold office for fourteen, and those in Pennsylvania for twenty-one years. In Switzerland, the Federal Legislature elects the judges of the Federal Court; in the Cantons, they are chosen by the Cantonal Council. In all other countries of primary significance, executive nomination, with or without legislative consent, seems the general rule.

What is to be said for the elective method? First, let it be noted that in at least three American States it is usual to be satisfied with the results of the system; in others, the degree both of professional and lay dissatisfaction varies enormously, New York, Minnesota, Missouri and Pennsylvania[1] being, it appears, the States in which least criticism has been aroused. In Switzerland, all competent authorities are agreed that the system works well; but here it should be remarked that the very limited jurisdiction of the Federal Court hardly makes it a likely subject of heated controversy.

For the election of judges by popular vote there is nothing to be said. In so far as its underlying assumption is the belief that the people should choose those by whom they are to be governed, it omits to note the vital fact that the qualifications for judicial office are not such as an undifferentiated public can properly assess. The constitutional qualifications, of age, citizenship, good character, and the rest have little meaning. Knowledge of the law, the balanced mind, the ability to brush aside inessentials and drive to the heart of a case—that a candidate will possess these qualities can, at best, be known only to a few. The people do not, in fact, choose their judges. They decide between the candidates of opposing parties, and, with rare exceptions, they merely vote for the colour they happen to prefer. It need not be denied that, under this system, extraordinarily eminent men have been chosen; it is only necessary to think of a man like Chief Judge Cardozo to see that this may be the case. But it is equally obvious that extraordinarily incompetent people, without any sort of pretensions to their function, can likewise be selected. This is, in fact, one of those cases in which a judgment by the public neither does nor can imply the existence of a public opinion. For we are here in a realm where the public, in any meaning sense of the word, is what Mr. Lippmann has admirably called a phantom.[2]

Nor does the difficulty end with the fact of choice. The system introduces the need of habits which ought con-

---

[1] *Cf.* Hall, in *Journal of American Judic. Soc.*, iii. 37-52; Hand, *Acad. Pol. Sci. Proc.*, iii. 130.   [2] W. Lippmann, *The Phantom Public* (1925).

sistently to be absent from the judicial mind. There have been judges who, while on the Bench, have looked to executive office when their judicial term is over. There have been judges, in North Dakota for example, who have sought to win favour from their electorate by the issue of weekly manifestos on the business of the court. There have been judges, as the trials under some of the "free speech" cases have shown, who have used their office to announce their possession of views unrelated to the issues before them. The method of election, if it is for a short term, means insecurity of tenure; and that position is fatal to a proper judicial habit of mind. It does not matter whether the power that can dismiss a judge be a sovereign one, like James I, or a sovereign many, like the modern democracy. The mere fact that to be on the Bench is, at least ultimately, to be in politics brings into play every factor which is ruinous to judicial independence. And, since judicial independence is the first requisite of judicial purity, it is the primary consideration to be satisfied in the making of selective criteria.

Little of this, it may be noted, would be remedied if the nomination of candidates for popular choice were made non-partisan in character. For many lawyers of eminence, particularly in equity work, simply do not come before the public at all, and would consequently be defeated because they were unknown; while others would be chosen either because a party was surreptitiously behind them, or because they were connected with some great interest, a business corporation for example, which knew how to exert its influence at the proper time. To the average voter, moreover, the great lawyer largely means the successful criminal lawyer; and while it is not a universal truth, the experience of England seems to suggest that the successful criminal lawyer very rarely makes a distinguished judge. From whatever point of view, in fact, the method of popular choice be regarded, even its occasional successes do not evade the essential fact that it is entrusting to the ignorant a task of the greatest delicacy and difficulty.

Election by the legislature is not open to the same objections; but it is still, I think, an undesirable method of choice. For, in the first place, the number of members in any legislature who are competent to choose is very small, and most will be swayed by exactly the same political considerations as the popular voter outside. If we consider what happens in a legislature that exercises this power, it becomes clear that the process is an undesirable one. If there is executive nomination, the name, as a rule, must spring from the party that is in a majority. If there is legislative nomination, the eligibility of members of the assembly produces an atmosphere in which a proper choice can hardly be made. Even if members of the assembly were, by a self-denying ordinance, excluded from the field of choice, the process of election would, to a sensitive person, be an intolerable one. If the voting were open, as all legislative voting should be open, it is hardly fair to the elector to announce his preference in a matter where personalities play so large a part. If it is secret, it opens the gates to illegitimate influence, to wire-pulling, and the use of political prestige in a fashion that would probably result in the choice not of the best, but of the most "available" candidate. I would, indeed, go even farther than this and suggest that the Senate's confirmation of presidential appointments is not a desirable system. The fight against the nomination of Mr. Justice Brandeis in 1916 was clear proof that, once a political assembly becomes involved in the system of choice, factors will enter in of a kind entirely unrelated to the necessary qualifications. And when that is set against the fact that the Senate has again and again confirmed the appointment of men about whom either nothing at all was known, or against whom everything could be said, it may be doubted whether its power to check presidential error is as valuable as general belief would seem to suggest.

I believe, therefore, that the nomination of the judges by the executive is the only feasible system of appointment. But it is clearly undesirable to leave it in the hands of the unfettered discretion of any executive politician to make a choice so momentous as this. Personal friendship and political eminence would exert far too great an influence upon him. In England, for example, it is customary to offer judicial posts as they fall vacant to the Attorney-General and Solicitor-General; and the Senior Counsel to the Treasury is generally, after a period of service, considered to have a claim upon such offices. It is notorious that Lord Halsbury used his position as Lord Chancellor to promote members of his own party; and it is seldom that an American President has the courage to nominate one of his political opponents.

It may be useful to illustrate the working of the system of unfettered executive nomination by an analysis of English experience from 1832 until 1906.[1] Out of the 139 judges appointed in that period, eighty were members of the House of Commons at the time of their nomination; eleven others had been candidates for Parliament, six of them on more than one occasion. Of the eighty who thus reached the Bench by the avenue of the House of Commons, no less than thirty-three had been either Attorney or Solicitor-General. Excluding from these men who became Lords Chancellor in this period, no less than fourteen were made, not merely ordinary judges, but heads of the court to which they were called. It is not, for instance, insignificant that, with one exception, every English Chief Justice for the last sixty years has been an ex-Attorney-General; and even the exception is explained by the notorious fact that his suc-

[1] The results which follow were compiled for me by Mrs. Annette Henderson through a grant made for this, among other purposes, by the Laura Spelman Rockefeller Foundation.

cessor could not be spared by the Government of the day when the vacancy occurred. Eight of the judges who had occupied political office before appointment later returned to politics as Lords Chancellor; though it should be added in fairness that no such case has occurred in the last half-century. Of the eighty judges who left Parliament for the Bench sixty-three were appointed by their own party while in office; the remainder are cases where an opponent was selected by the Lord Chancellor of the day. It is also significant that the average age of judges appointed from among Members of Parliament was less by six years than the age of those chosen solely with reference to their position at the Bar.

I do not infer from these results more than the fact that membership of Parliament is a distinct assistance to a lawyer who desires judicial appointment. It is also clear, and certainly it is significant, that the most important judicial posts are, in England, largely the appanage of the chief legal advisers of the Cabinet of the day. Practically, that is to say, if a vacancy occurs in the highest judicial offices, existing members of the Bench will find themselves barred from access thereto. At the present time, for instance, the Chief Justiceship, the Mastership of the Rolls, and the Presidency of the Probate, Divorce, and Admiralty Divisions are all held by men who played a great part in politics during the last half-dozen years; and, apart from membership of the House of Lords, these are the most eminent judicial posts in the gift of the executive. A consideration, indeed, of appointments to the Bench in the last hundred years would certainly suggest that, as a rule, the purely legal figure devoted thereto is likely to be more eminent at the Bar, and also more distinguished as a judge, than his political colleague. Certainly names like Bowen, Blackburn, Bramwell, and Farwell would be difficult to surpass in eminence; and it is possibly notable that men of equal quality like Watson, Jessel, Davey, and Hannen were judged by most of their contemporaries to have been out of their natural sphere in the House of Commons. Nor are there names among the non-political appointees which represent failure as complete as some of the political judges with one exception; and that, it is suggestive, is the name of a judge, appointed twelve years younger than the average, who was the son of a living ex-Chancellor of the time.

I do not suggest that lawyers who are Members of Parliament are ineligible for judicial office thereby; on the contrary it is probable that, *ceteris paribus*, a good lawyer who has won for himself an eminent place in public life would gain from that experience habits of mind of value upon the Bench. But the statistics here summarized seem to make it probable that political influence has been a factor to which undue influence has been attached in the selection of English judges. It has been, in some degree, a reward for political service, and it will, I think, be common ground that this is undesirable. It is, moreover, remarkable that the legal officers of the Government should have been so consistently promoted to high judicial position. More, it is probably undesirable that a man who has at all recently engaged in the task of advising Government departments should suddenly reach a position where the problems to which his work gives rise have to be analysed in an impartial way. It is not necessary to suggest that there will be conscious unfairness; but it is, I submit, possible that such judges will, particularly in cases where the liberty of the subject is concerned, find themselves unconsciously biased through over-appreciation of executive difficulty. Men, for instance, who are to decide cases like *R*. v. *Halliday* or *R*. v. *Casement* ought not, from the very nature of the issues involved, to have had recent affiliation with the executive department of Government. Nothing is more disastrous than that any suspicion of the complete impartiality of the judges should be possible. And it is a simple remedy against such misinterpretation to allow an interval to elapse before men who have held Government posts should be given judicial office.

There is also another reason of some importance. I have pointed out that the number of high judicial posts filled by members of the Government in England has been, and continues to be, exceptionally large. The same, it will be remembered, is true, though not in so large a degree, of the Supreme Court of the United States. Attorneys-General, Senators, and Members of the Cabinet have played an exceptionally full part in its composition. Such practical pre-emption of the higher posts means, inevitably, that men in lower judicial positions find access to promotion barred to them. The number of English judges who move from the first Bench of the High Court to the Court of Appeal or the House of Lords is less than the number promoted to the last two from outside; not only is that the case, but of those who did so move the larger number began as politicians. The same is true in the United States. It is fairly rare for a member of either the District Court or the Circuit Court of Appeals to be elevated to the Supreme Court. Yet few things can be so stimulating to a judge as to know that really eminent work in an inferior court will secure the reward of appointment to a higher one. Even the most energetic minds may after a time find the routine of *nisi prius* work a little deadening in character. There is an advantage difficult to overestimate in the creation for them of the prospect that the retention of energy and interest will not be overlooked when higher appointments are made. And it is, in any case, unfair that the more important posts should be in such large measure reserved for those who have turned to the Bench only after they have sought and obtained political success.

With the qualities that a man destined for judicial office

should possess I shall not here concern myself; they have, in any case, been discussed by Dean Wigmore with an authority to which few can pretend.[1] But certain facts about the English judiciary may be of value. The average age at which English judges are appointed is fifty-three; but it is notable that, with two exceptions, the great judges of the nineteenth century have as a rule been younger. Bowen was forty-four; Blackburn was forty-six; Jessel was forty-nine; Watson was exactly fifty-three. Over 40 per cent. of the judges were Oxford men; well over 70 per cent. came either from Oxford or Cambridge. In general, that is to say, the average English lawyer will have been over thirty years at the Bar before he reaches the Bench; and seven out of every ten will have come from a class which, as a rule, without being wealthy will at least be comfortable. They will have been educated under a system in which the influence either of classics, as in the case of Oxford, or of mathematics, as at Cambridge, will have been predominant. No judge in the period with which I am here concerned was trained in economic science; and none had the connection of intimacy or sympathy with the working classes which gave a man like Frederic Harrison a place apart among the lawyers of his time. Facts like these are, I think, significant in relation to cases like the *Taff Vale* case[2] and *Osborne* v. *Amalgamated Society of Railway Servants*.[3] In America, of course, the far greater fluidity of social classes does not reproduce the English position; but I am not, I think, wrong in saying that Mr. Justice Brandeis is unique among American lawyers in having reached the Bench after services to the organized labour movement somewhat akin to those rendered to it in England by Frederic Harrison. This is important for the simple reason that most judges,

---

[1] See the preface to his *Supplement to a Treatise on the System of Evidence* (1915).   [2] *Taff Vale Ry. Co.* v. *A. S. R. S.* [1901] A.C. 426.
[3] [1910] A.C. 27.

TECHNIQUE OF JUDICIAL APPOINTMENT 173

even in the case of the contemporary Bench, will have been trained at a period when their surrounding intellectual environment assumed, almost without discussion, the essential truth of economic individualism. With matters in which industrial law came to be interpreted, therefore, they brought to its analysis minds steeped in a tradition already partly obsolete. And if, as with many of the English judges, they had played a part in Parliamentary debates on Acts like the Trade Union Law Amendment Act,[1] or the Employers' Liability Act,[2] their minds would, almost unconsciously, have been swayed by considerations of which the urgency has been well emphasized by Chief Judge Cardozo and Mr. Justice Holmes.

From all this, I would venture to draw two conclusions, one of which is directly germane to the technique of appointment; the other, while so relevant only indirectly, has, I believe, an ultimate bearing upon it of grave import. It is dubious, on the facts analysed above, whether the uncontrolled discretion of the executive in choosing judges is desirable; it seems to leave too great play to political influence. There ought, therefore, to be some advisory body whom the executive would consult about appointments. That body should not be a committee of the legislature, since the latter would tend, in the very nature of things, to be composed mainly of lawyer members. In England, at least, it would be difficult to make up such a body from members of the Bar, since this is not organized with a view to work of this kind. The best body, I believe, would be a committee of the judges selected by themselves for some such term as three or five years. It would necessarily be a small committee, limited, at the outside, to seven members; and it would probably be necessary to make the Lord Chief Justice, the Master of the Rolls, and the President of the Probate, Divorce, and Admiralty Divisions *ex-officio* members

[1] 39 and 40 Vict. c. 22.   [2] 43 and 44 Vict. c. 42.

of it. The responsibility of appointment would still rest with the Lord Chancellor, or the Prime Minister, according to the post to be filled; but at least we should be certain of a thorough assessment of claims before an appointment was made by men thoroughly competent to assess those claims. We should thereby make choice on purely political grounds a matter of grave difficulty. The Lord Chancellor, doubtless, would still bring forward names of men whom it was desired to reward for political services. But the danger of their selection on non-legal grounds would be far smaller if it was known, *a priori*, that any suggested persons would be thoroughly criticized by a representative committee of legal experts.

It would be possible, I think, to adapt such a scheme to American conditions without much difficulty. In the case of federal judges, the President would confer with a committee composed of the Chief Justice of the Supreme Court, and, say, five other judges chosen by the Federal Bench, of whom three would be judges of the Supreme Court, and the others representative of the Circuit and District Court judges respectively. To them might be added, as representatives of the Bar, the Attorney-General and the President of the American Bar Association. It is not, I suppose, possible to abolish the right of the Senate to confirm. But a recommendation which came to the Senate with such authority would go far to make federal appointments to the Bench non-political in character and, I should expect, rapidly reduce the power of the Senate to a mere form. I believe this to be a desirable end. For a committee of the legislature in which one party is in a majority is, where patronage is concerned, a most undesirable body to have any control over its exercise; and so large a body as the whole Senate is bound inevitably to lack the opportunity of informal discussion upon which the proper character of appointments so largely depends.

TECHNIQUE OF JUDICIAL APPOINTMENT

It would, moreover, be simple to adjust such methods to the requirements of the States. The active power of nomination might be resident in the Governor; I have already given reasons why the power of appointment ought not to be left either to popular or to legislative choice. The Governor would be assisted by a committee of the judges of the State Supreme Court, together with the State Attorney-General and the President of the State Bar Association. It would be necessary, of course, to transform all State judicial tenure into a permanent tenure. The maxim that judges should hold office *quam diu se bene gesserint* is of the essence of their independent position; and the danger that they might cling to their position too long could easily be met by a provision for compulsory retirement at seventy or seventy-five. At that age, on English experience, the average judge will have sat on the Bench seventeen or twenty-two years; and, granted the exacting nature of judicial work properly performed, it is probable that, for all save the most exceptional cases, that is a long enough period of service. The heads of the permanent Civil Service in England retire, in general, at sixty; and, on this principle, the judge would be given at least a further ten years of office.

I am assuming, of course, that this advisory body is here concerned with first appointments; promotion, as in England to the Court of Appeal, or in America from District to Circuit Courts, raises somewhat different considerations. If I am right in assuming that it is desirable to hold out the prospect of advancement in return for work well done, it would follow that it is desirable to reserve the higher posts for men already on the Bench. That would be effected by asking the advisory body, in these cases, to submit to the proper authority a list of three names from whom he could select one. It is not difficult to devise safeguards against the danger that either undue influence or mere seniority would be the governing principle in advancement.

To safeguard against the first danger it could be provided that no judge should be promoted from a position he has not occupied for five years; and, similarly, to safeguard against the danger that excessive deference might be paid to seniority, it could be provided, further, that no judge should be promoted who is less than five years from the age of retirement.

I may perhaps illustrate the working of this system by some examples drawn from English experience. It would have prevented the appointment of Lord Carson to the House of Lords; it would not have prevented the choice of Lord Sumner, or Lord Blanesburgh. It would not have interfered with the advancement of Blackburn or Bowen; it would have stopped the appointment of Rigby, L. J., Lord Russell, and Lord Alverstone, directly to the highest judicial positions. It would not have hindered the advancement of men like Lord Parker or Lord Lindley; it would have asked from men like Jessel and Davey a period of judicial apprenticeship before their transference, on grounds of ability, to appeal work. The problem of the dual judicial system in America could be met by providing that transference between the State Supreme Court and the Federal Supreme Court should be permitted; but from inferior State tribunals transference should be made only to the Federal Circuit and District Courts. A foreigner may perhaps be permitted to observe here that on such a system there would be a real possibility of men like Learned Hand, Hough, and Mack, J.J., reaching the Supreme Court for which their legal distinction makes them so eminently fitted. On the present system their merits seem inevitably forgotten by the appointing authority. Where transfer from a lower Federal Court does take place it seems as a rule to be on political or personal grounds. It is possible to recall an instance of such a choice where the judge promoted was explained to the outside public as "the most gifted orator

TECHNIQUE OF JUDICIAL APPOINTMENT 177

in the State of ——." That is, of course, a high merit; but it is not necessarily related to judicial fitness.

One other analogous remark may perhaps here be made. It is, it may be suggested, vital to judicial independence that once a man has accepted a position on the Bench, a political career should be closed to him; or, if he choose to go into politics, that he should not return to the Bench. Six English judges in the nineteenth century accepted the Chancellorship after a period of office on the Bench; others, right down to our own day, have been in the position of Lord Langdale who was offered but refused that post. Since the Chancellorship is very partially a judicial office,[1] it is as undesirable for it to be within the grasp of a judge as it was for Ellenborough, while Chief Justice, to be a member of the Cabinet. Nor must it be forgotten that ex-Lords-Chancellor remain members of the Supreme Appellate Tribunal. They gain, that is to say, all the advantages of being judges without being subject to the self-denying ordinances which the latter are compelled to make. And it is not, perhaps, in this regard insignificant that the judicial members of the House of Lords, as with Lord Sumner and Lord Carson, have taken a direct part in ordinary political controversy. It is an infectious example; for in the present year a judge on assize, in his charge to the Grand Jury, suggested that an increase in crime was possibly due to communist propaganda. Certainly a judge of forty years ago would not, however eager his political convictions, have attributed a heavy criminal calendar to a growth in the Liberal or Conservative vote. If he had, he would have met with severe censure from the House of Commons.

What is here urged about the English judiciary applies not less truly to that of the United States. I do not doubt

---

[1] See the comments on his functions by Lord Haldane, himself an ex-Chancellor, in the *Machinery of Government Committee's Report* (1918), p. 66 f.

M

that Mr. Taft was an eminent and successful Chief Justice; but it would have been better for him to have reached that position from the Circuit Court rather than from the Presidency. Judges who fight for the presidency and governorships of States, others who take part in political campaigns, cannot adequately have realized that, whatever is untrue in the doctrine of the separation of powers, this at least of truth it contains that the absolute independence of the judiciary from politics is essential to the maintenance in it of a full and lasting confidence.

To a very different range of questions the problem of judicial appointments also gives rise. It is practically impossible, outside the lowest categories of police-court work, to confide judicial authority to anyone who has not had a legal training. The judge may be assisted by non-legal assessors, as in the English Admiralty Court; and one hopes that in certain types of criminal cases, he will soon be assisted by medical assessors. But the trained legal mind is alone competent for the decisions of the problems which arise, and even more, for the statement of the grounds of decision to an inexpert body like a jury. It is, therefore, of importance for those interested in the judiciary to consider how the lawyer should best be trained for the end he is ultimately, if contingently, to serve.

Into the vast subject of legal education I do not propose here to go. But there are certain hypotheses which arise from what has already been said that it is desirable to set down. In general, first of all, it is important that a legal training should not be purely legal in character. Any jurisprudence that is to work must be sociological in essence—as men like Montesquieu, Mr. Justice Holmes, and Eugen Ehrlich have insisted. It is therefore urgent not to separate a body of legal teachers from their colleagues in economics and politics; and the courses followed by the student should include a thorough training in these sciences. For, otherwise, it will generally be inevitable that the lawyer will later accept the crude economics of the business community as the final word of economic science, which they are not; and he will further tend to believe that the political institutions by which he is governed represent the final institutions of Utopia. It is important that he should be trained at an early age to scepticism in these matters. Otherwise, from the general habits of his professional career, he will be incapable, when he reaches the Bench, of appreciating the novelties that will be urged upon him. The mere fact, for example, that Mr. Justice Brandeis' historic brief in *Miller v. Oregon*[1] should have been taken to mark an epoch in juristic science is evidence of how separated law has been from kindred disciplines of great importance to its welfare.[2]

Secondly, it seems to me vital that schools of law should also be schools of law reform. Their teachers are not merely to explain what the judges say the law actually is; they must also insist, by constant reference to principle, what they themselves think the law ought to be. Certain American academies of law, and notably Harvard, have in this respect a tradition which an Englishman can only envy; but it is well for the student of the Common Law to realize that the record of France and Germany is even more remarkable in this respect. At a time, for instance, when Professor Dicey was instructing Englishmen that they were free from the trammels of administrative law—at best a half-truth which ministered only to a dangerous complacency—French teachers and German teachers of law were purging their administrative systems of what features a common lawyer might regard as dubious.[3] And if it is the business of the law school to teach law reform, it is the business of the body which selects judges not to overlook the work of the

[1] 208 U.S. 412. [2] *Cf.* my *Grammar of Politics* (1925), p. 574 f.
[3] *Cf.* my *Foundations of Sovereignty* (1921), chap. iii, and the interesting remarks of Professor J. H. Morgan in *Robinson, Public Authorities and Legal Liability* (1925), p. xlvii. f.

law teachers in the work of choice. Harvard and Cambridge might have been poorer if Ames and J. C. Gray, Maitland and Sir Frederick Pollock, had been on the Bench; but it is difficult to doubt that the official legal tradition would have been incomparably richer. The modern *responsa prudentum* must penetrate beyond a handful of scholars if they are to be effective agents in a process of control which works in narrower limits than geological time.

VIII

THE PERSONNEL OF THE BRITISH CABINET, 1801–1924[1]

I

A FULL history of the British Cabinet would be one of the seminal works on the technique of representative government; for, as Bagehot was the first to point out, the Cabinet has been the primary source of decision in the modern English institutional system. Few books, it must be added, would be so difficult to write. Until 1917 the Cabinet was without a secretary or authentic records; and there are even to-day purists who regret these obvious innovations. What account we have of its working is thus necessarily spasmodic and partial in character. A statesman who took a note of some meeting where his department was affected, a debate in the House of Commons after some dispute which has entailed resignation, a chance entry in a diary, the occasional revelation of autobiography—it is upon materials such as these that we are largely dependent for our knowledge. Even semi-official accounts, like those of Lord Morley and Mr. Gladstone, hardly give us more than the formal outline of the Cabinet as it functions.

Yet one clue to its character has been curiously neglected; and it illustrates, as it happens, the nature of the social system in England in a quite special way. We know the men who occupied Cabinet office; and by a careful study of who they were we can at least draw some inferences of interest and even importance. These inferences, let it be said at once, will not explain in any way the technique of

[1] I am indebted to Mrs. A. Henderson and Mrs. L. Turin, of the London School of Economics and Political Science, for much help in the preparation of the tables presented in this chapter.

the Cabinet system. But at least they will serve to measure the way in which the changes in the structure of English social life are reflected in the choice of those responsible for the nation's effective governance.

The notes which follow are not intended to do more than point a way to the much more detailed analysis which requires to be made. They deal only with what may be called the modern period. They begin, that is to say, with the formation of the Addington Administration in 1801; and they end with the Baldwin Government of 1924. They seek to answer certain obvious questions. Who were the men who entered the Cabinet in this century and a quarter of history? Were they aristocrats or plebeians? What were their professions? Where were they educated? Is there a difference in the personnel of the Cabinet at one period and another? Does, for example, a widening of the franchise mean a widening of the area from which Cabinet Ministers are chosen? Is there any difference in the type of men attracted to the service of the two parties which, until 1918, were the major political organizations in England? What is the main burden of the results discovered? What suggestions do they imply for the coming years?

Let us be clear, in the first place, about our definitions. The tables which follow will show how considerable and how prolonged has been the place of the aristocracy in the British Cabinet. How are we to fix the limits of that class? In England, very fortunately, there has never been an aristocracy of blood; all save the actual holders of peerages are, like the greengrocer and the bricklayer, commoners devoid of legal title to privilege. The English aristocracy, moreover, has always had a singular capacity, elsewhere unequalled, for absorbing external elements; lawyers, doctors, soldiers, sailors, business men, and civil servants have been admitted within its confines. For the purposes, therefore, of this study, the category has been defined as containing those Cabinet Ministers who have been the sons of men possessing hereditary titles. On this definition, Sir Robert Peel was an aristocrat and Lord Brougham was not; the first Lord Selborne was not an aristocrat, while his son, the second Lord Selborne, was. It follows that the tables below are to some extent weighted against the aristocracy; for there are men who belong to ancient families, like Mr. Chichester Fortescue and Sir William Harcourt, who are excluded from that class.

A word is necessary also upon the assignment of Cabinet Ministers to their various professions. Those who are called lawyers, for example, do not include any except the men who definitely earned their livelihood as barristers or solicitors. Mr. Gladstone, for example, was called to the Bar, but as he never practised he finds no place among the lawyers. And, similarly, Macaulay, who practised on the Northern Circuit for a few years (without success), is put, not among the lawyers, but, with Disraeli and Bulwer Lytton and Morley, among the men of letters, on the ground that this was in fact his effective vocation. So, also, the category of soldiers and sailors includes men like St. Vincent and Wellington and Kitchener who were warriors *de carrière*; but it does not include the very large number of peers and their sons who spent a few brief years in the Guards or the Hussars without seeking seriously to make the naval or military profession their life task. Where a Cabinet Minister went to any British university, account has been taken of it; and where, as in the earlier part of the period was not unusual, a statesman went both to Oxford or Cambridge and to a Scottish university (like Lord Henry Petty) he has been credited to both. For the category of public schools, apart from Eton and Harrow, nine of the principal schools have been investigated. Finally, in discussing the distribution of types among the political parties, Mr. Gladstone's first Administration of 1868 has been taken as the starting-point, on the ground that the present political labels date most effectively from that period.

II

In the period 1801–1924, a total of 306 persons held Cabinet offices.[1] Table I gives the salient particulars.

TABLE I

Sons of nobility	182
Sons of other parents	124
Educated at Oxford	118
Educated at Cambridge	81
Educated at other universities	26
Educated at Eton	83
Educated at Harrow	36
Educated at other public schools	53
Lawyers	42
Soldiers and sailors	8
Business men	23
Civil servants	3
Men of letters and journalists	9
Trade unionists	8

The interest of this table is considerable. Nearly 60 per cent. of Cabinet Ministers were born of immediately aristocratic parentage; nearly 80 per cent. were either at Oxford or Cambridge; 23 per cent. were Eton men, and over 10 per cent. from Harrow, while 17 per cent. were from eleven great public schools. Only 30 per cent. were dependent upon their own efforts for a livelihood, and of these nearly half were lawyers. In part, the latter fact is to be expected, since the legal profession, as organized in England, is much the most compatible with a parliamentary career; while business men are, as a rule, able at only a comparatively late stage of their careers to devote themselves to politics.

[1] The Lloyd George War Cabinet is counted as having contained five members only. This seems the fairer procedure, since many of the offices were temporary and many of their holders took no part in politics after the war.

It is noticeable that very few civil servants have ever attained the eminence of Cabinet rank; and that, thus far, the number of trade unionists is very small. Had this analysis, indeed, ended in 1905, it would have contained the name of no working man.

Speaking broadly, the aristocracy with which we are concerned consists of a thousand families; but the actual number from which Cabinet Ministers have been drawn is much smaller. The Cecil family and its relatives, for example, have contributed six Cabinet Ministers to the total; the House of Grey five; the House of Stanley four; four families have three Cabinet Ministers each, and twenty-seven families two each. Among commoners, not unnaturally, no such persistent attainment of office exists. Two Gladstones, three Chamberlains, two Harcourts, and two Balfours exhaust the list. The explanation, of course, is largely personal and economic. A considerable section of the English aristocracy enters Parliament at an early age; and these persons are thus able to take advantage of both family prestige and freedom from material care. With commoners this is much more rarely the case, unless, as with the Chamberlains, the creation of an independent fortune makes devotion to business unnecessary.

The mere totals of this personnel do not, however, give an adequate picture of the evolution that has taken place. The period from 1801 to 1924 is divisible into certain well-marked epochs. There is (1) the period from 1801 to 1831 —the *ancien régime* of modern English politics. There is (2) the period from 1832 to 1866, marked by the first Reform Act. There is (3) the period 1867 to 1884, marked by the second, and (4) the period from 1885 to 1905, marked by the third, Reform Acts. In 1900 came the *Taff Vale* decision and, as a consequence, the entry of the trade unions into politics as the Labour Party. This gives us another well-defined period (5) from 1906 to 1916, when the emergence of Mr. Lloyd George as Prime Minister reaped the fruits of the war period; the final epoch (6) from 1917 to 1924 saw the acceptance of the Labour Party as the official Opposition and its first experience of office. Each of these periods deserves separate analysis. In our treatment of them it should be noted that each Minister is counted separately if he held office, as did men like Gladstone and Disraeli, in more than one period. A number of Ministers, therefore, appear more than once in the tables which follow.

TABLE II

Period I. 1801–31. Total Number of Ministers, 71

Sons of nobility	52
Sons of other parents	19
Educated at Oxford	24
Educated at Cambridge	24
Educated at other universities	2
Educated at Eton	20
Educated at Harrow	9
Educated at other public schools	13
Lawyers	4
Soldiers and sailors	2
Business men	1
Civil servants	1
Men of letters and journalists	0

Seventy-three per cent. of the Cabinet were, therefore, in this period aristocrats. Every Cabinet Minister was a university man, and some 60 per cent. were public-school men, of whom Eton provided half. Only one business man attained high office; and the small number of lawyers—all of whom held legal posts—is explained by Lord Eldon's long tenure of the Chancellorship. Obviously, in the first period the Cabinet was a closely guarded preserve of the aristocracy. The period shows a slight decline (73 per cent. to 64 per cent.) in the proportion of aristocrats; a slight decline, also, in the proportion of university men; as also a slight increase in the proportion of public-school men. There is a perceptible increase in the number of lawyers (partly accounted for by rapid changes in the Chancellorship) and in the number of

TABLE III

Period II. 1832–66. *Total Number of Ministers*, 100

Sons of nobility	64
Sons of other parents	36
Educated at Oxford	38
Educated at Cambridge	30
Educated at other universities	10
Educated at Eton	27
Educated at Harrow	11
Educated at other public schools	17
Lawyers	12
Soldiers and sailors	3
Business men	5
Civil servants	2
Men of letters and journalists	3

business men. Men of letters, also, appear effectively in the Cabinet for the first time. But, taken as a whole, it cannot

TABLE IV

Period III. 1867–84. *Total Number of Ministers*, 58

Sons of nobility	35
Sons of other parents	23
Educated at Oxford	29
Educated at Cambridge	12
Educated at other universities	3
Educated at Eton	20
Educated at Harrow	5
Educated at other public schools	9
Lawyers	9
Soldiers and sailors	1
Business men	6
Civil servants	1
Men of letters and journalists	1

be said that the Reform Act of 1832 exerted any remarkable influence on the character of the Cabinet.

There is, again, in this mid-Victorian period, a slight decline in aristocratic personnel (64 per cent. to 60 per cent.)

TABLE V

Period IV. 1885–1905. Total Number of Ministers, 69

Sons of nobility	40
Sons of other parents	29
Educated at Oxford	35
Educated at Cambridge	17
Educated at other universities	5
Educated at Eton	25
Educated at Harrow	9
Educated at other public schools	12
Lawyers	9
Soldiers and sailors	0
Business men	6
Civil servants	0
Men of letters and journalists	1

as compared with the second period; although, after two Reform Acts, the degree of its influence remains remarkable.

TABLE VI

Period V. 1906–16. Total Number of Ministers, 51

Sons of nobility	25
Sons of other parents	26
Educated at Oxford	20
Educated at Cambridge	16
Educated at other universities	5
Educated at Eton	12
Educated at Harrow	5
Educated at other public schools	8
Lawyers	9
Soldiers and sailors	1
Business men	5
Civil servants	0
Men of letters and journalists	3
Academic	1
Trade unionists	2

Seventy-seven per cent. of Ministers were university men, and 60 per cent. public-school men. There is again, proportionately, a slight increase in the number of lawyers and business men.

The proportion of the aristocracy (58 per cent.) is practically identical with that of the third period. The percentage of university men is 83—an increase probably due to the reforms of 1854—and of public-school men, 65. The other figures show no considerable divergences from those of the previous period.

In this period the most notable fact is that the number of

TABLE VII

Period VI. 1917-24. Total Number of Ministers, 52

Sons of nobility	14
Sons of other parents	38
Educated at Oxford	18
Educated at Cambridge	9
Educated at other universities	4
Educated at Eton	6
Educated at Harrow	8
Educated at other public schools	11
Lawyers	8
Soldiers and sailors	1
Business men	4
Civil servants	1
Men of letters and journalists	3
Academic	0
Trade unionists	8

aristocrats is, for the first time, less than the number of commoners. The number of university men remains broadly constant, but the number of public-school men shows a distinct decline (from 65 per cent. to 50 per cent.). There is, also, an increase in the number of lawyers, and the category of trade unionists makes its first appearance. Broadly, it may be said that this is the first of the periods under discussion in which the commoners begin obviously to gain upon the aristocracy. Until 1906, the broadening of the franchise and the improvement of the means of education had not, in one hundred years of Cabinet history, seriously affected the hold of the aristocracy upon the pivotal posts of government.

The changes represented by the foregoing table, which includes the members of the first Labour Government, are obviously profound. The aristocracy represents only 27 per cent., the universities 60, and the public schools only 50 per cent. of the total. There are as many trade unionists as lawyers; and there are twice as many lawyers as business men. Obviously enough, had there been two Labour Governments within the period, the influence of the aristocracy on the personnel of the Cabinet would have been small indeed. It is clear, further, that the position of the Labour Party in the House of Commons means that the decline in the percentage of university men is likely for a considerable period to be large; as also that the number of trade unionists is likely to remain fairly stable, at some such size as at least one-third of each Labour Cabinet.

III

The statistics may now be analysed from the angle of party. In the period since 1868 (omitting the Coalition Government of 1917–22) there have been seven Conservative Governments, seven Liberal Governments, and one Labour Government; to which must be added the Asquith Coalition of 1915 in which only experienced and, so to say, professional parliamentarians found a place. Table VIII presents the same statistics as in previous tables for the different parties involved.

These figures suggest that no very considerable difference has existed between the Liberal and Conservative parties in the period under review. A Conservative Cabinet tends to be slightly more aristocratic than a Liberal Cabinet and to specialize in the possession of ministers who have been at

PERSONNEL OF THE BRITISH CABINET 191

the great public schools. The only man of letters in a Conservative Cabinet was Disraeli, but the Liberals have five who earned their living by writing. The Labour Cabinet contained three aristocrats, one of whom (Lord Chelmsford) was not a member of the Party; and it is notable as having been the first Cabinet since 1801 which contained no Eton men. Certain other conclusions suggest themselves. Apart from Mr. John Burns—since Mr. Arthur Henderson's

TABLE VIII

1868-1924

Name of Party	Conservative	Liberal	Labour
Sons of nobility	40	31	3
Sons of other parents	40	42	16
Educated at Oxford	38	28	3
Educated at Cambridge	16	23	2
Educated at other universities	4	3	1
Educated at Eton	31	14	0
Educated at Harrow	15	6	1
Educated at other public schools	13	12	3
Lawyers	15	17	2
Soldiers and sailors	1	1	1
Business men	6	9	1
Civil servants	0	1	1
Men of letters and journalists	1	5	3
Academic	0	0	0
Trade unionists	0	2	7

appointment was an accident of the war period—no trade unionist has ever sat in either a Conservative or a Liberal Cabinet; and there exists to-day no Member of Parliament belonging to a trade union who, apart from a Coalition Government, would be likely to find a place there.

It is interesting from this angle to take a number of Cabinets in detail since 1868 and to compare them with one another. For this purpose I have tabulated (Table IX)

Mr. Gladstone's Cabinet of 1868, Mr. Disraeli's of 1874, Mr. Balfour's of 1902, and Mr. Asquith's of 1908; Mr. MacDonald's Cabinet and Mr. Baldwin's of 1924 being put alongside for purposes of comparison.

Obviously, there are no very great differences among these Cabinets, apart from the Labour Government. It will be noticed that, apart from the Asquith Cabinet of 1908, and that of Mr. MacDonald, the number of Ministers dependent

TABLE IX

	Gladstone (1868)	Disraeli (1874)	Balfour (1902)	Asquith (1908)	MacDonald (1924)	Baldwin (1924)
Sons of nobility	8	10	12	6	3	9
Sons of other parents	11	7	11	14	17	12
Educated at Oxford	10	9	11	7	3	12
Educated at Cambridge	3	2	6	8	2	4
Educated at other universities	1	1	1	1	1	1
Educated at Eton	3	9	11	4	0	5
Educated at Harrow	0	1	2	3	2	6
Educated at other public schools	5	2	5	4	4	4
Lawyers	3	2	4	6	2	6
Soldiers and sailors	0	0	0	0	1	0
Business men	4	1	2	2	1	2
Civil servants	1	0	0	0	1	0
Men of letters and journalists	0	1	0	1	3	0
Trade unionists	0	0	0	1	8	0

for their living upon their vocation is small; in no case other than the two noted is it more than one-third of the total. Again, there is a tendency for Liberal Cabinets to be slightly less aristocratic than Conservative. The predominance of Eton men among Conservative Ministers is remarkable, and it is amusing to note that a Conservative Prime Minister educated at Eton, Lord Balfour, had colleagues almost half of whom were Eton men, while the

PERSONNEL OF THE BRITISH CABINET 193

Cabinet of a Harrow Prime Minister, Mr. Baldwin, had in it the largest number of Harrow men ever collected in a single Cabinet. Mr. Gladstone's administration of 1868 was the first Cabinet in which no Harrovian, that of MacDonald the first in which no Etonian, found a place.

IV

Certain general characteristics of the figures here collected may be noted. In our period, 306 persons held Cabinet office, and of them 182 were aristocrats. But if we subtract from the 306 the 93 who earned their living, no less than 213, or practically 70 per cent., were rentiers. Not less remarkable is the small number of professions from which the Cabinet has been drawn. Outside the rentiers, practically

TABLE X

Parental Occupation	Number
Soldiers and sailors	6
Lawyers	18
Business men	36
Clergymen	20
Teachers	2
Doctors	4
Men of letters	1
Artists	1
Civil servants	1
Rentiers	23
Working men	12

five categories exhaust the list. No scientist, no engineer, and no doctor[1] has ever been a member of the Cabinet; and, with the exception of Mr. Herbert Fisher, whose appearance was an accident of the War, no academic person, though for a brief period both Robert Lowe and Viscount Gladstone were university dons.

It is interesting to discover the parental occupations of

[1] Dr. Addison was, of course, Minister of Health under Mr. Lloyd George; but his appointment was hardly less abnormal than that of Mr. Fisher.

the non-aristocratic members of the Cabinet in the period. Table X gives these for the 124 persons who form this class. From this table certain obvious conclusions emerge. It is clear, in the first place, that the distribution of occupations among the parents of Cabinet Ministers is wider than among the Ministers themselves. That business men should form the largest parental class is notable. But it is probably explained by the fact that most of them, like the Goschens and Chamberlains and Peases, were successful business men who were able either to support their sons during a parliamentary career (as Tierney) or to give them an education which permitted an alternative career like the law. The number of clergymen is explained partly by the fact that some of them, as Sir William Harcourt's father, were connections of ancient families and thus able to command political influence, and partly by the fact that all of them were able to give their sons a university education; most, in fact, were comfortably endowed. The number of rentiers, which here includes members of "county" families, is comparatively small; although had this investigation been concerned only with membership of the House of Commons, or even with minor ministerial posts, it would have been very much larger. It is worth remarking that, apart from Mr. John Burns and Mr. Henderson, no member of any Cabinet previous to that of Mr. MacDonald was the son of a working man.

I have spoken of the educational training of Cabinet Ministers, and it is perhaps worth while to examine the statistics in some little detail. Among the 118 Oxford men in the list, no less than sixteen colleges are represented. But sixty of the Oxford Cabinet Ministers were at Christ Church; and Balliol, which is next in the list, has only seventeen, being closely followed by Oriel with twelve, and University with ten, respectively. On the basis of these figures, one or two facts are worth noting. The predominance

PERSONNEL OF THE BRITISH CABINET 195

of Christ Church is almost entirely due to its aristocratic connection, particularly in the period before 1867; since that time its degree of representation has declined. Of the Balliol men, all except one date from the epoch of Jowett. The Oriel men are mostly confined within the period when Hawkins and Copleston made it the outstanding college in Oxford; while nearly half of the representation from University College is due to the Cecil family. Of the

TABLE XI

	1801–67	1867–1905	1905–24	Government of Mr. MacDonald	Government of Mr. Baldwin (1924)
Age of entrance of aristocrats into the House of Commons	25.6	26.5	29.0	32.5	31.2
Age of entrance of aristocrats into the Cabinet	45.9	43.4	44.5	55.0	44.0
Age of entrance of commoners into the House of Commons	35.9	38.7	40.0	43.4	42.8
Age of entrance of commoners into the Cabinet	55.0	52.7	54.4	57.6	51.1

Cambridge results, somewhat similar remarks may be made. Of the eighty-one Cambridge men who attained Cabinet rank, fifty-four came from Trinity alone. St. John's has eleven and Trinity Hall five, the remainder being distributed among six colleges. In view of its influence in the University, and especially its connection with Eton, it is a little surprising to find that only two Cabinet Ministers came from King's College. Of the Ministers educated at other universities nine were from Edinburgh and six from London. It is notable that, except for Mr. Neville Chamberlain's brief attendance at Birmingham, no Cabinet Minister has so far been produced by one of the newer universities.

There is another interesting angle from which these figures may be analysed. Dividing Cabinet Ministers into aristocrats and commoners, Table XI gives their age at entrance into the House of Commons and the Cabinet in three periods within the last century and a quarter.

From Table XI three obvious conclusions can be drawn. Aristocrats, firstly, enter the House of Commons and the Cabinet ten years earlier, on the average, than commoners. The average age, secondly, at which men enter the House of Commons is rising for both classes; for aristocrats it has risen from 25 to 29, and for commoners from 35·9 to 40. The average age, thirdly, at which aristocrats enter the Cabinet has slightly declined during the period, as is true also (the MacDonald Cabinet apart) with commoners. The high average age at which aristocrats in Mr. MacDonald's Cabinet first received such office is, of course, due to quite exceptional circumstances. What is mainly remarkable in the whole table is the immense differential advantage in time which an aristocratic politician receives by reason of his birth.

V

"In England," wrote Matthew Arnold some fifty years ago,[1] "the government is composed of a string of aristocratical personages, with one or two men from the professional class who are engaged with them." Of the British Cabinet system until 1905 this is no unfair account; and if since that time the generalization has lost some part of its force, it is still by no means negligible.

For anyone who reflects upon the statistics here collected will be driven to certain irresistible inferences. The three Reform Acts of the nineteenth century had little effect upon the position of the aristocracy in politics. Policy may have changed, but the men who made policy came, in much the

[1] *Mixed Essays*, p. 164.

same degree, from the same origins as their predecessors. Even to-day the aristocracy, together with the lawyer and the rentier, possesses a predominance in the personnel of English politics. Though the advent of the Labour Party has altered for the moment the proportion of that predominance, it is by no means certain that it will not continue. For, in the first place, the Labour Party needs lawyers and accordingly offers better prospects of speedy appointment to office than either of its rivals. If, moreover, Labour remains the alternative Government, it will attract the more radical-minded members of the aristocracy in the same way that the Liberal Party used to do; and in that event, especially if the House of Lords remains unreformed, the aristocratic member of the Labour Party will have the same, if not greater, opportunities than he enjoys elsewhere. This thesis, of course, rests upon the assumption that there will be no drastic alteration in the laws of property and inheritance.

For the root of the hold retained by the members of the aristocracy is economic in character. In part, and perhaps mainly, it is derived from the possession of an income which renders these persons independent of the need to earn a living. In a lesser degree, the territorial influence of the aristocracy enables it to find seats for its members with less difficulty, and at an earlier age, than is possible for other classes. The only real competitors of the rentier in the Conservative Party are the lawyers; for, as has been pointed out, the number of vocations compatible with politics is small, and unless business men have independent means they enter the House of Commons (even more, the House of Lords) too late to embark upon a political career which may lead them to the Cabinet. It is worth while noting, moreover, that until 1905 this was also true of the Liberal Party; and, since that date, it is significant that the leaders of that Party were either lawyers or men of independent means. Nor are there signs that, so far as the Conservative Party is concerned, the change is a great one. The Party had, in November 1926, 410 members in the House of Commons. Of these, 53 were lawyers, 53 aristocrats, and 129 rentiers, while 18 were retired soldiers and sailors, and, of the remainder, more than 80 were possessed of means other than their vocational source of income. As in the case of Cabinet Ministers, there was a difference in average age in the Party between aristocrats and commoners of more than ten years, nor is it without significance that most of those likely to attain office in the Cabinet in the coming years belong to the three special classes noted.

The position of the business and working classes in the system is peculiar and interesting. The House of Commons has always, since 1832, contained a very considerable proportion of business men, and since 1895 an increasing proportion. There is, however, no sign that they are likely to enter the Cabinet in any increasing degree. They enter the House too late to make a sufficient impression upon its leaders; and they cannot, like adherents of the Labour Party, rest satisfied with the standard of life which a member's salary makes possible. Where they are outstandingly successful, on the other hand, their sons not seldom enter the House and, later, the Cabinet. A business man, therefore, can, within the ambit of our system, found a dynasty of rentiers to whom the Cabinet will lie open, even while he can hardly hope to enter it himself.

The position of the Labour member is different. The salary of a member of Parliament, with the possibility, further, of a supplementary income from his trade union, offers the very considerable trade-union section of the Party the chance of a fairly long parliamentary career at a standard of life which they regard as comfortable. For this section, however, the drawbacks, from the angle of office, are two in number. The period which must elapse before the average trade unionist can hope for a safe seat from his Party sends him into the House later than most other members; while defeat at a general election may, unless he is an official of his union, leave him without employment.[1] He is, moreover, rarely in a position to send his children into the House of Commons; Mr. Henderson was, until 1924, the only Labour member who had sat in the House with his own sons. The non-trade-union section of the Labour Party is, with the exception of the Clyde group, in much the same position as members of the other parties. They are lawyers, rentiers, teachers, doctors, and their ability to pursue a parliamentary career depends upon the same considerations as affect the Conservative or the Liberal. The number of professions compatible with a political career is limited; and, broadly, the trade-union official in the Labour Party has the same kind of advantage as the rentier or the lawyer.

A word should be said about the influence of the universities. It has obviously been profound. But, also, it is in a large degree secondary in character, since the men who went to the universities are, for the most part, the men who would in any case have entered the House. Where the university has counted is in the connections it has formed for men who, otherwise, would not have found the avenue to the House as direct as they did. Gladstone's Oxford friendship with Lord Lincoln gave him the opportunity of Newark; without it, he might have had to wait much longer for a seat. And it is clear that neither London nor the provincial and Scottish universities carry with them the same social connotation as Oxford and Cambridge. The claim that the latter are the nurses of statesmen means but little in the sense that the art of government can be acquired there. But in the sense that they open avenues more easily for those not of the aristocracy, the claim is not to be denied. They

[1] One former Labour member was compelled, in 1924, to apply for unemployment relief.

are an integral part of that Government by connection which is still influential in England.

The broad fact is that, even yet, political democracy in England has developed very imperfectly. There is no large equality of opportunity. Were tables similar to the above to be compiled for the Cabinets of France since 1870 and the United States since 1789, the results would show an immense difference. In France the Government of the Third Republic has been drawn almost entirely from the professional and middle classes; in the United States, although there was a considerable aristocratic and rentier element before the Civil War, the basis of government has been even wider than in France. Neither in America nor in France have the mind and imagination of the middle and working classes been subdued by the aristocracy as they have been in England. English liberty has not been paralleled by equality; and the conditions of English political institutions maintain that submission to the aristocracy by reason of the economic system they involve.

It is, of course, idle to seek to measure the degree of permanence in present English methods. Any aristocratic system which, like the English, has had a considerable degree of public spirit has obvious and great advantages over a purely democratic system. Its members are trained to the art of politics at an early age; and they acquire more easily than others the faculty of command and the ability to use other men gracefully, which are so important. Yet they possess it at a heavy price to the rest of the community. For an aristocracy, however public-spirited, is by its nature exclusive; and the experience it possesses at first hand is bound to be unduly narrow. In a State like Britain, where the equal claim of men on the common good is the touchstone of policy, the differential advantages which the present order implies make against the full understanding of wants by those who are called to rule. The English aristocracy, moreover, has long passed the zenith of its power. It no longer has a monopoly of the qualities which make for effective governance. It may even be said that the problems which confront civilization to-day are of a kind which call less for the qualities of an aristocracy than almost any others that can be imagined.

If we in England are, indeed, to place the full experience of our society at its service, the barriers of privilege which, as here shown, we still retain are not merely anomalous but undesirable. We are still living by what Matthew Arnold called our religion of inequality. We still offer special advantages in the search for power to those whose interest it is to prevent the democratization of the present order. To change this order is, doubtless, a delicate and difficult business, since it involves an alteration in the distribution of wealth and inheritance. Yet no society can genuinely humanize its institutions save as it becomes a community of equals. Equality alone breeds responsibility and elevation of mind in the multitude. Our system confers those habits upon a small number of men, but the privileges it offers to birth and wealth prevent their extension to the masses. For when new ideas are changing the perspective of men's habits of thought, those people can most usefully exercise power who see the implications of such ideas. It is the thesis of our system to open the road to authority less to these men than to those sections of society which have most to lose by their introduction and acceptance.

IX

JUDICIAL REVIEW OF SOCIAL POLICY

A STUDY OF ROBERTS v. HOPWOOD et al [1]

THE fiction that judges do not legislate has long since been abandoned by all who care for a conscious and realistic jurisprudence. To apply precedent and principle to new systems of fact is inevitably to extend their boundaries; and the men who interpret the meaning of clauses in a constitution or a statute are, in truth, bound to be the masters of them. It is clear, in such a background, that the duty of the judge is one of peculiar delicacy and complexity. He has to be sure that he is not mistaking his private desire for the public welfare. He has to be confident that he has taken pains to realize the implications of the environment about him. He has, above all, to be sure that his interpretation of that environment has been reached only after the widest possible study of the relevant material. "Something of Pascal's spirit of self-search and self-reproach," writes Judge Cardozo,[2] "must come at moments to the man who finds himself summoned to the duty of shaping the progress of the law."

This "spirit of self-search and self-reproach" is especially urgent where the policy of an elected legislative body is in question. It is a commonplace in a democratic society that to entrust powers of self-government to small areas is the surest way to breed habits of responsibility in the population. Commonplace is it also that few things are more difficult than to persuade men to voluntary political service unless the powers they can exercise are sufficient to lead to important results. Men enter a legislative assembly because they have their hands there upon a great machine; and the

---

[1] [1925] A.C. 578.   [2] Cardozo, *The Nature of the Judicial Process*, p. 172.

JUDICIAL REVIEW OF SOCIAL POLICY 203

knowledge that they can encompass great objects is always likely to attract the efforts of public-spirited men with views for which they seek the substantiality of statute. But, conversely, they will not be so attracted if the effort they can make is liable to nullification for causes other than those of strict legality. When, consequently, the results of their action come before the courts, it is gravely urgent that the judges should be moved by considerations of which no complaint can be made. We need to feel certain that public opinion can say of their judgment that it has been built upon the obvious meaning of constitution or statute; it is fatal if men can infer from judicial decisions a system of economic or political habits in the judges that are, at best, matters of grave difference of opinion, and, at worst, the outcome of prejudice built upon ignorance. It is possible to say of *Rex* v. *Halliday*[1] that the result could have been reached reasonably by men willing to scrutinize with liberal minds the executive interpretation of statutes; it is hardly possible to say other of the famous *Osborne* case[2] than that it represented the

[1] [1917] A.C. 260. In this case the validity of an order made by the Home Secretary for the internment of a naturalized British subject, was in issue. The Defence of the Realm Act (5 Geo. V, c. 8, § 1) gave to His Majesty in Council the power to issue regulations for securing the public safety and the defence of the realm, and provided for the trial and punishment of persons committing offences against such regulations. The King in Council issued a "regulation" empowering the Home Secretary to intern persons of hostile origins or associations, if such a course appeared expedient for the public safety. The order in question was made in pursuance of this authority. The House of Lords held that the regulation was authorized by the Act of Parliament. I should myself, however, agree with the dissenting judgment of Lord Shaw.

[2] [1910] A.C. 87. The plaintiff Osborne, a member of the Amalgamated Society of Railway Servants, sought a declaration of the invalidity of a rule of the Society, providing for the levy of contributions for payment of salaries or maintenance allowances to members of Parliament pledged to observe the conditions imposed by the constitution of the Labour Party. A majority of the House of Lords held that such a rule was beyond the powers given to trade unions by the Trade Union and Trade Union Amendment Acts (34 & 35 Vict. c. 31; 39 & 40 Vict. c. 22). Lord Shaw and Lord James of Hereford concurred specially on the ground that certain conditions imposed upon members of Parliament by the constitution of the Labour Party were contrary to public policy.

views of men at once ignorant of, and prejudiced against, the methods of trade unionism in the modern state.

The judge must be sceptical of his own beliefs; for he cannot but be aware, if he has at all that mood of which Judge Cardozo has written, how subtly and unconsciously they will colour his decision once a case raises political issues. No case in modern times, in England at least, illustrates this thesis better than the recent decision of the House of Lords in what is called the *Poplar* case. I propose here briefly to narrate the facts of the case, to consider the judgments to which it has given rise, and to draw certain general inferences as to the relation of judicial control to legislative action.

Poplar is one of the twenty-eight boroughs into which the administrative county of London is divided for the purpose of local self-government. In 1914, its borough council was paying a minimum wage of 30s. a week to men, and 22s. 6d. to women. From May 1, 1920, a minimum wage of £4 a week was paid to men, and £3 10s. to women. In auditing the accounts for the year 1920–21, the District Auditor did not challenge these rates on the ground of the increase in the cost of living since the War. When, however, he came to audit them in 1923, he found that the same minimum rates were being paid even though the cost of living had fallen in the interim. These rates were very considerably in excess of wages paid for similar work in London under industrial agreements between employers and employed, notably including the agreement arrived at between the members of the Joint Industrial Council and the Public Works Conciliation Board. The District Auditor thereupon disallowed to the extent of £5,000 the wage-charges included in the borough accounts on the following grounds:[1]

(*a*) Because, though private employers may make *ex*

---

[1] I quote from the brief submitted to the House of Lords, p. 11 (Appendix J. S. 1). I owe a copy of this to the courtesy of Mr. W. H. Thompson.

gratia payments to employees, the Council cannot, as a fiduciary body, expend sums "so largely in excess of those which were needed to obtain the services required."

(b) Because, at least to the extent of that sum, "they [the wages] were unnecessary and unreasonable charges, and therefore items contrary to law as charges upon the funds in the custody of the Council."

(c) It should be added that, in arriving at the figure of his surcharge, the District Auditor did not merely subtract the difference between the rates paid by the Poplar Council and those agreed upon by the Joint Industrial Council, but gave the Poplar Council the advantage of assuming a higher rate to be within the limits of reasonableness.

The surcharged councillors then applied to a Divisional Court for a *certiorari* to remove the District Auditor's certificate into the King's Bench Division to be quashed. The Divisional Court unanimously discharged the rule *nisi*.[1] The councillors appealed to the Court of Appeal and obtained there a majority decision.[2] The District Auditor appealed to the House of Lords, which unanimously reversed the court below. A similar decision has recently been handed down in the case of the borough of Bethnal Green; and a case in which, though a lower scale is involved, the principle is identical, is at present pending in the case of the borough of Woolwich.

It will be best, first, to consider the grounds upon which the House of Lords based its decision. Its guiding principle seems to have been the thesis that whatever in the making of policy is left to the discretion of an elected body acting under powers delegated by Parliament must be made in a "reasonable" way and be "reasonable" in its results; the cost of services maintained by such a body must, therefore, be built upon the payment of "reasonable" rates of wages. "Reasonable" wages are, as Lord Wrenbury

[1] *Rex* v. *Roberts*, [1924] 1 K.B. 514.   [2] *Ibid.*, [1924] 2 K.B. 695 (C.A.).

stated in his opinion,[1] "such sum as a reasonable person, guiding himself by an investigation of the current rate in fact found to be paid in the particular industry, and acting upon the principle that efficient service is better commanded by paying an efficient wage, would find to be the proper sum. . . . It is such figure as is the reasonable pecuniary equivalent of the service rendered. Anything beyond this is not wages. It is an addition to wages, and is a gratuity. The authority is to pay not such sum but such wages as they think fit." Lord Sumner put a similar view even more forcibly than his colleague. "The auditor," he said,[2] "is not confined to asking, if the discretion, such as it may be, has been honestly exercised. He has to restrain expenditure within proper limits. His mission is to inquire if there is any excess over what is reasonable. I do not find any words limiting his functions merely to the case of bad faith, or obliging him to leave the ratepayers unprotected from the effects on their pockets of honest stupidity or unpractical idealism."

These are vigorous words; but before we begin to assess their significance, it will be well to realize something of the history and nature of the District Auditor's office. Its origin lies in the period of poor law reform inaugurated by the famous report of 1834. To prevent the wastage that had occurred under the earlier system the new office was created and its occupant was to investigate the accounts of Boards of Guardians, the Poor Law Audit Act[3] giving to the Central Commissioners the power to hear appeals from his decisions. The Public Health Act of 1875 applied the system to a variety of old and new *ad hoc* authorities[4]; and the Local Government Acts of 1888 and 1894 extended the area of its operation to the County, District, and Parish Councils.[5]

[1] [1925] A.C. 578, 612.   [2] *Loc. cit.*, at p. 604
[3] 4 & 5 Will. IV, c. 76; 7 & 8 Vict., c. 101.
[4] 38 & 39 Vict. c. 55.   [5] 51 & 52 Vict. c. 41; 57 & 58 Vict. c. 58.

JUDICIAL REVIEW OF SOCIAL POLICY

Nor did its growth stop there. By the London Government Act of 1899[1] the system was applied to the metropolitan boroughs of London; and though the general accounts of other municipalities, through historic survival, are not subject to its control, their education and housing accounts are specifically subject to inspection.[2] The District Auditor has been, since 1879, appointed by the Local Government Board (now the Ministry of Health), which can also remove him. The Ministry assigns his task to him, and may make regulations concerning the method of audit; it also inherits the powers of the old Poor Law Board in being an alternative to the courts as a source of appeal from the Auditor's decisions. Technically, the auditors are paid from funds provided by Parliament; but a complicated system really involves the local authorities in reimbursing the Ministry for this expenditure. Lastly, it should be pointed out that whenever the District Auditor takes legal action to enforce the payment of surcharges, he is entitled to the recovery of his costs, whether he is successful or no. It does not matter whether the legal action brought is frivolous, or biased, or unwise. "It would, however," said Mr. Justice Mellor,[3] "be hard upon that officer if he were to lose his costs because he did not take the most judicious course in performing his duties." If, however, he is guilty of legal negligence or misconduct, the court may, by specified order, make him responsible for his own costs.

The functions of the District Auditor are set forth in the Public Health Act of 1875; but, for the purposes of the *Poplar* case, it is necessary to read his powers in the context of the Metropolis Local Management Act of 1855, under which the Borough Council takes power to fix its scale of wages. The functions allotted to him are described so clearly in the first of these Acts that it is worth while setting out the

[1] 62 & 63 Vict. c. 14.   [2] 11 & 12 Geo. V, c. 51, §§ 3, 70.
[3] *Prest* v. *Royston Union*, 33 L.T. (N.S.), 564, 566 (1875).

relevant section in full. "Any auditor acting in pursuance of this section," it reads,[1] "shall disallow every item of account contrary to law, and surcharge the same on the person making or authorizing the making of the illegal payment, and shall charge against any person accounting the amount of any deficiency or loss incurred by the negligence or misconduct of that person, or of any sum which ought to have been but is not brought into account by that person, and shall in every such case certify the amount due from such person, and on application by any party aggrieved shall state in writing the reasons for his decision in respect of such disallowance or surcharge, and also of any allowance which he may have made." It will be convenient, finally, to quote the relevant section in the Act of 1855 relating to wages.[2] "The ... Board of Works ... shall appoint or employ, or continue for the Purposes of this Act, and may remove at pleasure, such Clerks, Treasurers, and Surveyors, and such other Officers and Servants as may be necessary, and may allow to such Clerks, Treasurers, Surveyors, Officers and Servants respectively such Salaries and Wages as the Board ... may think fit."

These are the material factors out of which the House of Lords arrived at its decision. Certain preliminary observations may first be made. It is clear (1) that the Act of 1855 has in mind a Board which fixes salaries and wages in its discretion; no words suggest that it is answerable, except politically, for any "reasonable" interpretation of this power. It is clear (2) that the intention of the Act of 1875 is that the Auditor, in his scrutiny of accounts, is concerned to see that payments made have been made (a) for legal objects, (b) in good faith, and (c) with due care. He is concerned, that is, not with policy, but with administration. This has been well emphasized by the courts on a variety

[1] 38 & 39 Vict. c. 55, § 247 (7).
[2] 18 & 19 Vict. c. 120, § 62.

of occasions. "The auditor," said Lord Justice Farwell,[1] "does not claim, nor could he (in my opinion) properly claim, to exercise any control over questions of policy; but he does claim the right to check and challenge all items of administration."

The Auditor, in fact, is in relation to the local authorities as the Comptroller and Auditor-General in relation to departments of State. It is the latter's business to see that moneys authorized to be spent by Parliament are spent in good faith, without negligence, and upon objects of permitted expenditure. When that has been done, his functions cease, so far as Acts of Parliament define them.[2] So, too, with the District Auditor. If a local authority, or its servants, be negligent or dishonest, if, further, they go beyond their powers, he is legally bound to make them pay. But if the actions involved are within the area of their competence, there is nothing on the statute book which suggests that he has a power of challenge.

The reasons for this limitation are clear enough. Could the Auditor go further, he could challenge the actions of an elected body, not on grounds defined by statute, but because he did not happen to agree with what it was doing. He would be seeking to replace its view of its duty by his own view. A person, that is, responsible to no one, could seek to destroy the policy of men who have been returned by the electorate to exercise, within the limits of law, the power confided to them. That would be a situation as inconceivable and intolerable as if the Comptroller and Auditor-General were to seek, let us say, to prevent the Board of Education from spending money on its system of inspection, or as if he sought to secure a reduction in the salaries of the civil service on the ground that similar work could be done at lower pay. It is obvious that he is not entitled to such an attitude.

[1] *Rex* v. *Roberts*, [1908] 1 K.B. 407, 435.
[2] *Cf.* Durell, *Parliamentary Grants*, 155 *et seq.*

The courts themselves have, on other occasions, taken exactly this view. "The true mode," said Lord Justice Fletcher Moulton,[1] "of securing the good management of municipal affairs is to induce the best men to take part in them, and to give their services to the community in this way. The task is at best unremunerative, and often thankless; but if those who accept it are to be liable to have their conduct pronounced upon and their character and property injured by decisions, not of any Courts of law of the country, to which they are of course amenable, but of a special tribunal consisting of an official chosen by a Government department without any powers or qualifications for holding a judicial inquiry, and discharging these functions without any of those securities which protect the individual before our Courts, and if the jurisdiction of that individual is not to be limited to requiring an account of municipal money for which the accused has made himself responsible, but extends to calling him to account for the reasons and motives of all his actions, no self-respecting man will take part in municipal affairs." Nor do the English courts stand alone in this attitude. "A body such as the applicants," said Chief Justice O'Brien, in an Irish case,[2] "are responsible only for *crassa negligentia*. Certainly the standard of care exigible from them is not higher than what is exigible from paid directors of a Company. The degree of negligence which subjects such a body to responsibility is *crassa negligentia*.... 'Mere imprudence' is not enough; 'want of judgment' is not enough; 'grave error of judgment' is not enough."

The implications of these views are surely clear. A "reasonable" interpretation of a discretionary power by an elected body means an interpretation arrived at after proper consideration of the facts involved in its particular

[1] *Rex* v. *Roberts*, *supra*, p. 209, note 1, at 433. And note the strong remarks of Cozens-Hardy, M.R., in the same case.
[2] *Rex* v. *Browne*, [1907] 2 I.R. 505, 518.

JUDICIAL REVIEW OF SOCIAL POLICY

exercise. So long as it is made legally and in good faith, the District Auditor has no ground for intervention. He may, in his private capacity, disagree or disapprove. He may believe that the policy of the Council is contrary to all right judgment. Nevertheless, in his public capacity, he has no concern with these matters. In their local significance, they are the business of the electorate by whom the Council is chosen to pass judgment on matters of policy. He is not entitled to protect that electorate from the "honest stupidity" or the "unpractical idealism" of its elected representatives; nor is he entitled, by his intervention, either to anticipate or to prejudice subsequent electoral judgment. The Council does not owe him any obligation in matters of policy.

It is the more important to stress this view, because District Auditors have always taken a high view of their powers; and the authority both of the courts and of Parliament has been required to check their exuberance. In 1887 an Auditor surcharged a Board of Guardians for paying a commission of $1\frac{1}{4}$ per cent. in raising a loan.[1] In 1887 it was necessary to pass an Act of Parliament to lay it down that no expenses shall be disallowed by the Auditor which have been incurred under sanction from the Ministry of Health.[2] In 1908 an Auditor sought to compel a local authority to accept only the lowest estimates offered.[3] But perhaps the apogee of this audacity was reached in a conflict between the District Auditor and the London County Council in a case which was settled before legal action.[4] Under the Education (Provision of Meals) Act an education authority may provide meals free of charge for necessitous school children. In 1912, the District Auditor ruled that such items as cod-liver oil, malt extract, and fruit did not come within the definition of food; and it was only after a struggle that

[1] Regina v. Haslehurst, 51 J.P. 645 (1887).   [2] 50 & 51 Vict. c. 72, § 3.
[3] Rex v. Roberts, [1908] 1 K.B. 407, 435.
[4] See Robson, The District Auditor (Fabian Society, 1925), 7—an excellent pamphlet to which I am much indebted.

he was persuaded to abandon his objection to fruit in return for the surrender by the County Council of its enthusiasm for malt extract and cod-liver oil. It did not seem to matter to him that fruit is with many people, Mr. Bernard Shaw, for example, a staple article of diet; nor was he moved by the unanimous opinion of the school medical officers that his views were wrong. Every one of these cases is, surely, an example of the folly of allowing the mind of an appointed official to supersede the careful judgment of a responsible elected body. They are equalled only by the insistence of the courts that attendance by children at performances of Shakespeare's plays is not an educational activity.[1] A school may, it seems, study the works of Shakespeare, and even act them; but if a form of educational technique was not in usage when the judges were at school, the joint opinion of an elected body and its expert advisors cannot prevail against them. It would be difficult to find a better illustration of the grounds for making "reasonableness" simply the observance of a standard of due care in arriving at a decision.

Cases such as these, then, go to show that the District Auditor is not at all likely to belittle his office; and the courts, clearly, should be on their guard to prevent him from usurping legislative authority. Unfortunately, however, judges have not taken any consistent view of the proper limits of his function. I have already quoted the opinion of men like Lord Moulton; but the latter's clear sense of the importance of leaving the elected person unfettered where he is given discretion by the law has not been unanimously held. Mr. Justice O'Brien, for example, does not desire "to derogate from the authority of the auditor . . . or to narrow his authority so that he could not . . . deal with all payments of an unnecessary or extravagant kind."[2]

---

[1] *Rex* v. *Lyon*, 38 T.L.R. 62, (1921).
[2] *Regina* v. *Calvert*, [1898] 2 I.R. 511, 525.

"What is a reasonable sum," said Chief Baron Palles of subsistence allowances,[1] "is a matter of fact which the Auditor must himself determine." This, obviously, is to change the standard of "reasonableness" completely. It would broadly mean that whenever there is a broad difference of opinion between the Auditor and the elected body, it is the duty of the former to surcharge the latter. He has open to him, nevertheless, only the same body of material as the local authority. He may be satisfied as to its good faith, its zealous scrutiny of the facts, the legality of its object. Yet once this criterion is admitted, the Auditor's standard of "reasonableness" will become the law, so long as the courts lean to his view of the facts. Since, moreover, on the cases, the Auditor is a person unlikely to approve of experiments in policy, it will mean that these will become "extravagant" or "unnecessary" expenditure, and will be condemned by judges who do not know at first hand the social problems which are the efficient cause of the experiment involved.

This, at bottom, is the basis of the view taken by the House of Lords. What, broadly, their decision amounts to is the view that whenever expenditure lies at the discretion of an elected body, the District Auditor must test its exercise in terms of his own criteria of "reasonableness." "The Auditor," said Lord Sumner in the *Poplar* case, "is not confined to asking if the discretion, such as it may be, has been honestly exercised. He has to restrain the expenditure within proper limits. His mission is to find if there is any excess over what is reasonable." But Lord Sumner does not provide us with definitions of words like "proper" and "reasonable." Either there is some quantitative standard from which they may be deduced, or they mean only that due care has been observed in exercising the discretion. The first test does not exist; and since the House of Lords rejects the second,

[1] *Rex* v. *Newell*, [1903] 2 I.R. 335, 344.

it can only mean that the courts admit that the real test is, in their view, the social ideal of the appointed official. And this, it may be suggested, was the perhaps unconscious end Lord Sumner had in view; for while he does not deny that the Auditor has no powers over policy, he defines policy in a manner which would otherwise be, I venture to think, almost unique as an example of misplaced judicial levity. He denies, first of all, that the elected members of local authorities "are to be guided by their personal opinions on political, economic, or social questions in administering the funds which they derive from levying rates." By whose opinion they are to be guided, he does not say. He admits that they are to decide matters of policy which he defines as "such matters as the necessity for a urinal, and the choice of its position, provided no public or private nuisance is created." It is difficult to draw from this any other inferences than that either Lord Sumner is not aware of the powers conferred on local authorities by Acts of Parliament or that he regards all policy with which he is in political disagreement as necessarily "unreasonable."[1]

The test of reasonableness is, of course, one that it is seldom easy to apply in a court of law. For it always raises issues which in their nature are ultimately questions of opinion, and it tempts the judge to believe that he is simply finding the law when in fact he is really testing and rejecting other men's views by the light of his own. In arriving at the meaning of this conception, it is therefore urgent for the judge to be certain that he has surveyed the whole ground. This, at least, is a view for which there is the highest judicial authority. Reasonableness does not mean what a court feels other men ought to believe. "It is a misfortune," Mr. Justice Holmes has said,[2] "if a judge reads his conscious or unconscious sympathy with one side or another prematurely into the law, and forgets that what seem to him to be first principles

[1] [1925] A.C. 578, 604.   [2] Holmes, *Collected Papers*, p. 295.

are believed by half his fellow men to be wrong." That was the spirit in which the Supreme Court of the United States acted in *Noble State Bank* v. *Haskell*.[1] It was not concerned with, even while it plainly doubted, the wisdom of the measure involved. The power to enact was there; and its exercise could be nullified only if it transgressed the plain letter of the Constitution. The English Courts, on occasion, have taken a similar position. "A by-law," said Chief Justice Russell,[2] "is not unreasonable merely because particular judges may think that it goes further than is prudent or necessary or convenient, or because it is not accompanied by a qualification or exception which some judges may think ought to be there. Surely it is not too much to say that in matters which directly and mainly concern the people of the county, who have the right to choose those whom they think best fitted to represent them in their local government bodies, such representatives may be trusted to understand their own requirements better than judges."

It is, I submit, from this angle that such cases as the *Poplar* case should be approached; and it is worth noting that it was so approached by a judge not less eminent than Lord Justice Atkin in the Court of Appeal. "Where a case is admittedly near the line," he said,[3] "I can hardly conceive the circumstances in which the Court would allow the opinion of the auditor to over-rule the honest decision of the council." For consider the substance of the matter. The Poplar Council is a body of persons chosen to carry out certain functions delegated to them by Parliament. There are various ways of carrying out those functions, and each way, ultimately, expresses a philosophy of life. Those who are chosen by the electorate are chosen, presumably, because the electorate prefers their view of those functions to that of their opponents.

[1] 219 U.S. 104 (1911).   [2] *Kruse* v. *Johnson*, [1898] 2 Q.B. 91, 100.
[3] *Rex* v. *Roberts*, *supra*, p. 205, note 2, at 728.

In exercising them, they use the discretion allowed them by statute to pay certain rates of wages to their servants. It is admitted that they arrived at those rates honestly and after due deliberation; but it is charged that the rates are higher than those paid by other councils and higher than are strictly necessary to obtain the required service. It is agreed that other councils fix their rates in terms of an award made on a scale of living costs compiled by the Ministry of Labour and that the Poplar Council should, broadly speaking, have accepted this scale. Unless it does so, the House of Lords argues, rates of wages may be whatever the Council pleases; and it is thus the business of the courts to protect the pockets of ratepayers "against honest stupidity or unpractical idealism."

But the matter is not so simple as the House of Lords supposed. It is perhaps of minor importance that, as Lord Justice Atkin pointed out in the Court of Appeal,[1] the cost-of-living index of the Ministry of Labour has not only no statutory authority, but is also challenged as inaccurate by reputable authority. What is important is that the Council's theory of what is "reasonable" in the exercise of discretion is, even though affirmed by its constituents, seemingly inadmissible if it does not square with the economic preconceptions of the House of Lords; it is, it appears, a function of the courts to protect the electorate from the consequences of its own ideas. That is, surely, opposed to the essential thesis upon which the idea of local self-government rests. Men who serve on elected bodies go there to bend the powers confided to them to the service of their theories. They have never had to assume that they are limited in so doing by the degree to which these agree with the views of an official who, to them, is simply a person put there to test their efficiency and good faith. They know

[1] *R.* v. *Roberts, ut supra,* at p. 728. "The official figures as to cost of living have no statutory authority and are not universally accepted as accurate."

that if they do not please their constituents, they may be rejected at the next election. They know, further, that above them is Parliament which can always alter the sphere of their activities. They realize that, in particular matters, they must co-operate with, and even defer to, the views of the central government. They admit that if they exercise a power they do not possess, the courts will call them to account. But, subject to these exceptions, they have believed, with a great body of precedent and experience behind them, that they can make the powers vested in them the instrument of the political philosophy they hold.

This, I may point out, has been the historic basis of the Anglo-American idea of local government as opposed to the continental notion. It has also been the underlying thesis of American federalism. It is, avowedly, an experimental philosophy of government. It entrusts certain powers to a body of men chosen by their fellows, and asks them to see what can be made of those powers. It does not deny that mistakes will be made, and that responsibility will, often enough, be unwisely conferred. But it argues that, on the balance, by throwing open the gates of experiment as widely as may be, a greater maximum of knowledge will be gained, and a greater interest in the process of government stimulated. Particularly, the theory insists that in matters of local concern there is a fund of special knowledge in a given locality which can alone treat properly any special local circumstances. It does not deny that a central government, even a uniform standard of effort in local government, may be more efficient than a system which deliberately leaves room for local variation. But it insists that the cost of this efficiency is more than counter-balanced by a loss of interest and responsibility in the electorate involved.[1]

This theory may be wrong, but it is at least the historic legal theory of the British system. It ceases to be so if the

[1] *Cf.* Laski, *A Grammar of Politics*, pp. 60, 411 *et seq.*

decision of the House of Lords in the *Poplar* case remains unchanged by Parliamentary action. That decision means that whenever the District Auditor disapproves of the view taken by a local authority of its discretionary powers, he will prevail against it if the courts agree with him. "Reasonableness" then means not a view arrived at by men who, having taken steps to inform themselves of the facts relevant to a decision, arrive at a considered view, but what the courts think they should have come to hold; and they will have to pay out of their personal fortune for acting upon a faith different from that of the House of Lords. Surely it is obvious that men of conviction and energy will not embark upon the difficult task of local government under these conditions. If "policy" were to mean what Lord Sumner insisted it does mean, the life of a councillor would never have attracted the devoted service it has secured. No one who knows anything of the history of English local government can have failed to observe that it is exactly because the central government has left to local authorities a wide field of experiment that men have sought to control that field. On any other hypothesis its character is inexplicable.

It was said by Lord Sumner that if the view here urged were to prevail, local bodies would pay what wages they pleased. That would, of course, be logically possible; but it is the kind of logical contingency that is directly antithetic to actual experience. For the question of what is a "reasonable" wage is already subject to two controls. Those who fix it must satisfy their constituents, and, further, they act always in the knowledge that Parliament can, if need be, temper the wind to any lamb that is unduly shorn. Many economists of high repute would not think a minimum wage of four pounds "philanthropy." Many social philosophers have insisted that it is the business of governmental agencies to set an example to private employers in the conduct of their enterprises. No one suggests that the

Poplar Council acted without good faith or proper care. Their view may, to the House of Lords, seem "mere imprudence" or even a "grave error of judgment," in the standards of *Rex* v. *Browne*[1]; nobody ventured to urge that it was *crassa negligentia*. And it is my submission that only at the point where it is demonstrable that fault may be imputed with general approval in judging of the exercise of a discretionary power is a judicial authority justified in seeking to overturn the acts of an elected body. In any other circumstances, the proper sources of control are the electorate on the one hand, or the appropriate legislature on the other.

For the alternative, I venture to urge, is always fatal to the esteem in which it is essential judges should be held. They are, in the exercise of their functions, enacting into law a system of social philosophy; it is inevitable, accordingly, that they should be judged by the social philosophy they enact. Nothing is more dangerous than their use of the authority committed to them to suppress views or experiments they happen to dislike. That is always, ultimately, to bring the judicial office into controversy, and when that occurs, it is always a sign of *malaise* in the life of the community. When the judge, in particular, has to interpret a view of law taken by an elected body, he must always approach it upon the basis that he is not less likely than its members to be mistaken. He must be sure that he is not denying a power because he dislikes the use to which a power has been put. He must be sure, also, that what seems to him novel or outrageous does not commend itself to others as well-informed as himself as both obvious and defensible. He must bear in mind, as Mr. Justice Holmes has warned us,[2] that "judges are commonly elderly men, and are more likely to hate at sight any analysis to which they are unaccustomed, and which disturbs repose of mind,

[1] *Rex* v. *Browne*, [1907] 2 I.R. 505, 518.   [2] Holmes, *op. cit.*, p. 230.

than to fall in love with novelties." He should, above all, remember that what seems to him to-day hateful may to-morrow be one of the commonplaces of jurisprudence. When he searches for the light by which to see, he must take account of elements he would fain ignore not less than elements he is anxious to approve.

Yet it seems as though, at least in matters of economic philosophy, the House of Lords is incapable of learning this lesson. The *Taff Vale* case,[1] the *Osborne* case,[2] and the series of decisions which centre about the policy of Poplar, are all examples of an outlook which seeks to insist that views not cherished by the Court shall not, for reasons which it is difficult to term judicial, find the avenue of legality open to them. In each case, the theories rejected happened to be those of a class which, thus far in history, has not been able to shape the substance of English case-law. In both the *Taff Vale* case and the *Osborne* case, the decisions of the Lords were not only overridden by Acts of Parliament, but did more than any propaganda could have done to strengthen the theses they were intended to destroy. It is not improbable that the *Poplar* case will have the same result. It persuades many, even among those who do not sympathize with the policy of Poplar, that the House of Lords cannot be expected to approach an economic problem in a judicial spirit. It suggests that the court holds itself free to check economic solutions of which it happens to disapprove.

I am not questioning for a moment the sincerity of the House of Lords. But more harm has been done in legal history by the prejudices of sincerity than was ever achieved by the receptivity of scepticism. It is an easy step from the *Poplar* judgment to the conclusion that the House of Lords is, in entire good faith, the unconscious servant of a single

[1] *Taff Vale Ry.* v. *Amalgamated Soc. of Ry. Servants*, [1901] A.C. 426.
[2] *Amalgamated Soc. of Ry. Servants* v. *Osborne, supra*, p. 203, note 2.

class in the community. For such a belief to become widespread would be disastrous. The esteem in which the courts are held is always a measure of well-being in the community; and nothing so increases that esteem as the evidence of a large-minded and catholic temper in those who make the law.

X

PROCEDURE FOR CONSTRUCTIVE CONTEMPT

EVERY ground which exists for entrusting power to a body of men is a ground also for erecting safeguards against their abuse of the authority confided to them. This is true in a special measure of the judiciary in the modern State. The power exercised by judges grows with the enlargement of the province of legislation; and the careful scrutiny of, and comment upon, their habits becomes proportionately more important. That men so placed should be independent of passing opinion is now a proposition too well established to need discussion. That this independence is best secured by making entirely free the right of judicial comment in court is an obvious corollary. Nor is it less clear that only the gravest misconduct can ever justify the removal of a judge from office. To strike at his security is to undermine his independence; and we have the amplest proof from the history of the bench that an insecure judiciary tends inevitably to corruption. No theses in political science are better established than these; and none is more universal in its acceptance by the modern world.

It is, however, one thing to make the judge secure; it is another thing to protect him from just comment by the citizen-body. Everyone can see that for the proper performance of judicial work it is necessary to prevent such interference with justice as is exemplified by the interruption of a court proceeding or the comment upon a case while it is still under discussion. Contempts of this kind are properly forbidden and promptly punished. So to act is essential to the fairness and dignity of judicial proceedings.

Issues of a quite different kind arise, however, when a

decision has been rendered and effect is given to the findings of the court. There is general agreement, at least within the jurisdiction of the common law, that once this stage is reached, the judge, in Bentham's phrase, is "given over to criticism." The examination of what he has done, the analysis of his reasoning, the weighing of his results, the discussion of his conduct are essential to the formation of the opinion which, in a democratic State, ultimately determines the trend of legislation. It was criticism, for instance, of the long line of cases which began with *Priestley* v. *Fowler*[1] which resulted in the Employers' Liability Act of 1880.[2] It was criticism of the *Taff Vale* case[3] which produced the Trades Disputes Act of 1906.[4] It was criticism of a number of miscarriages of justice which culminated in the establishment of a Court of Criminal Appeal. Without scrutiny of this kind, the dangers of judicial conservatism, particularly in a system which, like the common law, so largely lives by precedent, would be immeasurable.

But it is not less important to remember that criticism of judges is, though less grateful a task, one not less significant than the analysis of the work they do. Judges, of course, are removed from the multitude; but they remain not the less human, and therefore fallible, beings. Like Lord Braxfield, they may be incapable of common decency;[5] like Mr. Justice Grantham, their political convictions may be imported into their judicial findings.[6] There has been a notable tendency in recent years for some of the most distinguished English judges to make political pronouncements relating to matters which might easily become problems of

[1] 3 M. & W. 1 [1837].
[2] [1880] 43 & 44 Vict. c. 42.
[3] *Taff Vale Ry. Co.* v. *Amalgamated Soc. of Ry. Servants*, [1901] A.C. 426.
[4] [1906] 6 Edw. VII, c. 47.
[5] 1 Cockburn, *Examination of the Trials for Sedition in Scotland* (1888), p. 85 *et seq.*
[6] See Lord Oxford (then Mr. Asquith) in 22 *Hans. Deb.* (5th ser., 1911), p. 366; also 160 *ibid.* (4th ser., 1906), p. 370.

the courts;[1] and it is not without significance that their decisions have not seldom been attacked as biased in that field where the social interest of the result imports a political context into their work.[2]

It is obvious enough that nothing is more likely to keep the judicial temper at its proper level than the habit of urgent criticism when it overflows its boundaries. There must, for this reason, be ample scope to criticize the judge whenever, to the observer, he seems to have strayed beyond the system of habits marked out for him by the character of his function. To secure for the public the certainty that this criticism will be made is therefore important. Whatever unnecessarily interferes with its production means that a safeguard of judicial adequacy is deprived of its proper opportunity to function. And nothing, clearly, is so likely to interfere with its production as an attitude to criticism which fails to provide occasion for its proper explanation and defence. That attitude is necessarily present whenever the judges themselves decide upon the fitness of criticism passed upon them. It is the more certain to be present when, in addition to the power to decide the fact, they can also, if they deem it to pass beyond reasonable bounds, decide the sentence and judge if, and when, the offence has been purged. An authority so wide and so uncontrolled must necessarily act as a limitation upon the willingness of men to criticize at all. The knowledge that the person challenged is to act as the judge of whether the challenge be reasonable, or, at the best, that his colleagues are so to act, is a dangerous hindrance to the need for effective public criticism. No one will deny that attacks upon the judges must be susceptible to the same kind of punishment as

[1] See, notably, a speech on Communism by Lord Hewart, *The Times*, August 29, 1927, and a pronouncement by him that he did not propose to abstain from political discussion, *ibid.*, December 10, 1927.
[2] See, e.g., Report of a Special Conference of Trade Union Executives, reported in *The Times*, April 30, 1927, p. 17.

attacks made without justifiable cause upon other persons. But no one, either, will deny that just as in an ordinary action for libel the defendant is entitled to put his case, as best he may, to an independent jury without direct interest in the result, so also, where it is felt that a judge has been unduly assaulted, the defendant is similarly entitled to the amplest protection our procedure has evolved.

Yet no such protection is afforded him in English law. Punishment for constructive contempt remains an anachronism which few persons, not themselves judges, have found themselves able to defend. It is a system in which the defendant is haled before the court, even, upon occasion, before the judge he has attacked, and those who are parties to the suit decide whether the offence has been committed and to what punishment it should fittingly give rise. The punishment is fine or imprisonment or both, and there is no limit to the amount of the one or the duration of the other. No prerogative of pardon exists to mitigate judicial error or prejudice; and, at least in theory, a defendant committed for a contempt of this kind might remain in prison for the whole of his life.

Let us be clear as to that in which the offence consists. The defendant has not directly interfered with the course of justice. He has, when a case is over, so commented upon it as to traduce the character of the judge concerned; or—though this type of case is more rare—he has, in some way deemed scandalous, called into question the character of the judiciary as a whole. He is, in either case, given no opportunity to justify his act. He cannot call witnesses in an attempt to prove his position. He does not have the protection of a jury, nor the safeguard of carefully defined penalties. The man or men whom he has attacked decide what they will do about the attack he has made. They may warn; they may imprison; they may fine; they may do all of these or any combination of them. From the decision they make, no appeal of any kind will lie; and a defendant who, in the best possible faith, has been adjudged guilty of such a contempt will, on the evidence of the cases, escape penalties only by an apology of the most abject and humiliating kind.

The history of this procedure has recently been investigated by a distinguished lawyer who was himself a high official of the courts.[1] It is significant that Sir John Fox declares the present English procedure for constructive contempt to be an innovation of the eighteenth century without sanction in earlier history. It appears, in fact, to be a Star Chamber procedure transferred to the ordinary courts at a time when, under the dubious leadership of Wilkes, public opinion was emerging into English history before an aloof and astonished aristocracy.[2] It appears, moreover, at a time when the judges were still fighting to retain the right to judge the facts, as well as the law of libel; and by the time that Fox's Libel Act[3] had become a settled part of the legal tradition, this dubious procedure had passed insensibly into the law.[4] Protests against it, indeed, there were, one at least from the most eminent legal scholar of his time, Francis Hargrave;[5] and the regrettable insistence of the House of Commons upon a similar procedure in *Burdett's Case*[6] led to a noble attack upon its underlying principle from Sir Samuel Romilly.[7]

Sir John Fox has shown how ill-rooted historically is the present procedure in constructive contempts; but it has probably become too well rooted in judicial practice for other than legislative action to abolish its anomalies. How

---

[1] Fox, *The History of Contempt of Court* (1927). I cannot too fully acknowledge my debt to this admirable book. [2] Fox, *ibid.*, at 5–15.
[3] [1792] 32 Geo. III, c. 60. [4] Fox, *ibid.*, at 16–33.
[5] 1 Hargrave, *Collectanea Juridica* (1791), p. 16; *ibid*, p. 204, cited in Fox, *op. cit., supra*, note 1, at 41. [6] 8 How. St. Tr. 14 (1680).
[7] 2 Romilly, *Memoirs* (1841), p. 32, 101. See 16 Hans. Deb. (1st ser., 1810), p. 484.

dubious a procedure it is, is evident enough from the remarks applied to it by judges even at the moment of its use. "It is a jurisdiction," said Chief Justice Russell,[1] "to be exercised with scrupulous care, to be exercised only when the case is clear and beyond reasonable doubt," and he insists that the law ought not to be "astute" in this class of case. Mr. Justice Stephen went even further and urged that it "ought to be used as seldom as possible, and almost entirely with reference to the interests of justice."[2] The Privy Council have gone even further still, and in the well-known case of McLeod v. St. Aubyn,[3] Lord Morris, on behalf of the court, said emphatically that the procedure was "obsolete."

There has, moreover, been parliamentary protest against its character. On five occasions Bills have been introduced into the House of Commons or the House of Lords for its abolition;[4] and only pressure of business or a change of administration has prevented their passage. Eminent legal figures, Lord Bramwell,[5] for instance, and Mr. Birrell,[6] have emphasized the unhappy nature of the method; and no resolution or Bill of this kind has ever been opposed in Parliament. In 1906 and 1908, indeed, two resolutions condemning the procedure were carried, one unanimously, in the House of Commons.[7] It is significant that from 1900 until 1928 no case of this type has been before the courts.

A recent decision,[8] however, makes it clear that the procedure is, so far from being dead, not less likely to be used than in the past. It is, therefore, worth while to examine

[1] *Queen* v. *Grey*, [1900] 2 Q.B. 36, 41.
[2] *Dallas* v. *Ledger*, 4 T.L.R. 432, 434 (1888).
[3] [1899] A.C. 549, 551.   [4] 1883, 1892, 1894, 1896, 1908.
[5] 277 *Hans. Deb.* (3rd ser., 1883), 1615.
[6] 125 *Hans. Deb.* (4th ser., 1903), 1419.
[7] April 4, 1906, 155 *Hans. Deb.* (4th ser., 1906), 579-611; March 10, 1908, 185 *Hans. Deb.* (4th ser., 1908), 1394-1431.
[8] *Rex* v. *Editor of the "New Statesman." Ex parte* the Director of Public Prosecutions, 44 T.L.R. 301 (1928). See the verbatim report published in a supplement to 30 *New Statesman*, February 18, 1928, No. 773.

the limits within which the judiciary ought to be criticized and, further, the method by which unjustifiable attacks should be punished. In so far as it is possible to follow the somewhat vague reasoning of Lord Chief Justice Hewart in Rex v. Editor of the "New Statesman,"[1] he and his colleagues seemed to feel that the procedure may be justifiably applied in two classes of cases: (1) where the judicial impartiality of a particular judge is called into question, and (2) where words are used which tend to undermine public confidence in the judiciary as a whole. For the court, it appears, the "gravamen" of these cases is "that by tending to lower his (the judge's) authority, it does tend to interfere with the due administration of justice."[2]

Quite clearly, so simple a dismissal of the issue cannot be regarded as satisfactory. Let us take each of the classes of cases separately. The procedure, it is argued, is justifiable when an attack is made upon the impartiality of a particular judge. But it is clear enough that there are cases in which such a charge should be made without any penalty of any kind. No one who examines the conduct of the court in the treason trials of 1794 but must feel that in those cases the judges were incapable of impartiality; nor, to take certain American instances, would it be difficult to draw up an indictment against the impartiality of certain American judges in Espionage Act cases during the War period.[3] To argue that the expression, even the strong expression, of such doubts is an "interference with the course of justice" because the result is to undermine public confidence in the judiciary is to forget that public confidence is undermined not so much by the comment, as by the habit which led to

[1] *Supra*, p. 227, note 8.
[2] 30 *New Statesman*, February 18, 1928, supplement, p. viii. The report in 44 T.L.R. at 303, reads: "The gravamen of the offence was that by lowering his authority it interfered with the performance of his official duties."
[3] *Cf.* the citations *passim* in Chafee, *Freedom of Speech* (1920), and Nelles, *Espionage Act Cases* (1918).

the comment; and the position is only made worse by the procedure which must be employed. Were a newspaper to say that a liberal candidate could not have hoped for an impartial hearing from Mr. Justice Grantham in an election petition, it would have said no more than the strict truth; it would also have been well within the ambit of the court's decision in *Rex* v. *Editor of the "New Statesman."* Yet, what would have undermined the confidence of the public would not have been the comment of the editor, but the habits of Mr. Justice Grantham.

It is, moreover, easy to imagine a series of cases in which the impartiality of particular judges might well be open to doubt. It would not be easy to have confidence in the conduct of a birth control trial by a Roman Catholic judge. It would be clearly unfitting for an Attorney-General responsible for the Trades Disputes Act of 1927[1] to preside over a case in which its interpretation was involved; for he has been committed during its debate in Parliament to an attitude of mind to which he is necessarily a prisoner in any subsequent proceedings. It may even be suggested that a judge who has attacked communism in public is unsuited to the trial, even more, to the sentence of communists charged, say, with a violation of the Seditious and Blasphemous Libels Act.[2] On any one of these situations, strong comment could justifiably be made in the interest of the standing of the courts themselves; yet, on the theory of *Rex* v. *Editor of the "New Statesman,"* the commentator is guilty of constructive contempt and lies in the mercy of the very court he may be seeking by his criticism to protect.

Even worse is the position when we pass from contempt of a particular judge to criticism of the judiciary as a whole. Here, upon the very threshold, we are met by the position that, to the communist, a fair trial from the judiciary of a capitalist State is *a priori* impossible; it is an opinion

[1] (1927) 17 & 18 Geo. V, c. 22. [2] (1820) 60 Geo. III, c. 8.

sincerely held, and, at the least, arguable; but it is, clearly enough, constructive contempt. Or take the attitude of the court in labour cases. An ex-Attorney-General of England has said that the courts are prejudiced in labour cases.[1] Mr. Winston Churchill has said the same thing;[2] and so eminent a legal scholar as Professor Geldart has insisted upon this thesis with great emphasis.[3] Yet no one has ever suggested that their observations ought to be followed by proceedings for contempt. The whole underlying note of the campaign against the Trades Disputes Act of 1927[4] was the insistence of its opponents that the courts were unfitted by the natural bias of their members for the resolution of the problems it would involve;[5] yet no single prosecution for contempt has followed. Nothing, indeed, would have been gained by pretending that a widespread suspicion of judicial impartiality is not characteristic of the trade unions both in England and America; and prosecution for contempt, so far from removing the suspicion, would only have confirmed it.

It is not, it must be remembered, as though the judges are not possessed of ample protection outside the procedure with which we are here concerned. They have the ordinary machinery of the law of libel at their disposal; they have, as a collective safeguard, the very ample aid of the Seditious and Blasphemous Libels Act; and the Attorney-General can always proceed upon their behalf—as before *Almon's*[6] case seems to have been the general rule—by means of information. If it is true, as was said by Lord Justice Cotton,[7] that "unless the thing done is of such a nature as to require

[1] 154 *Hans. Deb.* (4th ser., 1906), 1928.
[2] 26 *Hans. Deb.* (5th ser., 1911), 1022.
[3] Geldart, *Present Law of Trade Disputes* (1914), p. 44.
[4] (1927) 17 & 18 Geo. V, c. 22.
[5] See the Report of a Special Conference of Trade Union Executives, *The Times*, April 30, 1927, p. 17, and the file of the *British Worker* (1926), Nos. 1–10.   [6] *Rex* v. *Almon*, Wilm. 243 (1765).
[7] *Hunt* v. *Clarke*, 58 L.J. Q.B. (N.S.), 490, 493 (1889).

the arbitrary and summary interference of the court in order to enable justice to be duly and properly administered," then the alternative machinery in existence fulfils all the purposes a reasonable man could desire.

We can, indeed, go farther. Once the machinery implied in *Almon's* case is invoked, it is almost impossible for a prosecution to fail. For that would be tantamount to a statement by the court that the accusations complained of were reasonably made; and this, clearly, would render impossible the position of the particular judge concerned. Obviously a procedure is unsatisfactory in which there is little hope that the prosecution may fail. Nor is it right to omit the fact that the association of the Attorney-General with the case lends it, as a rule, an importance which may go far beyond the actual facts involved in it; for the almost inevitable assumption therein is of a specially serious *prima facie* case against the accused because the chief law officer of the Crown has chosen to take part in the proceedings. In short, the judges are, in cases of this kind, asked to protect themselves, either as individuals, or as a body, against the rare occasions in which their fitness is called into question. They do so under a procedure which prevents any defendant from doing himself justice. Every safeguard of an ordinary trial is suspended; and there is no means at hand for the correction of error. It is difficult to see upon what possible basis such a method of trial can result in justice.

The classic American experience in this regard is worth recalling.[1] Judge Peck issued an attachment for contempt against an attorney practising in his court for having published in a newspaper a letter deemed by the judge a libel upon him in his judicial capacity. The attorney was sen-

---

[1] *Cf.* Fox, *op. cit. supra*, p. 226, note 1, at pp. 202–26; Frankfurter and Landis, *Power of Congress over Procedure in Criminal Contempts* (1924), p. 37, *Harvard Law Review*, 1010, 1024, *et seq.*

tenced by the judge to a day's imprisonment and eighteen months' suspension from practice in that court. Judge Peck was immediately impeached; and though he was acquitted by a single vote,[1] his attempt to apply the doctrine in *Almon's* case to the federal courts was immediately prohibited in a statute[2] which broadly sought to abolish constructive contempt of the English kind.[3] Nor is it insignificant that in *Cooke* v. *United States*,[4] Chief Justice Taft has laid it down that the commission of an alleged contempt in the presence, but not the actual view, of the Court, shall not be followed by the summary mode of process applicable to contempts committed in open court. The accused is to have reasonable opportunity to prepare his case; if he so desires, he may have the assistance of counsel; and he is permitted to call witnesses either in total disproof or partial mitigation of his alleged offence. In *Ex Parte Grossman*,[5] moreover, the noteworthy decision was reached that the pardoning power of the executive extends to this class of case. While it is true that some of the State courts follow the English doctrine—several go so far as to hold contrary legislation unconstitutional[6]—their reasons, as Sir John Fox has shown, are grounded in a too confident acceptance of Mr. Justice Wilmot's historical inaccuracies.[7]

What appears to be required is a fourfold change. It is desirable, in the first place, to abolish completely procedure by attachment. It places both judge and accused in an impossible position. The former is at once a combination of prosecutor, jury, and court, while the latter is given no

[1] Frankfurter and Landis, *supra*, p. 231, note 1, at 1027.
[2] 4 Stat. 487 (1831). See *Ex parte Robinson*, 19 Wall. 505 (U.S. 1873).
[3] But see *Toledo Newspaper Co.* v. *United States*, 247 U.S. 402, 418 (1918); Frankfurter and Landis, *supra*, p. 231, note 1, at 1029-38.
[4] 267 U.S. 517, 532 (1925). [5] 267 U.S. 87 (1925).
[6] *Carter* v. *Commonwealth*, 96 Va. 791, 32 S.E. 780 (1899); *State ex inf. Crow* v. *Shepherd*, 177 Mo. 205, 76 S.W. 79 (1903).
[7] See Fox, *op. cit. supra*, p. 231, note 1, at 226n; (1924) 37 *Harvard Law Review*, 1010, 1042.

adequate opportunity of self-defence. The trial, secondly, should be in the form of an ordinary process for libel. The accused should be entitled to all the usual advantages (and dangers) inherent in trial by jury. The onus of pronouncing a verdict should be upon an independent body of persons. There is no danger to the prestige of the courts in such a change. So long as judges are honourable men, their fellow citizens will have an equal interest with themselves in maintaining their dignity; and where punishment is desirable, the decision that this is the case will be far more convincing from the independence of its source than where it emanates from those against whom the attack may have been made. The penalties, thirdly, should be made definite, and provision should be made for a right of appeal. The present system is unfair to all parties, especially upon the first head; for it is an elementary principle of penal law that the ultimate limits of punishment would not be a matter of judicial determination. The need for an appeal is born of the obvious possibility that here, as elsewhere, there may be misdirection of the jury. There should, finally, be a right in the executive to pardon. A single case will suffice to prove the necessity for such a provision.[1] During the Irish land troubles of the last century, the empanelled special juries were almost as invariably Protestant as the prisoners were almost equally invariably Roman Catholic. One Delany, a juror, protested against the deliberate exclusion of Roman Catholics from the panel of special jurors and was at once fined for contempt of court. Such a decision is clearly undesirable. Equity, trial by jury alone, would not necessarily provide a safeguard against such a result. It is therefore essential to have a reserve authority outside which can, where desirable, undo the possible mischiefs of human prejudice.[2]

[1] 155 *Hans. Deb.* (4th ser., 1906), 582.
[2] Compare Birrell's proposals in Parliament in 1905. 107 *Hans. Deb.* (4th ser., 1906), 107, 193.

In changes such as these, there is nothing likely in any way to undermine the necessary prestige of the judges; and the history of procedure before *Almon's* case in England does not suggest that information, as distinct from attachment, is likely to multiply offences of this kind. It may, indeed, be argued that the number of cases of constructive contempt in the last half century is proof both of the high reputation which the English courts enjoy, and the consequent infrequency with which it has been necessary drastically to comment upon them. Nor has any case in the record been such that, where punishment was desirable, it would have proved impossible to obtain a conviction from a jury.

It is unnecessary here generally to argue the case for a wide freedom to criticize in a democratic State. Its corollary is the clear inference, insisted upon by Mr. Justice Holmes in a classic opinion,[1] that the boundaries to the expression of opinion ought only to be set by the imminent danger of public disorder. Against such a canon the present English procedure seriously offends. While the privilege of Parliament would leave its members free to speak strongly upon matters concerning the judiciary, all other persons who, even from the highest motives, may choose to criticize the courts, find the scales heavily weighted against them. For, as has been argued, there is an inevitable corporate interest in the judiciary which makes it difficult for them to act independently and impartially in cases of this kind.

It may be said, of course, that the very rarity of this type of case is proof that the power will not be abused. But to such an argument there are at least two answers. When, in the first place, there are proceedings by attachment for constructive contempt, the defendant is in fact deprived of all real opportunity to defend himself adequately; and, secondly, no one can read the accounts of actual cases

[1] *Abrams* v. *United States*, 250 U.S. 616 (1919).

CONSTRUCTIVE CONTEMPT

without the sense that, as Blackstone himself admitted,[1] the procedure is wholly alien from the genius of the common law. The essential fact is that judges in these cases tend to take a very high view of their prerogative; and that they cherish the power implied in the procedure seems to be shown by the insistence, already remarked upon, of certain State courts in America that legislation which seeks to abolish it is unconstitutional.

Nor is it a valid argument that the power to punish in this way for contempt is inherent in the Houses of Parliament. Most cases in which that power has been used display every unsatisfactory feature of the proceedings in an ordinary court of law; and it is reasonably clear that public life would be impossible in England if Parliament sought to vindicate its reputation from every contemptuous attack made upon it. Nor should it be forgotten that one of the greatest of modern authorities upon the privileges of Parliament has expressly put on record his dissatisfaction with the existing method of vindicating, where required, its reputation from attack.[2] That, too, was the view of Sir Samuel Romilly. "The power of commitment for censuring past proceedings," he said in the debate on *Burdett's Case*,[3] ". . . was in contradiction to the most sacred and important principles of positive law. It confounded in the same tribunal the discordant characters of party, accuser, and judge. It deprived the accused of that which every legal jurisdiction secured to him, the power of being heard in his own defence."[4]

One final remark may be made. The dubious character of Chief Justice Wilmot's opinion has been demonstrated by Sir John Fox; and it has been severely criticized by judges upon other occasions. Nevertheless, the main weight of judicial opinion is probably on its side. Yet when the

[1] 4 *Bl. Comm.* 287.
[2] May, *Parliamentary Practice* (12th ed., 1917), p. 138.
[3] 8 How. St. Tr. 14 (1680).
[4] 16 *Hans. Deb.* (1st ser., 1810), 480–84.

substance of the doctrine has been discussed in Parliament, it has found few either able or willing to defend it. Every Bill which has sought to change the law has been supported by eminent legal names. It was resoundingly condemned by Lord Selborne; Lord Fitzgerald, with the warm support of Lord Bramwell, spoke of it as "exceedingly objectionable . . . uncertain, undefined, and dependent upon capricious discretion."[1] Those who apply it have never sought a defence other than its supposed basis in historic fact, or its supposed necessity for the adequate functioning of the courts. The first has now been shown to be baseless; the second has been denied by everyone who has examined the assumptions involved, in that view. Indeed, it is unnecessary to maintain these contentions before lawyers trained in the traditions of the common law. A procedure stands self-condemned when it applies methods and ideas against which the whole of Anglo-American constitutional history has been a considered and masterly protest.

[1] 277 *Hans. Deb.* (3rd ser., 1883), 1611 *et seq.*

XI

LAW AND THE STATE

I

EVERY State in the modern world is a territorial community in the name of which some agent or agents exercise sovereignty. By sovereignty is meant the legal competence to issue orders without a need to refer to a higher authority. The orders so issued constitute law, and are binding upon all who come within their jurisdiction.

In some such way as this the modern analytical jurist defines the nature of the State for the purposes of his science. Any explanation of its character is, most usefully, of two kinds. It can be, on the one hand, historical. It is possible to trace the way in which the *Respublica Christiana* of the Middle Ages was slowly transformed into the complex of States we know in the modern world, and to show how the demands of unity and order gradually and painfully resulted in the attribution to them of the quality we call sovereignty. Such an explanation has the value of enabling us to see that the modern State is not, either in its form or substance, anything permanent or eternal: it is simply a moment of historical time, obviously born of special needs, and, equally obviously, destined to transformation either when it has ceased to satisfy those needs or when the needs themselves have passed away. The historical study of the State has the great merit of showing us the essentially pragmatic character of all theories about its nature. They are born of the need to satisfy a particular environment, and they die when they cease to render that satisfaction.

Alternatively, the jurist's explanation of the State may dwell in the realm of formal logic. Making entire abstraction of the facts of any given State, it may seek the quintessential form of which all States are more or less imperfect expressions. It may then say that where there is an authority which fixes the norms of all law, and beyond which, in the search for the origin of such norms, we cannot go, there we have a sovereign State. The content of the norms, or of the orders begotten legally of them, is here irrelevant. Neither political nor moral considerations have any bearing upon this aspect of statehood. We have not to consider the goodness or badness, the wisdom or unwisdom, of the norms; no problem arises for the jurist save whether the authority which has fixed them is or is not competent formally to do so, whether it is possible to go beyond that authority to one upon which it depends for its existence. If there is formal competence, if, further, that authority is ultimate in what may be termed the hierarchy of powers, it constitutes a sovereign State.

From a formal point of view, it is clear that the juristic theory of the State explains why commands which are issued in the name of the State are binding upon all who come within its jurisdiction. For it makes the ultimate source of reference from which all legal power to command is derived. But it is important to remember what the theory does not do. It explains how a complex of personalities, both corporate and individual, is geared into unity by subordinating them to a single point in the community. It does not explain whether the method by which this result is attained is good or whether its consequences are beneficial. It defines law as the will of the State without regard to the content of law. It makes that will binding upon the subjects of the State without regard either to what it does or to its power to get itself applied. It does not explain why the State has acted in a particular way, or whether it should have acted in a particular way. It is merely a descriptive technique of competence, independent of the actual world that competence will have to encounter. It is entirely fair, from this angle, to speak of the will of the State as absolute, indivisible, and inalienable. For were it none of these things, it would, in terms of its definitions, cease to be sovereign. Any formal juristic theory of the State conceived in this way must necessarily dwell in a pure world of categories. It is independent of the day-to-day stresses and strains which States have to encounter. The ideal State of formal jurisprudence need not consider public opinion, the wills of other States, the impact upon itself of internal and competing powers, ethical right, or political wisdom. Within the structure of the community of which it is the supreme expression, life is lived in terms of categories which it alone can make or alter. It determines the life of all other wills because it alone makes the principles of behaviour to which they must conform. For their law is conceived in terms of its law, since rules of conduct hostile to its law are illegal in the precise degree in which they depart from it. We are, indeed, entitled to think of them as valid only by reason of State permission, since the possibility that the State may deny them renders their right to be an exercise always in the conditional mood. The State giveth, and the State taketh away; whether we shall add the wonted blessing depends very largely upon our political philosophy.

II

In terms of its axioms, formal jurisprudence is completely justified in the whole of its procedure; in terms of its axioms, neither its method nor its results can be denied. By its own inherent logic, all that it makes law is necessarily legal, all in conflict with it is necessarily illegal; for it could not continue its sovereignty on any other terms. But a philosophy of the State can never rest satisfied with the axioms of formal jurisprudence. It must ask why they have been assumed, and what they do as a consequence of their adoption. It must seek a bridge between the purely logical world of ideal concepts, in which alone the juristic theory of the State dwells, and the actual world about us, in which the States that we know have to perform their function. It needs to know, accordingly, what that function is, and, independently of the juristic theory, to devise an institutional pattern which seems most likely to enable it to be performed to the maximum possible advantage. When the juristic theory is analysed from this angle, its nature and validity begin to assume a much more questionable form.

Let us begin by remembering two things. Every State, from the legal angle, is divisible into a body of persons issuing orders, and a body of persons receiving them and, presumably, acting upon them. The latter encounter the State always through its agents. It cannot act upon them except through its agents. For them, the State itself is an abstraction in the name of which those agents are entitled to speak. They make its will for the subjects of the State, in whom, of course, where the State is a *Rechtsstaat* they are themselves included. Save through them, the State has no means of declaring its will. It is simply a category of description, a method of attributing formal competence of a specially majestic kind, to certain persons and not to other persons. There is nothing about the State, in this context, which enables us to assume that it has special virtues or special wisdom, or an inherent right (apart from a formal legal right) to be obeyed. Its sovereignty is a method of conferring formal power upon men to whom functions of a special kind have been entrusted.

The way in which this kind of power developed is well known. When the Western World split up, at the Reformation, into a series of communities no longer recognizing either a single religious head, as in the Pope, or a vague and tenuous overlordship, as in the Emperor, religious conflict made necessary the unification of power within the State if it was to survive the consequences of that conflict. Sometimes the solution took the form of assuming that the decisions for making unity, and, therefore, order, should rest with the prince who became, as with Henry VIII and Elizabeth, the supreme head of the Church; sometimes the unity was made by recognizing papal power as invested with a right to command Roman Catholics, but, also, investing another authority with the right to determine, as in France under the Bourbons, the limits within which that power should be exercised. The Reformation, in fact, transferred to a person, whether individual or institutional, in each of the communities into which Europe was broken up the power to determine the rights of groups and persons in the interests of peace and order. Continuous warfare made men feel that peace was the supreme good; uncertainty whether the claim of a group or person was valid or no seemed to involve the risk of further conflict. To set the monarch, or, as in England the King in Parliament, above all other persons in the community, was a simple way of resolving what rights those persons should possess. None of them, legally, could appeal to a will beyond that of the King, or his analogue. They had, therefore, in the legal realm no alternative but obedience to his decision. The supremacy of the State was, internally, the necessary consequence of the breakdown of religious unity. Its right to determine the boundaries of power in any association or person within the community over which it presided followed directly from that supremacy. Once there was no appeal to Rome, there was no power which could compete with the authority of the State. But it must be remembered, once more, that in all these relationships, the State acted always through agents: it was, for its subjects, Philip in Spain, Louis in France, Cromwell and his major-generals, or William and his Parliaments in England. Their right to issue orders was the expression of a relational context between them and other persons so placed as to be unable, by legal means, to go beyond them. What is termed the personality of the State was, in point of fact, always the personality of the Government of the State. The distinction between State and Government was nothing more than the means of obtaining a sanction for the norms imposed by the Government upon the community.

The international situation greatly helped this development. The growth of commerce meant that, internally, the interests of peace were paramount; and the Government of the State, as the authority charged with the preservation of order, enormously increased its authority as a consequence. Once commerce passed, in fact, from the local to the national sphere, the Government was able, in the name of the State, to make regulations which, in the interest of the whole community, could be regarded as superseding merely local advantage. And where war was deemed necessary for commercial advantage, obviously it was to the economic benefit of the interests affected to strengthen the authority of the State, therefore, also, of Government, for their own sake. By the middle of the seventeenth century, Government and State had become so identified that even dynastic wars contributed to the interest of the State's authority. Its power grew by leaps and bounds simply because the purposes it represented were attained by its increasing assumption of authority.

That this is the history of its development is brought out clearly by the history of political philosophy since the Reformation. The classical theory of the State, as it passes from Luther to Bodin, thence to Hobbes and Rousseau, and ultimately to Hegel and his disciples, is essentially the history of an axiom and its justification. Luther vindicated the right of the secular power to be, independently of ecclesiastical trammels. Bodin and Hobbes, writing, each of them, in an age when the power of the Government to speak in the name of the State was challenged, insisted that anything less than a sovereign State meant anarchy, because there was then no final source of certain reference for the norms by which men's behaviour is regulated. Both Bodin and Hobbes wrote in an age when the monarchical principle seemed to most thinkers by all odds the most satisfactory. It was a principle Rousseau could not accept. But the real upshot of his work was, by making the State the repository of the general will, to give to its agents a moral sanction they could hardly have otherwise claimed. For his denial that representative government is valid was omitted from the synthesis built in his name; and once it could be stated that the people could act only through its elected representatives, a penumbra of prestige was added to their activity which could in no other manner have been obtained. The inference, in fact, was drawn by Hegel who made the State, and, inferentially, the agents who act in its name, not only the culminaton of the social process, but the embodiment of the highest purpose humanity could know. Thenceforward, to challenge the State was not merely to challenge the source of peace and order, but to challenge, also, that in which the highest end of man was incarnate; and since the State could be challenged effectively only by a challenge to its Government—since the latter only disposed of the State's sovereignty—the moral beatification of Government seemed to follow from the function it performed as the supreme agent of the State purpose.

III

The problem of the juristic philosopher, in short, is the difficult one of validating his purely formal analysis of categories for the actual world about us. Institutions justify themselves, not by their position in a logical hierarchy, and the claims that position formally entitles them to make, but by their power to satisfy effective demand. Once they fail in this, new institutions become necessary, and a new hierarchy is developed to make the logical hierarchy more adequate to our needs. And this, in fact, is what is happening to-day. Social changes, on the one hand, and scientific development, on the other, have operated to revolutionize the position of Government both in the national State and in the international community. An adequate legal philosophy, that is to say, must not only explain the legal right of a Government to obedience, but its ethical right as well. It must not only do this. It must explain, also, how the sovereignty of the State can be reconciled with a world in which the hinterland between States is organized, must show, therefore, how a State which is the subject of a vast range of determinate obligations can remain subject to no will save its own, and yet remain under compulsion to fulfil its obligations. Increasingly, the inadequacy of the classical theory of the State to express the needs of our time is evident to the new generation. Duguit in France, Kelsen in Vienna, Krabbe in Holland, are only the most eminent of those who, in various ways, have admitted its bankruptcy by seeking to build it anew on different foundations. None of the new answers may be adequate; but all of them represent a recognition that a purely formal jurisprudence which seeks to explain the State as justified to its members simply as the highest unity-making factor we know is without meaning for the problems of our time.

This can, I think, be demonstrated by an examination of the axioms on which formal jurisprudence has been constructed. Those axioms arose out of a supreme need for order which had to be established in a way which satisfied a set of given social conditions. The supremacy of the State was achieved because it enabled those who actually held power, those, also, whose tenure of power was accepted, to exert authority in a formal way. Their exercise of authority

LAW AND THE STATE

satisfied their subjects at any rate to the degree that, broadly speaking, was necessary to secure obedience. But power can only be retained upon the saving condition that its exercise continues to satisfy its subjects. Men who are conscious of wants ask themselves whether attention is paid to their wants. They scrutinize the forms of the State in order to see whether those forms are such as to offer them the maximum possible certainty that their wants will be satisfied by them. And, in the long run, the forms are judged by the opinion built out of their actual operation.

Law apart, every community is a congeries of men and associations seeking the satisfaction of wants. Not all of them are attainable; some, at least, are incompatible with each other. Some, by their nature, demand the imposition of uniform rules of behaviour either upon all members of the community or upon all members who fall within a particular category. The desire, for instance, for security of the person means the imposition upon all members of the community of the rule that murder is forbidden and will be punished. A group within the community is charged with the application of that rule. Men generally obey the orders issued for the prevention of murder because they are satisfied by the consequences of that prevention. It is clear that if the group entrusted with the application of the rule were unable to secure its observance, other men would be entrusted with the task so long as men continued to regard security of the person as a desirable object of attainment.

It is in these terms that we must approach the position of the State in society. It is entrusted with power in order that it may satisfy, or organize the satisfaction of, the wants of men on the largest possible scale. It acts through a body of agents, the Government, to that end and no other end. It does not possess power for the sake of power; it does not even possess power for the order which power enables it to enforce, since order is not the highest good, but merely a means to the attainment of goods regarded as higher than itself. For, clearly, a savage despot might establish a *régime* in which order prevailed, but from which freedom and justice and honourable dealings between men were all absent. Order, in that event, would be akin to the annihilation of personality and could hardly be regarded as an end. Power, therefore, is not good in itself; a Government which exercises power is not, either, good in itself. Its goodness, or badness, is a function of what it does. Its nature is dependent upon the results it secures by its operations.

Results for whom? I see no answer to this question capable, at least, of ethical justification, except the answer that it must be results for every member of the community. For the community is a body of individuals, and goodness for the community must mean goodness for those individuals or it means nothing; since, if those individuals are abstracted, no community is left. And since the humanity of men is dependent upon their recognition as ends in themselves, goodness for the community must mean goodness for me as well as for another; for, otherwise, I cease to be an end in myself and become merely a means to the ends of others, which, being the definition of slavery, is a denial of my humanity and a refusal to recognize my status as a member of the community. The State, therefore, as it operates, must treat my claim to good as equal to that of another unless it shows that differentiation in its treatment of me involves some good in which my good is involved.

The norms of law, therefore, that are established by the State—that is, established or maintained by the Government which is exercising sovereignty in its name—are norms the substance of which is of the first importance for the validation of its claim to my obedience. For its demand that I should obey any given norm clearly depends, at least in part, on my recognition that my good is involved in that obedience. Mostly, without doubt, I shall obey its demand whatever its substance, since the comparison between its power and my own leaves me little alternative. But the norms it establishes may arouse dissent not only in me but also, it may be, in a considerable number of persons like-minded with myself. I may dissent, for instance, as a member of the Roman Catholic Church in the *Kulturkampf*; or I may dissent as a member of the South Wales Miners' Federation in the munitions strike of 1915; or I may dissent as a citizen who, in Russia during 1917, accepts the principles of Revolutionary Communism. In these cases the formal capacity of Government to make law is challenged by a refusal to accept the law it seeks to make. In crucial instances, that formal capacity remains purely formal; an attempt by the Government to validate it in the event is met by a resistance which changes the Government of the State. The unity of the State, of, that is, the legal system summarized in its power, may remain; but it remains on the condition that it is used for different purposes.

From this I draw two inferences. In the first place I infer that the validation of law is not a matter of the source from which it emanates, but of the acceptance which it secures; and, in the second place, I infer that it is the part of wisdom so to organize the ultimate law-making body of the State—that is, the Government—that a maximum consent to its operations is assured before it embarks upon them. Consent to law is not merely a function of the source of law. It is doubtless true that innumerable men obey the State simply because the Government which issues an order is entitled in law to speak in its name. But analysis would, I think, show that most of such obedience is the product of habit or inertia, and that it is never creative. The obedience that counts is the obedience of an actively consenting mind; and such a mind is concerned less with the source of law than with what the law proposes to do. This is always evident when the will of Government is opposed by some powerful will which dissents from its conclusions. Governments, at the margin, are rarely able to get their way if a considerable body of persons announce their refusal to accept their proposals. They can then only exercise their sovereignty at the risk of losing it. The fact is that no Government represents the whole community in a way that ensures automatic acceptance of its will. What it represents is an outlook which, because it temporarily possesses effective power, is legally entitled to use the machinery of the State for purposes it deems good. If that outlook conflicts with the outlook of other members of the community, an attempt at its application may meet an attitude which varies from secret evasion, through passive resistance, to active rebellion. Law is made effective, that is to say, through the fact of consent in those to whom it applies. There are limits to effective legal action. This is another way of saying that the unity the State is legally entitled to make it cannot practically make except upon conditions. There is thus a serious disparity between the requirements of formal law and the necessities which actual law encounters.

It is easy to see why this is the case. Every community has groups of citizens to whom certain things are fundamental. They will fight for the preservation of those things, and any attempt to invade them by the sovereign power will result in a challenge to the sovereign power. There are Englishmen, I think, who would resist an attempt to abolish the enfranchisement of the working-class, or the right to industrial combination, or the re-establishment of limitations upon freedom of religious belief. Legally, the King in Parliament could do any of these things; politically, by doing so, it would probably cease to be the King in Parliament. Legally, I think, the King in Parliament has the formal right to resume an active control of the affairs of the Dominions; politically it must, as in the Declaration of 1926, treat them as equal and independent States individually entitled to make up their own minds about their own problems, capable, of course, of being especially influenced by the opinion of the British Government, but never subject to its legal control. Citizens, in a word, expect from Government certain standards of conduct; and it lives by its ability to satisfy those standards. Its legal capacity is always set in the perspective of the limitations those standards impose. They determine its will since, when they are set at nought, it ceases to have a will because it is driven to dissolution by refusal of allegiance.

Formal law makes this allegiance single; the facts make it multiple. Allegiance goes, not with the legal claim of the State, but with the conduct of the organization which demands it. A man may be with his Church and against the State, with his trade union, or his party, if the facts seem to him to warrant that answer to the call. He does not recognize an *a priori* hierarchy of claims, which receive their ultimate expression in the State. Law as form is psychologically neutral to him; what gives it the validity of right is its content upon a particular occasion where conflict has arisen. He does not assume in actual life that the State is entitled to his loyalty because, as the State, it is acting in his interest. He examines what is done in its name and makes a judgment upon the moral quality of the order he is asked to obey. He knows, that is, that legal power, as such, is at every instant subject to perversion. No Government is, for him, entitled to permanent credit merely because it is a Government. It is liable to error, to perversion, to deliberate misuse of power. It may, consciously or unconsciously, identify the interest of a class or a group or a party with the interest of the community, and legislate upon the basis of that supposed identity. It may do this in good faith; it may do this, also, in bad faith.

No Government can be known from the simple fact that it is a Government. It can be known only from the character of its acts. Nothing is more clear historically than the fact that men judge that character as the acts impinge upon them, as they respond or fail to respond, to the expectations they have formed. Allegiance as a psychological and historic fact is always contingent. It becomes actual and effective in terms of the quality of law rather than of its source.

It is because of this that men have sought in every age institutional means of limiting the power of their governors. They have wished to define what law shall be used for, to what purposes alone its coercive authority shall be devoted. Constitutions, Bills of Rights, and the rest, are, after all, nothing more than ways of declaring that the ends of law make law valid, and not the mere source from which it emanates. It is because of this, also, that every age has seen a revival of the idea of natural law. That revival is nothing so much as an effort on the part of thinkers to recall the State to the purposes by which alone the exercise of authority can be justified. It is an announcement that positive law must run in the leading-strings of principle, that it is the thing it is seeking to establish which makes it binding upon those whose behaviour it is to control. Men struggle, in fact, against being imprisoned in the categories of formal law because they realize that unfettered authority as such cannot give rise to an obligation which, *a priori*, is entitled to claim allegiance. The very ideal of a *Rechtsstaat* is an effort to make the legal sovereign the subject of purposes outside itself. It is a denial that it can will what it pleases. It is an insistence that it is justified in willing only what satisfies the demands of those over whom it rules.

IV

At this point, those who defend the classic theory of sovereignty, even in one or other of its contemporary attenuated forms, fall back upon a new line of defence.[1] They admit that the supreme power of the State is merely a description of capacity within the realm of formal law. They agree that such a view of sovereignty as formal law demands is politically inadequate and sociologically unsatisfactory. But they argue that its retention as a concept is necessary because society needs an organ formally entitled to resolve conflict between individuals and groups within itself. Unless there is to be anarchy in society, they say, there must be a highest power somewhere to which reference can be made where disagreement arises. "A political system," said Madison in the Philadelphia Convention,[2] "which does not contain an effective provision for the peaceable solution of all controversies arising within itself, would be a Government in name only." There must, therefore, be some body within the community which, when controversy comes, can say the last word. Or there may even be more than one body, each of which, as in a federal system, is final in the particular sphere in which it presides. Only so can we safeguard ourselves against the danger of particularism.

I am unable to see that the argument is a valid one, and I do not believe that its exponents have adequately examined the presuppositions upon which it rests. In so far as it is an insistence that the State must necessarily perform the chief part in co-ordinating social activities, and that it cannot accept dictation from any other authority

[1] Cf. Dickinson, in *Political Science Quarterly*, xlii, No. 4, and xliii, No. 1; McIlwain, in *Economica*, November 1926; Emerson, *State and Sovereignty in Modern Germany*, ch. vii; W. Y. Elliott, *The Pragmatic Revolt in Politics*, *passim*; Coker, in *American Political Science Review*, vol. xv, No. 2; I. Mattern, *State Sovereignty and International Law*, *passim*.
[2] Farrand, *Records of the Federal Convention*, iii, 537.

in performing that function, it merely repeats the argument of formal jurisprudence; and, as I have here sought to show, so long as it remains within that sphere, it is impossible to controvert the position it assumes from the very nature of the axioms upon which it is founded.

But its exponents go further than this: they claim that its solutions have a validity other than purely formal because, somehow, the State is a safeguard against particularistic interests. It is acting in the name of the whole community. It makes peace possible. It is free from the partial views which permeate—inevitably—the attitude of groups and individuals lesser than itself. The whole of this argument seems to me fallacious in so far as it seeks to make these qualities necessary and *a priori* attributes of the State. It omits certain relevant facts of the highest importance from the view it seeks to establish. It forgets, first, that the State of which it speaks is an abstraction; that what we have to examine are the acts of the Government which speaks in its name. We cannot *a priori* say that the decision of this Government, in any given instance, is in the interest of the whole community until we know what the content of the decision is. That judgment, obviously, must be pronounced by those who are to be affected by it. To say that they must accept it because its rejection imperils peace is to argue that order is, and always must be, the highest good. I do not see that it is possible to take this view on any scrutiny of historical facts. I do not find it possible to blame, for example, those who resisted Charles I in 1642, or the men who revolted in France in 1789, or in Russia in March of 1917. No Government acts in the name of the community save in a formal sense until the opinion of the community upon its action is known. Governments have exercised the sovereign power for particularistic ends in the past, and they will, doubtless, do so again in the future. When Louis XIV revoked the Edict of Nantes his action was dictated by the view that the interest of France demanded a single pattern of religious outlook; his action, we need not doubt, was both sincere and built upon high motives. But I do not see why the Huguenots were not, equally sincerely and from high motives, entitled to resist his decision. The order he sought to establish was, for them, the abrogation of all they held most dear; and their judgment, as with Jurieu, that this was a case where acquiescence in the will of the State merely because it was the will of the State was impossible, seems to me a justified one.

I entirely agree with the view that the cases where men or associations oppose the will of the State should always be cases of last instance; I do not need to be convinced that peace is almost always better than conflict. But it is not so always. Because it is not so always legal claims are merely legal, and, as such, have no necessary connection with justice. Every sovereign act of the State is always, equally with the judgment of every other element in society, someone's act, whether of individual or group. It may be made with good will; it may be made with bad will. It has no inherent virtue as a sovereign act. It draws its quality from its consequences. Both morally and politically, it is neutral save in the context of those consequences. Any theory of sovereignty which would make it more than this suffers from the fallacy which identifies a maintenance of the power of the State with the preservation of general social well-being. There is no way of knowing whether that correspondence is justified until we know what the State actually does.

Now the State, as I have pointed out, exists to satisfy the largest possible volume of demand in the community. It co-ordinates the bewildering mass of activities there to secure the greatest measure of common satisfaction. That is the justification of its legal authority, the sole ground upon which coercive powers are entrusted to it, and to no other group of persons within the community. The question of whether it fulfils its function adequately is obviously incapable of an *a priori* answer. Some of those who have sought to give the juristic theory of sovereignty a place beyond its formal sphere have seen this. They have therefore wished to transfer the argument to the way in which the sovereign power is organized. Obviously, if it is to fulfil its task adequately, it must be organized to that end. Let us so organize it, and it can then claim an authority to which, otherwise, it could not pretend.[1]

The argument is an important one, and it must be developed in some little detail if we are properly to appreciate its significance. Every community is so complex in its nature that except for the formal purposes of law, it cannot be reduced to the unity of a single common good. There are interests in it which are permanently antithetic, those, for instance, of a Roman Catholic to whom the propositions of the Syllabus of 1864 are ultimate truth, and those of a Marxian Communist who discovers ultimate truth in the pronouncements of the Third International. If there is never a unity of common good, no organ in the society can do more than partially express the common goods upon which men agree. We make unities; we can never make unity itself. What we attain, at best, is never total satisfaction of demands, but partial satisfaction, sufficient, at best, to preserve a working compromise which men accept as less inadequate than any other to which they can lay their hand. Now the State which has power to co-ordinate the demands that are made needs, if it is to be successful, the fullest possible knowledge of those demands. It must not, so to say, either ignore them, or legislate for them. It must legislate through them. The organ which exercises its sovereignty must be so constituted as to represent not some part, or aspect, of the demands to be satisfied,

[1] Especially Emerson, *op. cit.*, p. 272.

but the largest possible area of those demands. Society, if I may so phrase it, is federal in its nature; and the authority, accordingly, that is to co-ordinate its activities, must correspond in structure to that federal nature.

We have, therefore, to take steps to see that the decisions made by the State take full account of the interests that will be affected by those decisions. Whether the interest affected is individual, association, or territorial unit, it must be adequately and effectively represented in the making of the sovereign will. Wherever there is a real interest in the community, means must be found for eliciting the will of that interest before it is presented with a decision about itself by which the contours of its life will be changed. The organization of the sovereign power, that is to say, must, if it is to be adequate, be immensely more complex than in the past. It cannot legislate about trade unions or churches being compelled so to consult trade unions or churches that their will is fully known to it before it makes its solution of the problem before it. The sovereign power must be compelled, *a priori*, to make a comprehensive effort to embody the wills of those over whom it rules in its will before it is entitled to act upon them. Anything less than this is not truly a *Rechtsstaat*; for anything less than this has not truly sought that amplitude of knowledge without which, in any real way, demand cannot be satisfied at its maximum. Anything less than this means a failure to take into account the conditions of that successful coordination by which alone the authority of the State can hope for justification. Only in the degree that this is attempted can the State be called true to the law of its being.

I have elsewhere attempted to describe the kind of institutional pattern to which such a sovereign power must conform.[1] Here I can only say that, as a pattern, it seeks

[1] *Cf.* my *Grammar of Politics*, ch. vii, *passim*.

to build into the form of the State that reality outside by which the success of law-making is determined. Those who seek to retain the classic theory of sovereignty in new form are ready, it appears, to accept the view that the organization of its instruments stands in need of thoroughgoing revision.[1] They realize that a legal claim cannot hope for the validation of fact except by genuinely meeting the needs it encounters. They see that the historic formulae of representative government—whether in its parliamentary or congressional form—are no longer adequate to the kind of society in which we live. But they make, I think, the mistake of assuming that the problem is solved when a reconstruction of the pattern has taken place, however adequate that reconstruction may be. They believe that there is some mechanism for making sovereignty an expression of what Rousseau termed the general will of the community.

That belief, I suggest, is profoundly mistaken for the simple reason that there is no general will in the community at all. We never encounter any will that can be denominated good by definition. We do not, indeed, ever encounter in the community a will the unity of which is effectively comparable to the unity of will in a human being. A number of minds does not become one mind any more than a word is a tree or a hive a bee. The will of the State is the will of certain persons exercising certain powers. This will cannot be termed "general" in the sense that Rousseau gave it, until we know what it is seeking to do and the motives which underlie its effort. Its value becomes attached to it as we meet its nature and declare its character: it is not simply *a priori* there. The will of the State may be made to approach "generality" the better it is organized for that end. But organization as such can never assure it

---

[1] *Cf.* Elliott, *op. cit.*, especially the last chapters; and A. D. Lindsay, in *Mind, Matter, and Purpose* (Aristotelian Society), especially pp. 43–4.

LAW AND THE STATE

of generality until we know the purpose to which it proposes to devote its powers. It is not even decisive that a State should announce its will in full conformity with the terms of the Constitution. For before we could declare that it was entitled to obedience, we should need to know both the character of the constitution, on the one hand, and the purpose to which, on the particular occasion, it was being devoted upon the other.

No theory, in fact, which seeks to make the transference from State to Government can fail to admit the possible perversion of power. And no theory which scrutinizes the historical process to discover the conditions under which power is usually perverted can be satisfied to declare the inherent primacy of the State will in any other than a formal sense until steps have been taken to erect safeguards against those conditions of perversion. If, as I have argued, for instance, each member of the State has an equal claim with others to well-being, conditions which are historically incompatible with the realization of that equal claim must be removed simply because their presence alters the evidence of State action to the advantage of some special section of the community. The State becomes an instrument of that section. It has been, in the past, the instrument of the aristocracy, whether of race or birth, of a particular religion, of a special class. When the State undertakes to enforce its interpretation of social need, the validity of that interpretation depends very largely upon the influences to which those who make it are interpreted. In a State, for example, divided, like the modern capitalist State, into a small number of rich and a large number of poor, that unequal distribution of wealth inevitably introduces bias into the character of State action. *Mutatis mutandis*, the same is true of a community like Russia. There, the demands the State proposes to satisfy are the demands which the Bolshevik Party believe it is desirable to satisfy. That Party has identified its conception of good with the total well-being of the community. Its interpretation may be made from the highest motives; but it is a biased interpretation, which ignores the factor of consent and assumes that power as such creates right. I cannot accept that view. I should agree that when a constitution is built upon the wants of men and operates so as continuously to satisfy those wants, it is entitled to obedience. But this raises the questions: (*a*) What is a good constitution?; (*b*) who decides whether it is good?; (*c*) and who decides whether it is good in operation?

My own view is clear that these questions can only be answered in terms of the judgment of individual citizens. They are the persons who feel the results of State action in their lives; they, therefore, are the only persons who are entitled to pronounce upon its quality. They make the law valid by consenting to it. They consent to it as it satisfies their desires. A good law, therefore, is a law which has, as its result, the maximum possible satisfaction of desire; and no law save a good law is, except in a formal sense, entitled to obedience as such. This view, of course, involves an empirico-historical theory of politics. It means that a constitution is not likely to be good unless men equally co-operate in making it, and working it, for the simple reason that, historically, classes and persons excluded from a share in power are always excluded from a share in benefit. Because, therefore, each citizen is an end in himself, each citizen must know that his desires are so counted that, equally with other persons, he has a chance of self-realization. He is entitled to the conditions which assure him that his desires will be counted; and these conditions must be inherent in the fabric of any State which seeks to present itself as worthy of obedience. Where, alternatively, those conditions are absent those for whom they are absent are entitled to deny that the State is the

LAW AND THE STATE

guardian of their interests; and that denial carries with it a title to disobey.

I have termed this view the pluralistic theory of the State because it is rooted in a denial that any association of men in the community is inherently entitled to primacy over any other association. Neither legal authority nor width of declared purpose can give that primacy; title to it depends always upon performance, and of that performance individuals are always the judge, because it is in the quality of their lives only that it is in fact measurable. It is objected that this is a doctrine of contingent anarchy, that no State worthy of the name can be satisfied with a view which leaves open the possibility of dissent from its will. Such a State, it is said, will be, in Madison's phrase, "a Government in name only." But the objection, after all, is purely formal. Ever since Hume showed that even the most despotic of Governments is ultimately dependent upon public opinion, theories have been illegitimate which sought to confuse legal unity with moral unity. Pluralism is simply an explicit protest against that confusion. It is an attempt to recover the individual conscience as the only true source of a law which claims obedience from its subjects. It is a recognition that no jurisprudence can hope for adequacy which separates the idea of law from the idea of justice. It seeks the content of the latter conception in terms of the initial postulate that man is an end in himself and, therefore, entitled to the conditions which enable him to realize himself as an end; those conditions, where equally maintained for all, it equates with the idea of justice. It does not deny the need in society either for rules or for organizations to maintain those rules; but it does deny that such a need involves the concept of a sovereign State, or the attribution to that State of an inherent supremacy which enables it to dominate all other associations in the community. It insists that the right to make rules is always conditioned by the quality of the rules that are made.

To the critic who points out that someone must define the limits of authority in the individual and the group, that the sovereign State is merely a convenient hieroglyphic for this purpose, the pluralist has, I conceive, at least two answers. He can argue, first, that as a matter of history the function of definition is never wisely performed unless certain conditions are fulfilled, and, second, that once sovereignty is possessed by a State, those who exercise it in the name of the State always effect the transition from legal formality to moral right. Every Government claims that it is wrong to break the law. To the pluralist that judgment can only be made when it is known what law is broken and under what circumstances. There are realms of conduct, both individual and collective, into which, under circumstances, he would deny that the State has a right to enter. He would not merely question the wisdom of its entry; he would go even farther and argue that the organization of the power under which Government operates ought formally to deny the existence of such a right. Seeking, also, the realization of the individual as an end, he would postulate the conditions upon which that realization depends as principles which the ultimate authority, however organized, must respect, which, also, under all circumstances it must be powerless to change. The State, for him, is an organization, like any other, charged with the performance of certain functions. He cannot see that the character of those functions entails the right to sovereignty. For realism compels him to admit that this is the entrustment of unlimited authority to ordinary and fallible men. There are no guarantees possible that such authority will be justly used. The need, consequently, is paramount to deny title to its possession.

A right to sovereignty, moreover, does not exist for the

LAW AND THE STATE

sake of sovereignty; it exists for the ends sovereignty is to serve. A right to sovereignty must be correlative with the duty of fulfilling those ends. These, as I have said, are in their sum the maximum possible fulfilment of desires. The logical inference, therefore, from a right to sovereignty would be a duty so to organize and exercise the sovereign power as to secure the ends for which it exists. To argue, as Jellinek and his school argued, that the theory of auto-limitation fulfils this condition, is to miss the point that a will bound only by itself cannot be conceived as objectively bound; for an obligation of a form of conduct which the body obliged can alter at will, and yet never chooses to alter, either suggests a power outside that body and controlling it (in which case it ceases to be sovereign), or suggests the subordination of the body to principles inherent in human personality of which the State will is then the subject.

These dialectical tangles are unsatisfactory. It is better to say quite simply that the idea of a sovereign State is at variance with the idea of law once that idea is conceived as related to a moral end. For any other conception of law makes it unconnected with reason or good except by its own choice; and would leave unexplained why that choice should be made. The action of a sovereign State binds as such without regard to whether that action fulfils the obligation to which the State is bound by its inherent character. The character of such a State proclaims not only its inability to discriminate between right and wrong, but even a positive indifference between them. The sovereign State makes positive law; it does not make a law in which there is any inherent relation to justice. Such a positive law is merely an expression of power; power is morally neutral until its substance is examined. Since no State automatically wills that by which men ought to be bound, it is neither necessary nor desirable to accept its sovereign character. The State must derive its law from principles beyond itself, if the character of its policy is to have a morally valid claim upon the allegiance of men. In any other context, law is empty of all title to consent save the naked assertion of its power to enforce obedience.

V

Nor must we omit the international aspect of the problem. The doctrine of the sovereign State becomes a theory of international law in two ways. On the one hand, by the rigorous logic of its primary assumptions, since law is the will of the State, it is compelled to insist that no rules of international relations have the force of law save as the State consents to them; on the other, most largely through the influence of Hegel, by its argument that the State is the ultimate embodiment of moral values, it assumes that international rules are valid only in so far as the State chooses to accept them for its purposes. Since the State is the ultimate and highest form that allegiance can take, it either denies altogether the existence of an international community which is above, or beyond, States; or it argues that while the mutual life of States may make such a community, its rules cannot be binding upon them since the interests each State protects in that international community are the highest it can know. To bind the will of the State, therefore, to an objective international law outside its own will is both mischievous and undesirable.

It is difficult to put in moderate terms the degree to which either aspect of this doctrine is undesirable. By making the self-preservation of the State the highest duty it can know, it insists that the State is bound by no rules which it does not regard as serviceable to that end. International law merely becomes a body of convenient doctrines which a State is free to reject or accept as it pleases. It is

LAW AND THE STATE

not bound by any agreements or treaties; it is not responsible for any wrong; there are no moral obligations governing its relations with other States. As an eminent exponent of this view has pointed out,[1] its logic demands that right and wrong be the outcome of the exercise of successful force, and victory in war is made the true judge of international controversy. I reject this view of the State claim in the international field upon exactly the same grounds as in the municipal. The sovereign State in international relations is a body of persons making decisions. They have the legal right to make those decisions; but nothing is, or can be, *a priori* known of the moral quality of the decisions made until we know their content. That a State refuses to fulfil a treaty it has signed makes it no more valid that it should refuse to accept its obligation than that a merchant should refuse to fulfil a contract he has freely made. That a State should make war without provocation no more makes that war just than that a man should commit an unprovoked murder. A treaty forced upon a defeated State against its will is no more right than a contract forced upon one of the parties to it under consent. The goodness or badness of law is independent of the parties to it, or of their power. It is a function of the substance of law, a judgment upon what some decision actually proposes to do. It is no more logical to allow a State both to make its own law and then judge its validity than it is to allow the private citizen to be judge of his own actions. Law must be objective to the State in the international, as it is objective to the individual in the municipal, field. Adequate international relationships are impossible if on conflict law is merely to mean the rule of the stronger. For that is exactly the divorce of law from justice which defeats the whole purpose law is intended to serve.

Nor is it true to say that international law finds its

[1] E. Kaufmann, *Das Wesen des Völkerrechts*.

sanction in the sovereign will of States.[1] The recognition of a new State is not followed by an announcement from that State that it accepts the rules of international law; nor is it possible for the new State to pick and choose between them. To argue, as Oppenheim does, that a demand for recognition, by Communist Russia, for instance, is to be taken as an implicit acceptance of the binding force of international law, is to introduce fiction of a peculiarly unedifying kind. The facts have to be explained very differently. What we are presented with is a system of States equal in the sense that each has an identical right to the protection of the law. That is a position inherent in the notion of States as sovereign; for, logically, once sovereignty is in question there can be no discussion of superior and inferior. But this right to equal protection of the law is obviously incompatible with the idea of law as merely a subjective State right which each State imposes on others if it will or can. Law here must mean an objective body of principles above all States, laying obligations upon them they have no legal alternative but to accept. The very fact, indeed, of a need for recognition means that States cannot, in the international sphere, make or unmake law as they please. But the power to make or unmake law is what the formal theory of jurisprudence means by sovereignty, and if this power be absent in States it cannot be claimed that they are sovereign.

Or let us take a doctrine like the famous maximum *pacta sunt servanda*. The classic theory of sovereignty says that this rule is binding because States will to observe it, and they are equally free to refuse to will its observance if they so please. If we ask why States so will it as law we are told that it is because of the difficulties to which any other

[1] See all this put admirably in H. Lauterpacht, *Private Law Analogies in International Law*, ch. ii. I cannot over-emphasize my debt to this brilliant monograph—the most significant British contribution to post-war international law.

attitude would give rise. But that is an explanation which formal jurisprudence is not entitled to adopt. It can only say that the rule is binding independently of the will which accepts it, or the causes which make for acceptance. The will is in fact binding from its inherent nature. It is an objective norm of a legal order which must be postulated as underlying all States and providing them with the principles by which their life is lived. To say that States break the rule no more deprives it of its validity than the law against murder is rendered invalid because a man commits murder. Any other hypothesis, as Bluntschli saw long ago, would make international law not merely an inferior kind of contract, but one in which no agreement was ever binding when a State changed its mind, and in which, as he said, a change in the State's will produced a change in the law. Such an outlook results in impossible contradictions. Jurisprudence must be subject, not less than other sciences, to the maxim that no more causes are to be predicted than are necessary to explain the phenomena. To make international law the creature of the sovereign State's will is to pile the Pelion of fiction upon the Ossa of undemonstrable assumption to a degree that is intolerable.

The difficulties of the lawyer who insists that international law is merely the will of the State in the external field are by no means over even at this point. The whole history of the practice of international arbitration is the history of the adoption by tribunals of rules of international law the sourse of which cannot, even by the wildest use of fiction, be found in the will of the State. Phrases that desire a decision to be made in accord with "principles of justice," or "considerations of equity," or, again, "on the basis of respect for law," all clearly indicate that the idea of law is, for international purposes, outside and not inside the State's will. Nor, moreover, can one read the Statute of the Permanent Court of International Justice without seeing that its underlying assumption is the notion that the absence of a fixed rule must not mean a refusal to judge. The business of the Court is not to pronounce itself without jurisdiction, where the will of States is undiscoverable, but to make a suitable rule in terms of alternative sources which can only be explained as valid on the hypothesis of objective norms sanctioning inferences of the widest character in terms of the needs of an international legal order above individual States.[1]

Nor need we accept the view that only States can be the subjects of international law. The post-war world is littered with organizations which are certainly not subject States, but, equally certainly, are the subjects of international law. This is an antiquated view which flows from the assumptions of formal jurisprudence and not from the facts of international life. International law has to concern itself with the rights and duties of the League of Nations, of international unions, of the members of the British Commonwealth of Nations, of pirates, of rebels who are recognized as belligerents, none of whom possess the formal indicia of statehood. It is by no means inconceivable that, in the future, we shall see individuals recognized as possessing an international status, able, for instance, to sue a State that has done them wrong in an international court. International law is theoretically capable of laying rights and duties upon men as well as upon States; the present conception arises only from the way in which its foundations have been formulated and not from its inherent nature. For it is equally as valid to postulate the existence of an international community the character of whose law requires that every person who acts internationally shall be a subject of the law of that community as to postulate a society of States in which no persons save States shall be recognized as the subjects of rights and duties. The present system is

[1] *Cf.* Lauterpacht, *op. cit.*, p. 215 f.

a deposit of historic categories invented to explain a given body of facts. It is no more valid for all the facts we encounter, or all the needs we have to meet, than Euclidean geometry is valid for the total universe of geometry.

At this point, indeed, we can go farther. International law has been built upon the idea of the State as a legal personality the will of which embodies a will compounded from the separate wills of all its subjects. Now this view of the State is metaphorical only since the State itself can act only through persons. When we take a community politically organized into a State the will of that State is the will of the person or persons entitled to act in its name. There is not a single will in any other sense than that of a legal capacity attaching to some persons and not to other persons. From the angle of an international community concerned to maintain law as the inherent expression of its ultimate nature the will of the State must be a will for that law; a will against it cannot be legal in any sense which is valid. For that would mean a right in the State to will the absence of law, to overthrow the system of jural relations in which it is necessarily involved by the fact of being a State. From this angle it must follow that legal supremacy belongs to the body of rules which make up international law, and that the rules of any other society are of lesser significance than these. The State, that is to say, is bound in the rules it makes by the superior rules of the international community to which it belongs. It cannot make and unmake them any more than the individual can make or unmake the law of the State of which he is a subject. The personality of the State is, so to say, an inference from the fact that it is a part of the international community. It is a way of conferring legal capacity upon certain persons within a juridical community to enable them to formulate rules which have no validity if they conflict with the fundamental rules of the society in and through which its capacity arises. A State, therefore, cannot legally will what it pleases; it can only will what is consistent with the superior will of the international community. Its personality is a capacity in its rulers to act for that end, but for no other end.

From this, I infer the supremacy of international law over the law of any given individual State. I assume that a jurisprudence which seeks to be scientific has no alternative but to regard the community of States as what has been termed a *civitas maxima* the law of which is primary over all other law.[1] States, in this conception, appear to me as provinces of this *civitas maxima* whose authority is derived from the rules discovered to be necessary for the maintenance of the common international life. Apart from this conception, I see no way of arriving at a body of axioms capable of explaining the relationship between States assumed to be equal in international intercourse. No State can have a legal right to enforce its will upon another State if both are sovereign; force in the international sphere can only be valid upon the assumption that there is a body of legal rules over and above both to which each equally conforms. A State is then entitled to force in order that the legal rules may be maintained. Any other view must assume ultimately that force makes law; that what is alone valid in the international sphere is the rule of the strongest which is in fact law. I have already rejected this view as incompatible with the facts, especially with the doctrine of recognition, in international relations. International law cannot be, as Hegel argued, merely an external municipal law, since it would then be changeable, as it is not, at the will of each individual State. It is not merely, as Austin suggested, a "positive morality," since it is the rules of a

---

[1] *Cf.* Kelsen's famous monograph, *Das Problem der Souveränität*, 2nd ed. (1923); I. L. Kunz in *Proc. Grotius Soc.*, vol. x (1925), pp. 115–42; Verdross, *Die Einheit des rechtlichen Weltbildes*.

society which, even if more loosely and feebly organized than the State, is, in Westlake's phrase, "as necessary to human existence as the State itself."[1] Right and wrong are notions relevant to the relationship between States, and such notions predicate the existence of a society of which those States are a part. But a society without law is inconceivable. The norms, therefore, of that society are the necessary rules of its intercourse for the realization of right and the avoidance of wrong. The universality of this international society presupposes the primacy of its norms over those of its parts. The State, therefore, is a subject of law which presides over its being and limits the nature of the objects it can seek to attain.

VI

In the light of this conception let us return to the formal theory of law on its internal side. Law, it is maintained, is the will of the sovereign State; and the will of the sovereign State is law because it knows no superior. For jurisprudence, therefore, the content of law, the nature of the norms made by the State, is irrelevant. What it is concerned with is capacity to act, not what that capacity actually does. Any attempt to go beyond this view belongs not to the field of jurisprudence, but to politics, or morals, or psychology. No questions in these realms can, it is held, affect the validity of the formal conceptions of law. It is, indeed, even claimed that this methodology will have the desirable result of removing confusion from political theory.[2]

I suggest that this is an entirely mistaken point of view. Were the categories of formal law axiomatic in the sense of being inescapably necessary to the structure of a scien-

[1] *Collected Papers*, p. 13.
[2] Professor W. W. Willoughby, in *American Political Science Review*, x (1926), p. 510; and see his *Fundamental Concepts of Public Law* (1924), *passim*.

tific jurisprudence the problems they involve might assume a different character. But, in fact, they have an origin which is meaningless apart from a system of special historic conditions in Western Europe, and they only partially summarize those conditions. They make the construction of a philosophy of law impossible because they refuse to consider the relation of law to the totality of circumstances under which it must operate; they omit from their equations all the problems to answer which it is in fact necessary to construct a science of law. They refuse to consider the problems of conflict and valuation. They see no meaning in the grave issues which arise from the choice of a point of departure, and the application to life of its results. The validity of their results, therefore, holds only of a static world in which there are no stresses and strains with consequences which exist and alter life. If ethical conceptions have altered the law, if economic change has meant its adjustment, law cannot neglect either ethics or economic change. It is the static character of the formal theory of sovereignty which explains its helplessness before the phenomena of international law; these it can only resume by the invocation of fictions utterly unconnected with reality. The formal theory, indeed, is like the relation between the ceremonial and the operative parts of the British Constitution. The King may ride in the carriage, but it is the Prime Minister on the pavement who effectively makes the decision. A theory of the State which emphasizes formality at the expense of substance is not likely to possess final value. It abstracts the legal system from the context in which alone its meaning can be found.

Formal jurisprudence, therefore, is an answer to the problems of power existing at any given time; and even to that it is only a partial answer. The categories it employs are those which enabled effective demand to be satisfied roughly since the Reformation; but there is no sort of certainty that they will continue to provide that satisfaction. The new facts of a world-order both in the legal and in the economic sphere are making our political conceptions rapidly obsolete for the purposes they have to fulfil; and formal jurisprudence has been built by its makers in terms of those conceptions. Men live to satisfy demands, and they recognize as valid only the institutions capable of their effective satisfaction. Our system was constructed, by men like Bodin and Hobbes, and Hegel, at a period when the hinterland between States was not only not organized but was not unnaturally deemed incapable of organization. Our whole theory of the State has accordingly been conceived upon the assumption that it was the final form of institutional pattern, and even a body like the League of Nations was constructed by men faithful, in the main, to that ideal.

The facts, I suggest, have outgrown this view, and the developments require the construction of a new juristic edifice. The institutional pattern we need for an adequate theory of politics must take regard to the demands which require satisfaction and the way in which that satisfaction is to be attained. Here, surely, the unity we have to consider can only be properly understood in terms of the universe of facts to which it is relevant. If miners in England demand an adequate wage, it is the international coal problem and not the national that we must seek to compass. Stable financial conditions in London are a function of Chicago and Calcutta, of Berlin and Tokio. These interrelations have to be organized in order that we may render satisfaction to those who live by their results; and the inference that must be drawn herefrom is the need for a political philosophy, not in terms of the nation-State as the final source of unity but of a cosmopolitan order in which the nation-State is being rapidly reduced by the facts to the position of an uneasy and unsatisfactory province. The solutions made by the law-making body in any given State will only work in even the national sphere if they fit the facts of this cosmopolitan order. They have no assurance of adequacy save as they are built upon the working consent of at least its major part.

The inference from this is, I think, of supreme importance for a working theory of law. The epoch of Grotius, so to say, is drawing to a close. Instead of building up the conceptions of international law from the relation of States one to another, we shall, in the future, have to build up national law as a system of inferences from the rules of an international law far wider in its incidence than national law can claim to be.[1] It is not likely, in this new world, that any State will have, even formally, ultimate powers: it will be much more akin to the province of a federation, having authority over a defined sphere, but finding that its powers beyond that sphere are strictly limited. England, for instance, may well discover that while it may prescribe the penalties for murder, it cannot control the hours of work for miners; that while it may make its own traffic regulations, it cannot settle the scale of its tariffs. The process of government, in a word, has escaped from the categories in which the nation-State sought to imprison it. Some part of its functions, at least, is obviously destined to transference to a new authority by whose commands the nation-State will be bound. It will lack, from the very nature of the cosmopolitan order, the power to make final decisions in any sphere save that allotted to it by the needs of that order. It will fail to correspond to the formulae of classical jurisprudence, and new formulae will be developed more adequate to the needs jurisprudence must meet.

This indicates, I venture to think, that the approach to law cannot usefully be made in any terms which postulate

[1] I shall deal further with this problem in a work now in preparation on the necessary assumptions of international law.

the State as its ultimate source. Law is the operative satisfaction of effective demand, and its sources are as varied as life itself. The State is the organ through which the Government registers the fact that some given demand has secured a factual title to satisfaction: it is an announcement that behind this given demand there lies, prospectively, the coercive power of society. But, clearly, the State is no more than the form such registration now assumes. There is no *a priori* necessity that it should assume this particular form and no other form. That depends upon the character of social organization at the time when some effective demand searches for satisfaction. And the value of approaching the problem from this angle is that we are not compelled by our definition to put the orders of the Government into a category different from the orders of other organizations. We learn to see them, as we ought to see them, as species of a wider genus. Any association which issues orders to its members makes law for them which differs in degree rather than kind from the laws made in the name of the State. The power, also, of other associations is a power it is difficult to differentiate, again except in degree, from that of the State. It may be granted that the authority of the State is utilized to make its orders binding upon all within its jurisdiction: it seeks, within that jurisdiction, universality. But we must be careful not to mistake the character of that universality. It is a universality simply of formal reference. It makes unity upon the ground that unity in some given realm of conduct is held by those who operate the machinery of the State to be desirable. It does not tell us why it is so held: it does not tell us whether its recipients will so regard it: and it does not, finally, tell us whether it ought so to be regarded. Yet a true philosophy of law ought to explain all these things if it is to satisfy those over whom its sanctions operate.

A theory of law, in fact, which does not start by postulating an end for law, can never explain why law ought to be obeyed; and there is, surely, no point in making rules except upon the assumption that they are entitled to obedience. If we assume that law is made in order to satisfy human demands at that maximum which is socially possible we have at least a criterion by which to create an effective system of values. Therefrom we can infer a pattern of institutions which, at any given moment of historic time, enables us to explain the character of their operation. Such a theory of law has the merit of escaping subordination to the State. It attaches values to the institutions which satisfy its purpose, and to no other institutions. It explains why associations live and die, for it shows that their life is set by their ability to satisfy effective demand. It does not perish in the formalism of that categorical hierarchy which makes the State ultimate either on legal or on moral grounds. It makes the State ultimate only when its activity enables maximum demand to be satisfied. But it insists, as the facts insist, that maximum demand may be satisfied only by refusing obedience to the State, or, conceivably, by going beyond it to a cosmopolitan order which must make the rules if demand is to hope for satisfaction.

This is, of course, a pluralistic theory of law. It is so because the facts before us are anarchical. We reduce them ourselves to order by being able to convince men that some unity we make means added richness to their lives. We encounter everywhere not allegiance, but allegiances in men. We are not warranted in seeking their reduction to a Procrustes-like unity which is formal only in character. An institution cannot seriously expect to be obeyed merely because it is an ultimate point in a series where that series itself is a merely logical construction. Institutions can only secure obedience in terms of the values that obedience creates; and if the values are denied by those in whose ns they are to be effective in the long run, obedience will be denied also. From this angle, in short, we can make the necessary bridge between the formal demands of law, and those other contexts, ethical, economic, political, psychological, which give the abstract legal claim its validation in the event. Above all, such a view as this puts the source of law where it most truly belongs, in the individual consenting mind. For we each of us judge the commands we receive by their relation to our experience of life; and the success of the institutions which formulate commands is a function of their ability to convince us that their response to that experience is continuously and deliberately creative.

XII

JUSTICE AND THE LAW[1]

I

THE considerations I desire to place before you have not, I fear, the merit of simplicity. My thesis is the need for a movement towards law reform as vigorous and as far-reaching as that which Bentham inaugurated a century and a half ago. I am anxious to urge upon you the necessity, if we are to meet the requirements of our time, to reshape the foundations of our legal system that they may more fully satisfy the needs of a democratic society. I shall argue that too many of our laws bear upon their face an effort to meet social conditions other than those we confront. Above all, there is absent from its temper that spirit of deliberate equality without which no state can satisfy the aspirations of democracy.

I am not concerned to deny the reality of progress since Bentham's time. The immense improvement in penal methods will be obvious to anyone who has studied the noble work of John Howard and Elizabeth Fry. Much of the procedural inadequacy against which, in their different ways, Bentham and Dickens made so magistral a protest has been removed. Our judges are wholly free not only from the taint of corruption but also from that habit of erecting private prejudice into legal principle which characterized so many members of the Bench a hundred years ago. There is much less pleasure in the infliction of punishment for punishment's sake than was the case even in the later Victorian age. Even the justice of the country bench shows a definite decline in that spirit of class prejudice by which it was pervaded even in our own lifetime. Things like the

[1] A lecture delivered before the Ethical Union.

Court of Criminal Appeal, the new Law of Property Act, the Divorce Rules, the Poor Person's Rules, represent definite gains which I am as eager as anyone to recognize and to celebrate.

But the reality of improvement does not imply a title to quiescence. Law, by its nature, never changes as rapidly as the rest of our social habits; its need of certainty and stability always makes it lag behind the substantive requirements of a given period. By its nature, again, it is tough and technical; it is difficult to arouse a public opinion either to the consciousness of its inadequacies or to the knowledge of how these may be repaired. Its practice is a mystery which rarely yields its secrets to the outsider; and its habits are defended by a trade union of experts more powerful, in my judgment, than any other defensive association in the modern world. It is an arduous task even to understand the operations of the legal system. It is not, therefore, a matter for wonder that men should be satisfied with that which does not seem to provoke public outcry.

Yet I would remind you of three things; and upon their basis I shall invite you to reflect, first, upon the underlying philosophy of our law, and, second, upon the implications, this seems to me to contain. I choose my examples carefully, and I draw them deliberately from three quite different types of opinion. When, in 1910, the House of Lords decided, on grounds of public policy, that the trade unions had no right to impose a political levy upon their members, the late Professor Geldart, one of the first lawyers of our time, wrote that it was impossible for the English judges to understand trade unionism. Mr. Winston Churchill will not be suspected of revolutionary opinions; but he has said in the House of Commons that he fully understands why trade unions are suspicious of the courts. If you study, finally, the proceedings of Labour Party Conferences you will find that year after year there is an insistent demand for the appointment of labour magistrates; it is clearly and strongly felt that justice will not be done in the minor courts so long as its administration is mainly confined to members of the older parties.

It is important that these feelings should exist; what interpretation are we to place upon them? Here we must move into the difficult realm of legal philosophy and seek some principle whereby we can find the clue to the character of law in any given age. No subject is more controversial; in none, save perhaps theology, is it less easy to obtain agreement. I do not deny the audacity of my adventure if I try to lay down a simple hypothesis as the main guide to our problem. I suggest that the law of any given age is a function of the way in which economic power is distributed in that age. The substance of law, broadly speaking, will be determined by the wants and needs of those who dominate the economic system at any given time. In the balancing of interests which legal doctrine expresses the incidence of the result will be tilted to the advantage of the rich or the strong.

Law, that is to say, is not the embodiment of justice, or the voice of reason, in a simple and satisfactory way. There is justice in law, there is reason in law, but they are not, and never have been, interchangeable terms. What the courts do day by day is to apply rules the object of which is to protect the interests of the existing order. The maxims they invent, the principles they discover, are those which will satisfy the requirements of the dominant class in the society in which they function. In a bourgeois State you will get bourgeois justice; in a communist State you will get communist justice. Law, seeking order as its highest end, attains that order by satisfying the requirements of the stronger part of society.

I do not want you to think that I speak the language of cynicism; nor would I have you believe that I am denying the impartiality of the courts. I am saying only that legal

JUSTICE AND THE LAW 279

institutions, like all other institutions, take their main character from the economic system; where, therefore, this operates unequally, the law operates unequally also. The first need of any society is to make its obvious requirements postulates of the ideal; and judges, being human like ourselves, partake of, and are influenced by, its predominant mental climate in just the same way as other people. They have, at the back of their minds, what a great lawyer has termed an "inarticulate major premiss," which, all the more because it is usually unconscious, plays an essential part in determining their decisions. The results they reach seem to them the inescapable principles of justice; but they are, none the less, born of a special and limited experience which makes them weigh the interests in conflict with unequal force.

We should all agree that it is difficult for an Englishman to judge with detachment the social institutions of the Hindu. He brings to the effort to understand them prejudices, thoughts, ideals too different to make impartiality possible. There is poured into his mind a social and historic tradition which effectively prevents the possibility of detachment. So, also, with legal principles. A judge of the nineteenth century could not easily find place for trade union methods in his categories, partly because he had no experience of them, and partly because the atmosphere in which he lived was altogether unfavourable to the claims they put forward. He found it difficult, even in the face of statute, to sympathize with the purpose of Workmen's Compensation; he whittled it down to the narrowest margin, because it seemed to subvert the principle that there can be no liability without fault which time had made of the essence of the Common Law. The Supreme Court of the United States refused for many years to admit the constitutionality of a legal minimum wage on the ground that it is a violation of liberty of contract; though anyone can see, as Mr. Justice Holmes has so insistently taught, that true liberty of contract can begin only where equality of bargaining power begins. Clearly, as between the individual worker and his master economic circumstances make that equality impossible.

My point, then, is the simple one that where the effective claim of men upon the common good is unequal the response to that claim will be unequal also. This is as true of law as of every other aspect of social life. Our law, for the most part, was made by the owners of property in their own interest; and its character necessarily advantages them unduly as compared with their poorer fellows. This is not, I emphasize, because of any selfishness special to them. It is simply because those who dominate the State at any given time naturally equate the public welfare with their conception of good; and this conception, quite inevitably, is inextricably bound up with the preservation of their power. Exactly the same is true of Soviet Russia. Crime and its punishment are there so defined as to maintain the authority of the Communist Party. Examine, indeed, in any State the meaning of words like "constitutional," or "seditious," or "blasphemous," and you will find that they always are interpreted so as to protect some existing order from invasion of its privileges.

Such an economic interpretation of the law could be illustrated from almost every branch of English jurisprudence. I shall not attempt an exhaustive list of examples. I would remind you only that doctrines like that of common employment, which Lord Abinger invented in *Priestley* v. *Fowler*, are unintelligible on other grounds; and it is significant that when the working-class vote became a factor of importance the Employers' Liability Act should have put a term to its operation. So, also, the Osborne judgment can be explained only by the dislike of the House of Lords for the growing power of the trade unions; just as its amendment by the Trade Union Act of 1913 was the outcome of the Liberal relation to Labour support in the

JUSTICE AND THE LAW

House of Commons. I have already alluded to Workmen's Compensation; here I will only say that no one can read Judge Parry's admirable analysis of the decisions without seeing that, especially, the Court of Appeal was seeking deliberately to whittle down its consequences to a minimum in order to protect a social interest which, as it thought, had been unfairly invaded. I do not doubt the sincerity of the Court of Appeal; I only ask you to note the way in which its prejudices triumphed over the plain intent of statute.

II

Law, then, is a response to effective economic demand; in a society such as this I do not need to argue that there is no necessary relation between effective economic demand and justice. That is obtainable only where effective demands are broadly equal; where, further, differences of response are capable of rational explanation in terms of social good. That is not the case with contemporary England. A universal franchise has, so far, meant neither social democracy nor economic democracy. We are still a State in which privilege, both of wealth and place, assumes an importance that leaps to the eyes. We have not yet learned the truth of Hobhouse's great remark that "liberty without equality is a name of noble sound and squalid result."

But it is significant that, after the effort of a hundred years, we have at last recognized the right to political equality by the conference of universal suffrage. It is unlikely, I think, that this could be admitted without producing results in every other sphere of social life. You cannot confer the franchise upon the poor without inducing a demand for equality in other departments of effort to which, sooner or later, response has to be made. One of those departments is the law; and my anxiety for legal reform is born of the knowledge that, sooner or later, this demand will be made, and that it is a challenge to a large part of our present legal practices. For in any creative sense equality before the law is largely formal in England. Not only does treatment vary with social status; more important, access to the law is very largely a function of economic position. Our methods of legal training, moreover, do not breed lawyers who are adequately aware of the issues we confront. I am eager that measures of legal reform should anticipate a just popular demand, and not follow it as a sullen concession resented almost as much as it is welcome.

For let us realize that lawyers are not a popular race with the English people; it is significant that every great radical movement has been accompanied by an attack upon them. The rebels of 1381 hanged the chief justice; the first impulse of Cade and his fellows was an attack upon the lawyers; so, also, with the Cromwellian epoch and the Chartist period. There is, I think, a widespread feeling among the disinherited that the lawyer is their natural enemy; that he embodies, both in his principles and his technique, the main protective armament of the present social system. The hostility, like most hostility, is a little blind, and not wholly fair. But it has at least this important basis in fact, that the reforming lawyer is one of the rarest types in his profession. It is, for instance, significant that the Judicature Act of 1873 should have created a council of the judges, one of the purposes of which is the reform of the law. It has not, I believe, met half a dozen times in its history, and no legal change of any value is traceable to its influence. Yet few people are in so admirable a position to correct the anomalies of the law as the judges. Few people, either, could exert an influence so critical or so pervasive did they choose to bear a full sense of their responsibilities.

I cannot, of course, pretend here to do more than draw your attention to certain obvious aspects of the law in which immediate action is required. I ask you to take them as

JUSTICE AND THE LAW

symptomatic of wider issues which are certain, sooner or later, to call for examination. All of them I have chosen advisedly as examples of the unreality inherent in our belief that there is equality before the law. There is equality, doubtless, where there is equal wealth; but in most other aspects law, like any other commodity, is subject to purchase in terms of the litigant's financial status.

You know as well as I do that what is called petty theft in a poor woman, say in Whitechapel, too often becomes neurasthenic kleptomania in a rich woman in Kensington. What are called high spirits in University students on Boat Race nights becomes serious misconduct as we move east of Temple Bar. The poor man who is regarded as drunk when in charge of a car has nothing like the same chance of acquittal as a rich man who summons independent medical evidence and appeals to the Sessions against a conviction. The different treatment meted out to the sedition of Lord Carson and his colleagues during the Ulster Movement and that which characterizes our treatment of communists charged with the same offence is, I suggest, noteworthy. Nor is it, I think, without significance that every modern prosecution under the Blasphemy Laws has been against a poor man; eminent opponents of Christianity, whose criticism of its foundations has been far more powerful and influential, have not been touched in a single instance. Yet, as Mr. Nokes has shown in his admirable work, there can be no sort of doubt that they come equally within the ambit of the law.

I desire, however, to take my main illustrations from more homely realms. The Debtors Act of 1869 was intended to abolish all imprisonment for debt save where the defendant is fraudulent and dishonest. The measure was stoutly fought; and under the auspices of its critics a clause was inserted in the measure permitting the creditor to take out a judgment summons against the debtor. When this is granted, and the latter makes default, he may be committed to prison for six weeks if the court is satisfied that he either has, or has had, the means to pay. Under this system hundreds of thousands of summonses are taken out yearly, and thousands of persons go to jail. The system is automatic. An order is made for the payment of the debt by instalments; once there is default about these, the creditor issues a warrant and his debtor goes to jail. In theory, of course, the principle of the system is to make men recognize the sacred nature of commercial obligations. How does it work in fact?

It protects the tallyman, the moneylender, the cheap jewellers' tout, the vendor of petty business to those dwellers in mean streets who fail to resist a moment's temptation. Though much of the stuff sold is entirely worthless, the vendor is protected by the noble maxim *Caveat Emptor*. Husbands may be imprisoned because their wives have, in a weak moment, been foolish. The summonses are issued by the hundred in most courts; the defendant rarely is able to put in an appearance, partly because he dare not leave his work, partly because the summons is often made returnable, clearly with deliberation, in a place which would involve him in a railway journey. The system encourages that millstone of petty debts which hangs round the neck of the poor. It uses the blackmail of imprisonment to force men to pay for things they do not want, things they would never have bought had not the lure of instalment purchase got the better of their judgment. Anyone can see what a family must suffer whose wage-earner is taken to prison for six weeks. The economic loss, the psychological misery, the social danger involved, are all unthinkable. The system discourages wise thrift, and it puts a premium on the activities of the least desirable section of the trading community. It enables the reckless wife to pledge her husband's credit at the drapery store; it persuades a drunken husband, in a public-house over a glass of beer, to buy a watch which he cannot afford and will probably pawn later. In his evidence before the Royal Commission of 1908 the Governor of Worcester Gaol gave a typical instance of how the system works. A man was committed to gaol for twenty-one days in default of a payment of four shillings and costs. The debt had been incurred by his deceased wife. He had four children, all of whom became chargeable to the parish. He lost his work, the State maintained him in prison and had to pay his fares to and from Dudley where he lived. Is not such a system not merely a violation of justice, but also of plain common sense? Ought not a credit system to be based upon ability to pay, and not upon the power to use the threat of prison as blackmail? Perhaps I may add that since 1899 the State has still further tightened up the system by making the debtor do ordinary prisoner's work and wear prison clothes. The contrast between his treatment and that of the reckless commercial bankrupt who settles for two shillings in the pound is, to say the least, startling.

I add two other observations. The price paid by the debtor and his immediate family is heavy enough; but, what is worse, the creditor knows that the threat of imprisonment will enable him vicariously to blackmail the relatives and friends of the debtor. Unless they are themselves hopelessly poor or hard-hearted, he knows that he can count upon them. And England is, I think, the only first-class power which retains imprisonment for debt as a normal feature of its law. It has been abolished in most American jurisdictions; it does not exist in Germany; it ended in France in 1867. It has not existed in Scotland, except for Crown debts and those for maintenance, for just fifty years. Nowhere where it has been abolished has its restoration even been seriously suggested. To anyone who knows the system in its actual operation its persistence is literally incredible. It is a method of slavery which has not even the merit of refinement. Its only possible defence is that it enables a large class of mean traders to prey upon poor people who would not otherwise be able to pursue their parasitic vocation. And if it is said that it enables the working class family to enjoy services of which otherwise they would be deprived, I venture to point out that much the largest part of its income is spent on commodities for which a cash basis is the unavoidable source of payment. "He that trusts one whom he designs to sue," said Dr. Johnson, "is criminal by the act of trust." Here, as so often, the good doctor talked sound common sense; and I do not think the law should lend itself to the service of such persons.

The second illustration I ask you to examine is that of Workmen's Compensation; and I want you to look upon it from two angles. There is, first, the question of its legal interpretation; and there is, second, the question of the way in which it is best administered so as to secure its full objects. On the first head let me say this in preamble: the intention of the Act of 1897, which was badly drafted, was simply, as Lord Halsbury said in the House of Lords, "that there should be compensation given to every workman in certain trades when an injury happened to him in the course of his employment." It is no secret that the judges of the Court of Appeal did not like the Act, and in their efforts to restrict its scope they laid down doctrines (I add ultimately corrected by the House of Lords) which showed a complete inability to understand the purpose the Act was intended to serve. They first used the fact that the Act forbade the payment of compensation to men guilty of "serious and wilful misconduct" to hold that contributory negligence debarred a worker from benefit; though Mr. Chamberlain, the author of the Act, specifically explained, with the assent of Parliament, that this was not the case. Their next general determination (again upset by the Lords) was even more remarkable. The Act stated that benefit was contingent upon being incapacitated for more than two weeks. The Court of Appeal held that this meant that a workman who was killed or injured during the first two weeks of his employment was not entitled to compensation. Lord Davey's description of this decision as "startling and untenable" does not seem one whit too strong. The Court of Appeal again added a clause of its own to the Act which deprived a man of benefit if he did not start proceedings within six months. It held, further, that a rupture due to moving a heavy weight (one of the commonest of industrial accidents) was not an accident at all unless accompanied by a fall or a slip on the man's part; that an accident in the street when a man was about his master's business did not "arise out of his employment," since it could happen to him under other circumstances; that, notwithstanding Section 3 (1) of the Act which prohibits contracting out of its provisions, the workman and the employer could come to a private arrangement. I owe it to the House of Lords to say that, at long last, it reversed every one of these decisions. They are only samples from a vast mass, the application of which has done grave injustice to hundreds of injured workmen; and the House of Lords itself, in the recent *Bevan* case, has laid down an interpretation of the Act by a majority which will deprive hundreds again of compensation in quite obvious defiance of all that the Act seeks to perform.

My point is that if only the judges who did this understood the lives of the workers they could not have acted in this way; indeed, it is notable that some of the best County Court judges—a great humanitarian like Sir E. Parry, for instance—consistently carried out the original purpose of the Act until they were overruled. But let me ask you to note the history of its administration. Mr. Chamberlain's original intention was quite simple. All cases of accident were to be examined by State medical referees, and an independent arbitrator was to make a final decision upon their report. The lawyers, however, were horrified at their exclusion from a promising line of business, and their pressure in Parliament resulted in the present cumbrous and dubious procedure. It is costly, it is protracted, and it is vexatious; the Miners' Federation, in the *Lysons* case, spent over six hundred pounds, and the *Bevan* case cost much more. The system, moreover, is built upon the principle of insurance. What this means can be shortly stated by pointing out that in 1920 the companies collected eight millions in premiums and paid out three millions in profits. Out of £5·8 millions in premium income in 1925 they paid out three or 52 per cent. in claims (in which they include all costs of disputed claims), 9 per cent. in commission, 24 per cent. in expenses of management, and 16 per cent. in profits. Will you forgive me if I say that I do not find this a satisfactory result?

For compare it with the working of the Ontario system. Its Act is based on a report, made in 1915, of the Chief Justice of Ontario, who examined our methods and recorded that it was desirable "to get rid of the nuisance of litigation," and that his sense of justice was outraged by them. Ontario, accordingly, set up a special body called the Workmen's Compensation Board. It receives a report upon injury from a doctor agreed upon by employer and workman. Where the case is straightforward it affords immediate compensation; where it is complicated one of its officials can take evidence on oath, and there can be further medical examination. There are no lawyers, and no appeal to the courts. The medical and money benefits are greater than in England, and the cost to the employer is smaller: I add that the expenses of administration in Ontario are 2 per cent. of the assessments upon the employers. Practically speaking, that is, Ontario business men have insurance at cost against compensation. Can anyone who compares our system with that of Ontario doubt for a moment that, to serve the vested

JUSTICE AND THE LAW

interest of lawyers, its retention does a grave injustice to the working men of this country? Is it not significant that in England, in the search for law, we have too often omitted justice, while in Ontario, by evading the apparatus of law, they have secured it? I am, of course, only asking questions.

The third illustration for which I ask your attention is that of the costs of legal proceedings, and the quite inadequate steps taken to protect the interests of those poor who are charged with offences in the police courts. I recognize at once that something has been established in these realms in recent years. The Poor Prisoners' Defence Act of 1903, the Poor Persons' Rules of 1914, the committees appointed by the Law Societies since 1926, the work, as at Toynbee Hall, of the Poor Man's Lawyer—all these represent the slow dawn of a new social consciousness in these matters. But I suggest to you in all seriousness that they do not go to the root of the matter. They do not help the poor prisoner in the police court; no one who has watched its proceedings, especially before the voluntary magistrates, will doubt that this is a grave defect. They do not help the poor person in the County Court—the main refuge of the working class— since the rules are devised to facilitate access to the High Court only. And even there, if the local committee refuses its aid to a prospective poor litigant, he has no appeal of any kind from its decision. A recent report of the London Chamber of Commerce has stressed the immense and growing burden of law costs upon business men; how much the more, then, in time, in money, in the distress which comes from bewilderment, must they press upon the poor?

I cannot here attempt any detailed body of suggestions for the improvement of the position; that I have sought to do at length elsewhere.[1] But I ask you to note that we have done nothing towards the establishment of those Conciliation Courts which have, for nearly a hundred and fifty years, been

[1] *Cf.* my *Grammar of Politics*, p. 567 f.

so outstanding a success in Denmark; that we have nothing like the Bureaux of Legal Advice which are an integral part of German municipal life and deal annually with three hundred thousand cases; that, though we have a Public Prosecutor, we have no public defender. Judge after judge complains of the complexity of the Rent Restriction Acts, which touch very nearly the lives of the poor: we do nothing to simplify them. We have taken no effective steps to lower or remit fees in appropriate cases. The papers report the occasional incident of a dock-brief as though such counsel were public heroes; and I am unable to discover in the last half-dozen reports of the Bar Council the slightest pretension to any serious interest in the relation of their profession to the poor. Most of the judges, at least in their public utterances, seem well content with things as they are; men like Judge Parry who set out deliberately to measure the vastness of the problem are shining exceptions to a general judicial somnolence.

The poor, I think, could be pardoned if they had the impression that the law was an instrument rather for their control than for their service. For the most part, it is a luxury that they cannot afford; where they are parties to its operation they lack, as a rule, the skilled guidance necessary to a proper defence of their interests. That is why, despite all our protestations of equality before the law, no maxim is more deeply rooted in the mind of the masses than the belief that there is one law for the rich and one for themselves. Costliness and complexity make this belief true from one angle; the surprising limitations of judicial experience and imagination—I use advisedly moderate words—explain its significance from another. The courts of this country, for all the ability of the judges and their noble freedom from any hint of corruption, are, I think, feared rather than respected by the poor. I believe that this is a dangerous condition of mind, especially in a critical

JUSTICE AND THE LAW

epoch like our own. I can conceive few things more important than the effort to induce a different attitude by deliberate and wide-reaching reform.

III

I turn to a very different branch of my theme. Anyone who studies the history of law cannot help but be convinced of the futility of spasmodic movements for reform. We need something more than a Bentham every century to goad his fellow lawyers into a reconsideration of legal foundations. He cannot, even with Bentham's inventive genius, exercise an influence sufficiently wide and profound as to secure that continuity of creative change which is of the essence of successful reform. Much of his effort will be wasted, as much as Bentham's was, by heart-breaking and reactionary opposition; the kind of antagonism Sydney Smith depicted when he wrote of "the attorney-general and the solicitor-general for the time being always protesting against each alteration, and regularly and officially prophesying the utter destruction of the whole jurisprudence of Great Britain!" Is there any way in which we can assure to ourselves a steady and continuous improvement in the substance and administration of the law?

For myself, I believe that the high-road lies through an increasing equality among citizens. I doubt the possibility of really basic reform so long as the present immense disparities between rich and poor continue. But I venture to suggest that, even with that serious qualification, there are certain matters to which public opinion could be usefully directed with tolerable certainty that serious improvement would result. We need to reconsider the foundations of English legal education; at present our schools of law are woefully behind those of the major Continental countries and of the United States. We need, secondly, to organize the legal profession, not merely, as it is now organized, for the protection of its interests, but also for the improvement of their technique by research; we need bodies which shall do for the law what the Royal Society of Medicine does for doctors. We need, thirdly, as the Haldane Committee on the Machinery of Government pointed out, a Ministry of Justice in which there would be a small but permanent department continually engaged in seeking to improve the law. It would amass information upon foreign and domestic experience. It would investigate from time to time particular branches of the law; and it would receive from any relevant source criticisms and suggestions upon its working. It would serve, in fact, as the eye and ear of the Minister of Justice, and so prepare him for creative innovation. Finally, as I think, we ought to use the knowledge and experience of the judges much more fully than we do. If we required from them, for example, an annual report upon the working of the courts, with their view of defects which require remedy, I believe we should call into play a latent fund of suggestion of very high value. If, for example, the remarks made *obiter* by judges who sit in the Divorce Court were annually expanded into a full analysis, I do not think the Majority Report of the Royal Commission of 1909, an urgently needed change, would have had to wait so long upon ecclesiastical prejudice and governmental timidity.

I cannot here discuss these suggestions in anything like the detail I venture to believe they warrant;[1] but, because I am a university teacher, whose own subject borders at every point upon the law, perhaps you will allow me to explain why I emphasize the importance of reconstructing legal education. To make law a genuine intellectual discipline it must be taught as a science and not merely as a practical technique. It must leave the student with a sense that its problems are a vital tract of human experience the

[1] I have done so in my *Grammar of Politics*, p. 575 f.

solution of which definitely adds to the sum of human good. It must wrestle with principles as well as memorize conclusions. It must suggest vistas of change even while it seeks to convey the picture of the contemporary position. Our present system does not meet these requirements. It cannot be seriously considered as having in view the scientific study of its subject. Its aim is to enable the student for the Bar to pass, with a minimum of effort, a number of relatively simple examinations in which memory counts for more than insight, and an acceptance of judicial decisions for more than a philosophic scepticism about them. The average lawyer knows, when he is called, little of legal history and less of jurisprudence. He has been shown nothing of the interrelations of law with economics or political science. He is taught dogma and not inquiry; nothing is done to stimulate his curiosity. He learns the doctrines made by the courts without any attempt at their critical examination. I do not deny that successful lawyers emerge from the system. I do deny that it produces lawyers concerned to reshape the law to the needs of a changing environment.

I wish we could follow the example set us by the traditions and methods of the great Continental law schools, on the one hand, and the more important American law schools on the other. They train successful lawyers; but they also do more. For they learn that legal cases are legal problems, and that the judicial solution must be proved, like any other, in terms of principle. They learn from teachers continually engaged in remarking the foundations of law, whose views consciously influence the opinions of the Bench. A great teaching tradition, as the work of Maitland even in England shows, is a great reforming tradition; but there is no teaching tradition in the Inns of Court. The students of Harvard and Yale, Paris and Bordeaux, Berlin and Hamburg, go out not merely to practise, but also to improve.

They become missionaries for new ideas. They clamour for experiment. I do not discover men of this temper among the general run of English lawyers.

I am arguing that an attempt, to put it concretely, to make legal teaching in England emulate the spirit of Harvard would, on the basis of experience, build a better type of lawyer. But I am anxious for more even than the critical study of positive law. I believe that it is urgent to insist upon a serious training in jurisprudence, especially upon its comparative side, because without that training no lawyer, however practically eminent, really knows what is implied in the assumptions of his subject. Jurisprudence is the eye of the law. It gives law its insight into the environment it seeks to meet; without its pervasive influence positive law will always fail to meet the spirit of a new time. Is it not significant, in this context, that English jurisprudence, since the age of Austin, should have been incomparably poorer than that of France or Germany? Was not the failure of the courts to meet such challenges as the *Free Church of Scotland* case or the *Osborne* case the outcome of that poverty? Can lawyers decide cases rightly if they do not know, as in those cases the House of Lords did not know, the juristic significance of what they are doing?

One other point. Law is a part of life, and to be fruitful it must recognize its relationship to those other parts which fix its contours. No man can really understand law who lacks an intimate acquaintance with economics. Their present divorce in our legal education is calamitous. It explains the decisions I have discussed about workmen's compensation and the place of trade unions in the State. Contract, tort, property, these are legal categories which can be grasped only fully in their economic context. Constitutional law is only intelligible as an expression of the working of social forces which derive their meaning from the disposition of economic power. Can we not seek to do what France and Germany have done, and make a training in political economy an integral part of the lawyer's equipment? We shall not accomplish such changes as I have outlined by waiting for the Inns of Court to reform themselves. It is, I think, some seventy years since Lord Westbury urged them to set their house in order, and over fifty years since Langdell revivified the teaching of American law. The universities apart, the legal profession has learned little from the experience of other countries; it has not even sought seriously to examine the quality of its own effort. We are fortunate, at the moment, in having upon the Woolsack a Lord Chancellor who cares profoundly for ideals of legal reform.[1] Is it too much to plead with him to make his tenure of office memorable by setting up that inquiry into legal education which is so long overdue? At least I can put on record my own conviction that such an inquiry, seriously pursued, might well open a new epoch in the history of English law.

IV

One final word and I have done. Law, like life, has its periods of change and its periods of conservation; it is not a closed system of eternal rules elevated above time and place. The respect it can win is measured by the justice it embodies, and its power to embody ideals of justice depends upon its conscious effort to respond in an equal way to the widest demands it encounters. I do not deny the difficulty of the task, and I am anxious to recognize its nobility. I know how tremendous is the pressure of past tradition, how urgent, especially in a critical time, the need for stability. The lawyer's regard for precedent has been one of the great preservative forces of history; I do not for a moment deny the importance of the contribution it has made.

But there come epochs in the record of mankind when

[1] Lord Sankey.

a too strict regard for precedent serves to destroy rather than to preserve. When a new class of men and women, hitherto excluded by public policy from the benefits of the State, demand that they also shall share in its good, law cannot afford an undue emphasis upon stability. It is the lawyer's function to make his doctrines keep step with the spirit of the time. He must seek continually to reshape them to new needs and new compulsions; he must make the researches which can give to experiment the prospect of success. Our age is refashioning swiftly the foundations of its social life; law has no higher task than deliberate readjustment to this novelty. If I am told that law is not morals, I can only answer that it is then so much the worse for law, for the degree of their separation, as our law of divorce so notably shows, is always the measure of its failure. I do not ask the lawyer to be a knight-errant for dubious causes, I do not plead that he should be a fanatic for innovation. I ask only for the recognition that so long as men are gravely dissatisfied with the result of social operations his work as a lawyer cannot have been adequately performed. To find within his sphere the causes of this disharmony, to seek as best he can to remedy them at the source—this is to labour in the spirit of justice. It is a noble ambition, easier to record than to realize. But on its achievement there depends the quality of our civilization.

INDEX

Abinger (Lord), 280
Adams (S.), 121
d'Alembert, 18, 31
d'Argenson, 26, 42, 45
Arnauld, 15
Arnold (M.), 196, 201
Atkin, 215–16
Audiffred, 73
Austin, 268

Babeuf, 32, chap. iii, *passim*
Bagehot, 104, 181
Baldwin (S.), 193
Balfour (Lord), 192
Barbeyrac, 25
Barbier, 19, 26, 29, 43
Barker, 133
Baudeau, 41
Baudot, 84
Bayle, 13, 17, 22–5
Bentham, 131, 138, 160, 276, 291
Billaud-Varenne, 84
Birrell (A.), 227
Blackstone, 235
Bluntschli, 265
Boileau, 15, 18, 33
Boisguillebert, 25
Boissel, 86
Boissy d'Anglas, 83
Boulainvilliers, 17
Bossuet, 15, 16, 35
Bourdaloue, 35
Bramwell, 227
Brandeis, 167, 172, 179
Brissot, 31, 76, 78
Buffon, 33, 38
Burke, 38, 75
Burns (John), 191
Buonarroti, 88 f.

Calas, 23
Cardozo, 165, 173, 202

Carlyle, 59
Carson, 283
Caveyrac, 22
Chalier, 85
Chamberlain, 286
Chatham, 104
Churchill (W.), 230
Claude, 17
Condillac, 14, 20, 29
Condorcet, 15, 21, 31, 41, 78, 83, 121
Cournot, 32
Croy, 42

Darthe, 88
Davey, 287
du Deffand, 19, 49
Déverité, 71
Dicey, 179
Dickens, 276
Diderot, 14, 15, 20, 22, 28, 33, chap. ii, *passim*
Dolivier, 85–6
Dubos, 14
Dufourny de Villiers, 71
Duguit, 244
Dupont de Nemours, 33

Fauchet, 78
Fenélon, 16, 23, 35, 66
Figgis, 133
Fitzgerald, 236
Fletcher Moulton, 210, 212
Fontenelle, 13
Fourier, 38
S. Francis (Sales), 17, 35
Franklin, 120
Fréron, 43

Galiani, 62
Geldart, 230
Geoffrin, 49

Gérard, 15
Gladstone, 138, 181, 183, 199
Godwin, 38
Goethe, 59, 60
Gosselin, 71
Grantham, 223, 229
Gray (S. C.), 152
Green (T. H.), 131
Grey (3rd Earl), 120
Grimm, 51
Grotius, 25, 272

Halsbury, 168
Hargrave, 226
Harrison, 172
Hazlitt, 58
Hegel, 38, 131, 242, 262, 268
Helvétius, 20, 21, 24, 28, 43, 51
Henderson, 199
Hewart, 224, 228
Hobbes, 130, 242
Hobhouse, 281
Holbach, 13, 21, 24, 29, 30, 34, 41, 43, 51, 56
Holmes, 131, 146–62, 173, 178, 214, 219, 234, 279

Johnson (Dr.), 17, 286

Kaufmann (E.), 263
Kelsen, 244
Krabbe, 244

La Bruyère, 26, 35
Lacombe, 85
Lambert, 80
Lamennais, 38
La Mettrie, 20, 24, 56
Langdell, 295
Lange, 85
Lauterpacht, 284–5
Lees-Smith, 118
Lenin, 98 f.
Lessing, 59

Lezardière, 45
Lillo, 38, 59
Linguet, 31, 67
Lippmann, 165
Locke, 13, 22, 29
Louis XIV, 16–17
Loustalot, 75
Luther, 242

Mably, 18, 24, 28, 34, 41, 67
MacDonald, 196
Madison, 66, 251, 259
Maistre, 57
Maitland, 133
Malesherbes, 18, 27
Mandeville, 67
Marais, 26
Marat, 15, 71, 76, 79 f.
Maréchal, 88 f.
Marivaux, 15
Marmontel, 18, 37
Marx, 38, 67, 130
Massillon, 15
Mellor, 207
Mercer (S.), 15, 37, 67
Mercier de la Rivière, 33
Mill, 140
Mirabeau, 34
Montaigne, 13
Montesquieu, chap. i *passim*, 162
Moreau, 37, 43
Morellet, 18, 46
Morelly, 28, 32, 67
Morfontaine, 41
Morris, 227
Mun, 97

Naigeon, 21
Necker, 42
Nivelle de la Chaussée, 38
Nodier, 97
Nokes, 283
Nollet, 33

INDEX

O'Brien, 210, 212
Oppenheim (L.), 264
Ossian, 13

Paine, 121
Palles, 213
Parry, 281, 287
Peck, 231
Phlipon, 15, 44
Pupendorf, 25

Quesnay, 14, 67

Rabaut de S. Etienne, 79
Rabelais, 13
Racine, 15
Raynal, 31
Réamur, 33
Rétif de la Bretonne, 67, 72
Richardson, 13, 59
Robespierre, 76, 79 f.
Romilly, 235
Rousseau, chap. i *passim*, 51, 130, 242, 256
Roux, 85
Russell, 215, 227

Sadeur, 26
Saint-Évremond, 13, 36
Saint-Just, 82

Saint-Michel, 83
Saint-Pierre (Abbé), 15, 25, 41
Saint-Pierre (B.), 37
Saint-Simon, 25
Sankey, 127, 136
Selborne, 236
Shelley, 38
Smith (Sydney), 291
Spinoza, 152 f.
Stephen, 227
Sumner (Viscount), 206, 213, 218

Taft, 232
Taine, 32, 76
Temperley, 120
Tocqueville, 32, 103
Toussaint, 14, 24, 43
Turgot, 34, 41, 45, 121

Vairasse, 26
Vauban, 17, 25
Voltaire, chap. i *passim*, 51, 52, 67

Wells (H. G.), 129
Westbury, 295
Westlake, 269
Wrenbury, 205

Young, 13, 38

12756

JA
38
L35
1969

Laski, Harold
Joseph, 1893-1950.

Studies in law and
politics

DATE

© THE BAKER & TAYLOR CO.